NEW CAMPGROUNDS
THE STATEWIDE GUIDE

TEXT AND PHOTOGRAPHY
BY CHRISTINA FRAIN

WESTCLIFFE PUBLISHERS

westcliffepublishers.com

International Standard Book Number: 1-56579-436-2

Text and Photography: Christina Frain, © 2004. All rights reserved.

Editor: Martha Ripley Gray
Designer: Carol Pando
Production Manager: Craig Keyzer

Published by:
Westcliffe Publishers, Inc.
P.O. Box 1261
Englewood, CO 80150
westcliffepublishers.com

Printed in China by H & Y Printing Ltd.

Library of Congress Cataloging-in-Publication Data:
Frain, Christina.
    New Mexico campgrounds : the statewide guide / text and photography
by Christina Frain.
      p. cm.
    Includes bibliographical references and index.
    ISBN 1-56579-436-2
      1. Camping—New Mexico—Guidebooks. 2. Camp sites, facilities, etc.—
New Mexico—Guidebooks. 3. New Mexico—Guidebooks. I. Title.

GV191.42.N6F73 2003
796.54'09789—dc21   2003057664

For more information about other fine books and calendars from Westcliffe Publishers, please contact your local bookstore, call us at 1-800-523-3692, write for our free color catalog, or visit us on the Web at **westcliffepublishers.com**.

Please Note: Risk is always a factor in backcountry and high-mountain travel. Many of the activities described in this book can be dangerous, especially when weather is adverse or unpredictable, and when unforeseen events or conditions create a hazardous situation. The author has done her best to provide the reader with accurate information about backcountry travel, as well as to point out some of its potential hazards. It is the responsibility of the users of this guide to learn the necessary skills for safe backcountry travel, and to exercise caution in potentially hazardous areas. The author and publisher disclaim any liability for injury or other damage caused by backcountry traveling or performing any other activity described in this book.

Preceding Page: *Chaos, the dog, sits at watch at McCrystal Creek Campground*
Opposite: *Jemez Falls near Jemez Falls Campground*

CONTENTS

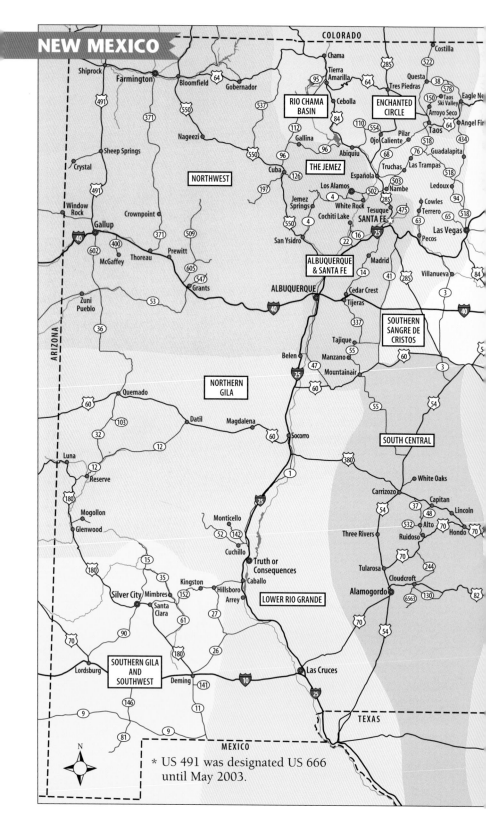

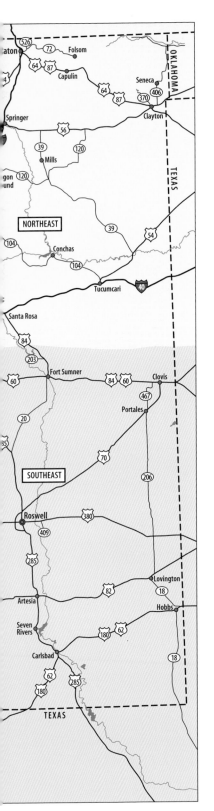

Dawn breaks on the glassy surface of Morphy Lake at Morphy Lake State Park

ACKNOWLEDGMENTS

I began to list everyone who had provided me with insight, offered me information, or otherwise helped me as I ran around New Mexico for two years—and realized that I might miss someone. To avoid offending through omission, thank you to all of the rangers, park personnel, volunteers, camp hosts, and fellow campers. Your stories and personal experiences helped me in many ways to try to document the remarkable places listed in this guide.

I also want to thank the people at Westcliffe Publishers who worked to make this book possible. John Fielder and Linda Doyle supported me in the project from the start; Jenna Browning and Craig Keyzer answered questions and offered advice and guidance regarding the book's form and scope; Carol Pando created its beautiful design; and Martha Gray edited, reshaped, and helped research the text to make it a better book.

Finally, although he can't read, Chaos needs to be acknowledged. He is my 110-pound yellow lab/shepherd that listened to me ramble, bounced in the back of the Wrangler, protected me from creatures of the night, and served as a constant companion without a whimper. May everyone have a critter of such caliber at some time in his or her life.

—Christina Frain

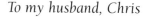

To my husband, Chris

Thank you for supporting me through this amazing journey

Opposite: *Late summer brings wildflowers to life along the South Fork Rio Bonito, near South Fork Campground*

PREFACE

Why are *you* camping in New Mexico? Are you heeding the call of the wild? Looking for a little hiking, fishing, or other outdoor fun? Exploring the state's amazing heritage and natural beauty? Taking advantage of an inexpensive educational vacation option for your family? Or are you simply looking for a clean, cheap place to bed down for the night while hurtling along New Mexico's highways? In these pages I have attempted to address the varied needs and interests of campers who want to pitch a tent or park an RV in the Land of Enchantment.

This book developed out of a personal need for comprehensive information on camping in New Mexico. When I moved to New Mexico several years ago, I looked for a guidebook on the state's public campgrounds that spoke to my interests—and came up short. I personally wanted to target the areas in New Mexico that most appealed to my aesthetic sensibilities and hoped to stay in campgrounds set in the middle of the landscapes I wanted to photograph. A pocket guide was available that covered the basics, but I was looking for a bit more. In the end, I decided to set out, usually accompanied by my dog, Chaos, to put a different kind of guidebook together.

Chaos patiently waits for breakfast on a frosty morning at Heron Lake State Park

Cliff-side ruins near Nutria Lakes, in the Zuni Mountains south of Gallup

During the research process, I tried to view a campground from a variety of angles. What are the main area attractions, and why would someone be drawn to camping there? What key natural, historical, cultural, or practical reasons distinguish that location? How long might someone stay there before becoming restless? How tough is the area to access? How likely is a camper to find a site without a reservation? By addressing such questions, this guidebook provides details that others do not.

As you read about these public campgrounds, I hope you look past the fire ring and explore the nature, history, and culture that might be right in your campground or just beyond your campfire's light. Don't be afraid to go off the interstates and explore the winding two-lane roads and thousands of miles of forest roads. You are guaranteed to encounter natural wonders and wonderful little towns. Just because a campground is simple doesn't mean that the journey to get there isn't going to be full of beauty and the pleasantly unexpected. I hope this guidebook helps you get the most out of your camping experience. New Mexico and her campgrounds have so much to offer. Bienvenidos!

HOW TO USE THIS GUIDE

The 175 campgrounds included in this book are divided among twelve chapters, reflecting regional areas defined primarily by natural features. New Mexico has vast tracts of mountains, canyons, deserts, and other areas that roads do not cross. The campgrounds are thus organized according to logical paths of travel based on New Mexico's system of roads. Beneath the name of each campground in its entry is a tagline that expresses briefly the camping experience there. Because people camp for different reasons and expect different things from their camping experience, I have also compiled an appendix called "Picks by Activity or Interest" (p. 274). These lists of campgrounds reflect my selection of the best camp areas sorted alphabetically by such criteria as fishing access, hiking opportunities, proximity to interstates, and historical interest, among others.

Since many of the campgrounds I have included are remote, with little signage to help visitors reach them, I urge visitors to take detailed maps in addition to the directions and maps provided in this book. The primary map tool I used to create this book was the *New Mexico Road & Recreation Atlas* from Benchmark Maps, now in its fourth edition (call 800-962-1394 to order). Forest Service maps provide even more detail and are available at map stores or from the USGS by calling 888-ASK-USGS or 303-202-4200. Another great product is the National Geographic Topo! CD-ROM series for New Mexico, based on the USGS 1:24,000 quadrangle maps and downloadable onto many GPS handhelds. You can also look for or order these products at many bookstores, map stores, and outdoor retailers.

Many maps, including the Benchmark atlas, will show most of the existing campgrounds but also a few that are closed or no longer exist for a variety of reasons. I have tried to update information through September 2003. After each fire season, a few closures typically occur. The only way to be completely sure that a campground is open is to contact the appropriate land-management agency and check. The appropriate contact phone number is listed at the end of each entry in boldface.

A note on selection: As you look at various maps indicating recreational areas around the state, you may find campgrounds on the map that are not in this book. Reasons for omission include changes in official designation (from a campground to a picnic area, for example), closure following a forest fire, or abandonment because of repeated vandalism. Conversely, there are some campgrounds in this guidebook that I never found on any map but do exist and are certainly worth visiting.

Opposite: *A stormy spring sky sets a dramatic scene for the canyons around Angel Peak National Recreation Site*

RECREATIONAL OPPORTUNITIES

Beneath each campground name and tagline are icons representing activities available in the immediate vicinity of the campground. Note that at certain remote campgrounds, the nearest activity may be an hour's drive from your location. In other cases, you may just have to go a few miles to a neighboring campground to reach a trailhead or other major local attraction. The activities are illustrated by the following icons:

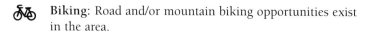 **Biking:** Road and/or mountain biking opportunities exist in the area.

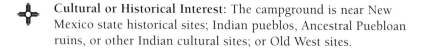 **Cultural or Historical Interest:** The campground is near New Mexico state historical sites; Indian pueblos, Ancestral Puebloan ruins, or other Indian cultural sites; or Old West sites.

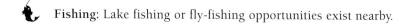 **Fishing:** Lake fishing or fly-fishing opportunities exist nearby.

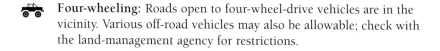 **Four-wheeling:** Roads open to four-wheel-drive vehicles are in the vicinity. Various off-road vehicles may also be allowable; check with the land-management agency for restrictions.

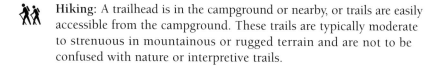 **Hiking:** A trailhead is in the campground or nearby, or trails are easily accessible from the campground. These trails are typically moderate to strenuous in mountainous or rugged terrain and are not to be confused with nature or interpretive trails.

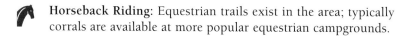 **Horseback Riding:** Equestrian trails exist in the area; typically corrals are available at more popular equestrian campgrounds.

Interpretive or Nature Trails, Exhibits: Perfect for families, interpretive or nature trails are typically short, on flat terrain, and equipped with signage explaining the natural, historical, or cultural significance of the area. Many such trails are paved and wheelchair-accessible. Many visitor centers offer interpretive exhibits as well.

Motorized Boating: The location allows boats that create a wake. Sometimes waterskiing is allowed at these locations; call for specific regulations. Personal watercraft are allowed in these lakes.

No-Wake Boating: The location is open to nonmotorized boats or small boats with electric motors; call for specific regulations. Personal watercraft are not allowed in no-wake lakes.

Photographic Opportunities: This reflects my picks for best photographic opportunities and great views.

Rafting or Kayaking: Whitewater runs are situated nearby for rafters and kayakers.

Sailing: The location is a good place for sailing or windsurfing.

Swimming: Swimming is allowed in designated areas.

A young angler fishing at Fawn Lakes

CAMPGROUND FACTS

The following headings of basic information appear under each campground description to simplify your planning.

LOCATION

Mileage from a nearby town by road, not as the crow flies.

ELEVATION

Elevation in feet above sea level. If you are planning to camp in the late spring or early fall, keep in mind that higher elevations frequently get snow. Also note that the higher the elevation, the more difficult it may be for some to breathe comfortably during physically strenuous activity.

NUMBER OF SITES

The number of individual, developed sites, sometimes including group sites, per land managers. A published number may be at variance with the figure given herein, because by the publication date, all sites may not be usable for various reasons. Sometimes a combination of developed, group, and dispersed sites may exist. Where I have given no number but just indicated "dispersed," I refer to camping areas made up of an indefinite number of primitive sites. (Dispersed sites can nevertheless be designated, rather than created; to keep overall impact low, please look for fire rings to find sites that have been previously used.)

RV NOTES

Information of particular interest to RV campers. Maximum lengths listed are recommendations offered by the land-management agencies based on parking area size and road conditions. In most campgrounds, a limited number of campsites can accommodate the very largest RVs. Those with larger RVs should always call ahead to confirm the availability of a spot in which their vehicles can fit.

FEE

I have just indicated "yes" or "no" here rather than providing explicit fee schedules, which are subject to change. Call the appropriate land-management agency or ranger district for the latest information before you set out.

SEASON

Many campgrounds are open year-round. If the description mentions snow, call ahead if you plan to camp during late fall through early spring and don't want to contend with snow camping.

Opposite: *Campsites edge the Red River Gorge in the Wild Rivers Recreation Area*

NEAREST SUPPLY CENTER

The town listed is the nearest reliable supply source that is open seven days a week. New Mexico is full of vast, sparsely populated areas. A dot on a map with a town name does not mean that an open store is there.

ACCESS ROAD

To get to many of the campgrounds in New Mexico, pavement must be left behind. The system of forest roads provides explorers the opportunity to venture into wild, natural areas that few people see. Road conditions vary greatly. In higher elevations, snow and snowmelt can make roads virtually impassable in the winter and spring. Late summer brings the monsoon rains, frequently leaving dirt roads a muddy quagmire. For questions about road conditions, contact the land-management agency beforehand; tow trucks can be very hard to come by.

MAP

The page number and map coordinates for the campground as found in Benchmark Maps' *New Mexico Road & Recreation Atlas*.

It's easy to find a pleasant campsite in Cimarron Canyon State Park

DIRECTIONS

These directions are as accurate as possible. Carry the pertinent U.S. Forest Service map or at least a good atlas such as the *New Mexico Road & Recreation Atlas*. Many campgrounds are in very remote areas, and road signs can sometimes be small or obscured.

DESCRIPTION

Each description begins with an overview of the campground environment and any highlights, natural or manmade, of the surrounding area. Campgrounds that are especially popular are noted; in those cases, I've tried to give an indication of how likely it is that a camper can arrive without a reservation and get a spot. I list any special facilities, such as marinas, designated group areas, and ADA-compliant amenities (see page 30). Depending on the size and complexity of a campground, a description may just sketch what is found in individual sites or may detail various different loops and camping areas. I have noted it if a pay phone is on the premises and if drinking water is available, but be prepared in case the phone is out, or if (off-season) the water is off or not potable for a variety of reasons. Since New Mexico is full of highly photogenic locations, I have sometimes offered photographic tips for capturing notable features near campgrounds.

In the last paragraph of each entry, gate times are noted where applicable. A number to call for reservations is given where these are required or recommended. Typically these reservation services lines cannot provide information on local conditions. For that information you need to call the contact number at the end of the listing.

CONTACT NUMBER

New Mexico has a wide variety of agencies that manage campgrounds, including the U.S. Army Corps of Engineers, the U.S. Bureau of Land Management, the U.S. Forest Service, the National Park Service, New Mexico Department of Game and Fish, New Mexico State Parks, and various Indian reservations, each with its own rules and regulations related to camping. Call, write, or stop by the agency office, or visit the land-management agency's website where available, to get your questions answered ahead of time about what is permitted in a particular area, such as ATV use or fishing.

I have listed a local phone number contact **in boldface** at the end of each entry. In some cases, you will connect to an on-site visitor center or park manager; in others, the number links to a ranger district or other appropriate agency. Note that Appendix B contains a list of contact addresses for all land-management agencies, as well as selected website addresses.

RATINGS

Meant to give potential visitors a quick feel for what they will find in a particular campground, these ratings are as objective as possible and reflect weighted averages for the campground as a whole. They are not necessarily indicators of quality.

SCENERY

★★★★★ The campground or the immediate area around the campground has phenomenal views or natural wonders within sight.

★★★★ The views are amazing, just not quite as jaw-dropping as a five-star site.

★★★ The campground is situated in a grove or stand of trees without any major distinguishing features but is still pretty.

★★ The area is nice, but there is some detractor like a nearby road.

★ Sites have no views and some major detractor exists, like a road that is too close and heavily traveled.

RVs

★★★★★ The RV sites have everything: water, electric, and sewer hookups; nearby dump station; and level, easy-to-enter parking with good surfaces.

★★★★ RV sites have electric and water hookups, and level, easy-to-enter parking spaces with good surfaces; a dump station is available.

★★★ RV sites have electric hookups and level parking spaces; water hydrants and a dump station are available in the campground.

★★ The campground can accommodate RVs and might have a dump station.

★ RVs can fit in the campground, but there are no RV-specific amenities.

NR (Not recommended): RVs are unsuitable for various reasons, such as road conditions or lack of room in the campground for maneuvering.

City of Rocks State Park offers camping in an unforgettable setting

TENTS

★★★★★ All sites have tent pads or well-graded, level, smooth tent surfaces.

★★★ Sites generally have level, relatively rock-free areas for tents.

★★ It takes some work, but level, rock-free tent sites are possible.

SHADE

★★★★★ Campsites are well shaded either by trees or shelters.

★★★ Some sites have shade. Bring your own shade in case your site lacks it.

★ Bring your own shade since no, or few, sites have any shade.

PRIVACY

Privacy criteria apply generally to tent sites that can be occupied by tents or RVs. RV sites, almost universally, are set close together with little privacy.

★★★★★ Virtually all sites have significant space between them and may include such barriers as trees, shrubs, or rocks.

★★★★ The majority of sites have space or barriers between them.

★★★ Sites are spaced reasonably far apart, but you may be able to see and hear your neighbors. This setup is typical.

★★ Only a handful of sites offer a significant degree of privacy, or sites are relatively close together.

★ Campsites are small and virtually on top of one another. You will probably share your camping experience with your neighbor.

FACILITIES

This is an indication of the types of facilities available, *not* the quality of the facilities. Across New Mexico, land-management agencies do a good job of maintaining their campgrounds. Any campground can be abused by visitors on a random basis. A note about the toilet criteria: "restrooms" have sinks with running water; "vault toilets" have no sink but are generally larger and typically cleaner than "pit toilets," or outhouses.

★★★★★ Showers, restrooms, picnic tables, and grills are available, and the campground overall is significantly developed.

★★★★ Restrooms, picnic tables, and grills are available, and the campground overall is significantly developed.

★★★ Vault toilets, picnic tables, and grills are available in a somewhat developed setting.

★★ Picnic tables, grills or fire rings with grills, and a pit toilet are available, in a rustic setting.

★ Fire rings and outhouse are available, usually in a dispersed camping area.

CAMPGROUND ACTIVITIES

Included are activities available in the campground or a short distance away, assuming that the camper is not planning to fish, hike, or engage in a single kind of activity every day. Winter activities at some campgrounds are not calculated into this rating, since they are seasonal and snow-dependent.

***** Visitors could camp for five or more days and do something different each day, since the campground offers numerous recreational or sightseeing opportunities, possibly including multiple trailheads or different fishing environments, or proximity to nearby towns or sites.

**** The campground offers at least four days of different recreational or sightseeing activities, possibly including multiple trailheads or different fishing environments, or proximity to nearby towns or parks.

*** The campground offers at least two to three days of different recreational or sightseeing activities, possibly including multiple trailheads or different fishing environments, or proximity to nearby towns or parks.

** The campground offers just one primary activity, such as fishing or a trailhead.

* The campground and the surrounding area do not offer any specific recreational amenities.

AREA ACTIVITIES

This indicates kinds of activities available within roughly a 30-mile radius. Campgrounds in remote areas, where the main highway may be 10 or 20 miles down rough forest roads, generally will not receive high marks in this category, since most people typically go to these places and stay put.

***** Visitors could camp for five or more days and do something different each day, since the surrounding area offers numerous recreational or sightseeing opportunities, possibly including multiple trailheads, different fishing environments, sites in towns, or national or state parks.

**** The area offers at least four days of different recreational or sightseeing activities, possibly including multiple trailheads, different fishing environments, sites in towns, and national or state parks.

*** The area offers at least two to three days of different recreational activities, possibly including multiple trailheads, different fishing environments, sites in towns, and national or state parks.

** A single day-trip would be possible.

* The surrounding area offers no specific recreational amenities.

WHEELCHAIR ACCESSIBILITY

The information below was provided by rangers identifying accessible facilities for those in wheelchairs.

***** A wide variety of accessible facilities are on-site, possibly including restrooms or vault toilets, interpretive trails, visitor centers, campsites, courtesy docks, marinas, playgrounds, group shelters, and parking.

**** The basic camping facilities are accessible, including restrooms or toilets, parking, and campsites, as well as one or more recreational facilities.

*** The basic camping facilities are accessible, including restrooms or toilets, parking, and campsites.

** Only the toilets or restrooms are accessible.

* No specifically wheelchair-accessible facilities are available.

Public Campgrounds in New Mexico

A mostly rural and long-settled state, New Mexico offers campers unique and diverse environments with various levels of amenities. The following summary of general distinctions among types of campgrounds can help you to predict the outdoor experience you might have at a given place.

BLM Lands

The BLM has just a few camping areas in New Mexico, but they're all big, diverse, and prime: Orilla Verde, Santa Cruz Lake, and Wild Rivers Recreation Areas. All three are in great locations and are well-maintained. And although some sections of these recreation areas are highly developed, primitive sections also exist in each of them.

Group

Group areas are typically large sites or areas reserved for multiple families or parties of 15 or more people who want to camp together. Amenities and layouts vary greatly, with everything from pavilions fitted with large grills and private bathrooms to just a standard pair of sites linked together. Frequently, group areas are set apart from the rest of the campground, in some cases several miles away within the same park. A universal rule is that group sites have fees and must be reserved in advance.

Indian Reservations

Some of these campgrounds are very nice and well-developed, particularly the Navajo's Bowl Canyon, the Mescalero Apaches' Silver Lake, and Isleta Lakes (with close-by golf and gaming), but you should expect amenities less deluxe than those of the state parks system. Cochiti Lakes, run by the U.S. Army Corps of Engineers, lies within the Cochiti Reservation, with golf nearby. Many other reservation campgrounds, such as those of the Jicarilla Apache, are primitive areas near fishing, so be sure to know the appropriate fishing regulations before you go. Usually, no New Mexico state fishing permit is needed. Some camping fees are included in the fishing fee; be sure to call ahead for details.

Fishing opportunities abound at numerous lakes administered by Indian reservations

NATIONAL FORESTS

National Forest campgrounds constitute the greatest number of campgrounds overall in the state and lie in many highly desirable outdoor locations. Conditions vary dramatically among them, however, depending on various factors, including location, heaviness of use, and amenities. Generally, the closer a campground is to an urban or resort area, the greater the impact on facilities you can expect to find. Some, like Paliza and Capilla, are well-maintained and have been recently renovated. Others, like Buzzard Park and Mora, are primitive or impacted, on account of factors such as extreme isolation or intense use. An isolated location does not necessarily mean a lesser-quality facility, however. In choosing an area, be sure to call the respective ranger district office to get the latest information.

NATIONAL PARKS

Like Forest Service campgrounds in New Mexico, National Park campgrounds are hard to generalize about. All are first-come, first-served except for group areas. Expect to pay entrance *and* campground fees, but economical park passes are available. The campgrounds at Bandelier National Monument and Chaco Culture National Historical Park are busy and relatively large; by contrast, El Morro National Monument has just nine sites and no overflow. Gila Cliff Dwellings National Monument and Dog Canyon, on the northernmost end of Texas's Guadalupe Mountains National Park, are seldom crowded. White Sands National Monument, which offers only remote, backcountry camping, has been included because of its singular setting.

STATE PARKS

Crème de la crème, these 31 parks represent the finest amenities available for campers in the state, whether beside huge impoundment lakes, nestled in mountains, or amid dramatic desert environments. Highly developed and kept immaculate, state parks offer showers, playgrounds, evening programs, wheelchair-accessible and RV-friendly facilities, and as clean an outdoor environment as you can expect to find. Reservations are available for hookup sites and should be made well in advance; expect to pay a reservation fee. A new annual permit program is a great money-saving option for qualifying campers.

STATE WILDLIFE AREAS

These campgrounds are uniformly primitive, although each has at least one toilet. Typically the locations offer good access to fishing; people don't come for the amenities. They are almost always free. Be sure to know the appropriate fishing regulations before you go.

MAKING RESERVATIONS

The typical camping season in New Mexico begins with Easter and ends around Labor Day. If you want a hookup site, you must reserve it in advance. Arriving early for a weekend stay affords those without reservations the best chance of getting preferred sites. Groups sites must always be reserved.

At all New Mexico state parks, there will always be some first-come, first-served sites and a limited number of reservable sites. Reserve hookup sites at www.icampnm.com or toll-free at 877-664-7787; expect to pay a reservation fee. If you show up at a state park campground without a reservation, you will likely be able to find a site, if only an overflow site—but you probably won't have a hookup. BLM- and Army Corps of Engineers–administered campgrounds have similar reservation arrangements. Forest Service campgrounds are generally all first-come, first-served except for the group sites, which must be reserved in advance.

Autumn color in the nearby Pecos Wilderness brightens Jack's Creek Campground

RULES AND A BIT OF ADVICE

CAMP ETIQUETTE

Always look over specific campground rules, usually posted near the entrance, including check-in and check-out times, day-use fees, and quiet hours, and respect these rules. Leave your campsite as clean as you found it—or cleaner. In primitive camp areas, use already-existing campsites rather than creating new ones, and pack out all of your trash. Watch pets and children closely around campsites.

CLIMATE AND WEATHER

The topographic variety often surprises first-time visitors to New Mexico. If you plan to head into any of the mountain ranges or unexpectedly high-elevation areas such as the northwestern corner of the state, pay attention to the weather reports. What may be rain in Albuquerque could well be snow at a higher elevation.

CRITTERS IN THE ROAD AND IN CAMP

Beware of livestock and wildlife. In New Mexico, virtually any road can be a crossing point for some kind of animal. This includes herds of cows, goats, and sheep. Deer, elk, and pronghorn move in small groups, so if you see one crossing the road, it is very possible that a second or a third may follow. Be vigilant. In camp, do not feed any wild animals, both for your safety and theirs. Food, toiletries, and coolers should be stored away from your living area and never inside a tent. Store all edibles, pet food, and trash in bearproof food containers, in a hard-sided vehicle or RV, or suspended from a tree.

The sun rises on Goose Lake at the remote Goose Lake Campground

DESERT PRECAUTIONS AND WATER

Consider almost all of New Mexico to be high desert. Respect the dry landscape as if your life depended on it. You never know what could happen to you or your vehicle. Know the symptoms of heat exhaustion and heatstroke, and bring clothing and headgear that can protect you from the sun. Consider taking a tarp for shade, just in case. Always be prepared with extra water, and always purify, or boil for 15 minutes, water gathered from streams and lakes. And although it may be hot during the daytime, temperatures drop drastically after the sun sets, often by 30 or even 40 degrees, so be sure to pack extra layers.

FIRE

In recent years, the fire dangers of the western United States have tragically extended beyond the typical fire regions. Fire restrictions and rules are serious matters of life and death for both people and the forests that surround them. New Mexico is a tinderbox. If fire bans are in effect, don't even think about breaking the prohibition. If you are heading into any of the national forests during New Mexico's fifth season—fire season—call ahead to the ranger station to see if restrictions are in place, or if districts are even open. Above all, use common sense. Don't ever make campfires if it's windy, don't set off fireworks, and don't ever leave a fire that isn't *dead out*. (Extinguish it by dousing thoroughly with water and dirt, then repeating.)

PETS

Developed campgrounds require that pets be leashed at all times; elsewhere you're on your own. Always clean up after your pets, and avoid taking loud pets to developed campgrounds. Just like with human food, remember to clean up and properly store your dog's food at night to avoid attracting coyotes, bears, raccoons, and any other local scavengers. Equestrians should look for campgrounds that have corrals; horses should not roam free by the picnic tables.

PROVISIONS ON THE ROAD

When you look at a map of New Mexico, you will see lots of dots for towns. Do not expect to head toward one of these and find gas, food, or any other supplies. The state is full of tiny hamlets that are simply clusters of people who live in the same area but go elsewhere to stock up on necessities. The campground descriptions include the most reliable, seven-days-a-week supply center. Make sure you are stocked up before you head into the backcountry or even along the many paved roads that traverse the great expanses of the Land of Enchantment.

SUPPLY EXTRAS

So you've packed your tent, sleeping bag, mattress, warm clothes, rain gear, stove, food, extra water, and utensils. A few other less-obvious items you don't want to forget include firewood, toilet paper, trash bags, shade (such as a tarp), an inflated spare tire, and sun protection. Insect repellent is also a good idea, to discourage not only mosquitoes but also fleas and ticks.

THE WEEKEND SCENE

Park rangers work hard with limited resources to keep the campgrounds under their supervision in good condition. The fact is, however, they have an enormous task with high-use facilities near major urban areas. Any campground locale just outside of urban areas may be a frequent party spot on the weekends. Unfortunately, at these times the areas are not always safe for campers and their property. On other days of the week, however, you might be camping almost by yourself. Plan accordingly around high-use times.

ABBREVIATIONS USED IN THIS BOOK

ADA: The Americans With Disabilities Act prohibits discrimination against persons with disabilities in, among other areas, public accommodations and other facilities open to the public. The law has brought changes in the design and construction of campground amenities to allow those in wheelchairs to have access to them.

CR   County Road
FR   Forest Road
NM   New Mexico state highway (preceding number)
US   Federal highway (preceding number)

Opposite: *Striped cliffs along FR 151 near the Rio Chama*
Below: *Natural arch in the Jemez near the Rio de Las Vacas*

ALBUQUERQUE AND SANTA FE

Home to the state's largest city and the capital of New Mexico, the Albuquerque and Santa Fe region offers the widest range of cultural and city-based recreation as well as plenty of outdoor activities from which to choose. Albuquerque, Santa Fe, Los Alamos, Bandelier National Monument, and Petroglyph National Monument (see p. 44) are all readily accessible from Cochiti Lake Recreation Area. The southernmost peaks of the Sangre de Cristo Mountains tower above Santa Fe. NM 475 begins near the famous Santa Fe Plaza and runs to the Santa Fe Ski Area. Numerous trailheads start from the roadside along the way, most leading into the Pecos Wilderness. Plenty of campgrounds dot the area.

Aspen canopy at Big Tesuque

Festivals and special events occur year-round. Santa Fe hosts annually the Indian and Spanish Markets, the Rodeo de Santa Fe, and a myriad of craft and art shows. The Albuquerque International Balloon Fiesta, Fiestas de Albuquerque, and New Mexico State Fair draw visitors from around the world to New Mexico's largest city. The many nearby Pueblo communities hold dances, fairs, powwows, and festivals, some of which are open to the public.

The Sandia Mountains border Albuquerque to the east, offering plenty of hiking trails that access the Sandia Wilderness and Sandia Crest, elevation 10,678 feet—but no designated campgrounds. South of Albuquerque lie the less frequently visited but equally beautiful Manzano Mountains. Along their eastern foothills sit old Spanish land-grant villages and the ruins that make up the Salinas Pueblo Missions National Monument. Forest roads and trails lead up through canyons and ultimately to the edge of the Manzano Wilderness. In addition to hiking, the area is particularly popular for mountain biking and horseback riding. A trip to Capilla Peak affords a 360-degree view of the area. The Manzanos and the Sandias sit on the migratory path for a variety of raptors and are home to black bears, mountain lions, and deer.

Area Campgrounds

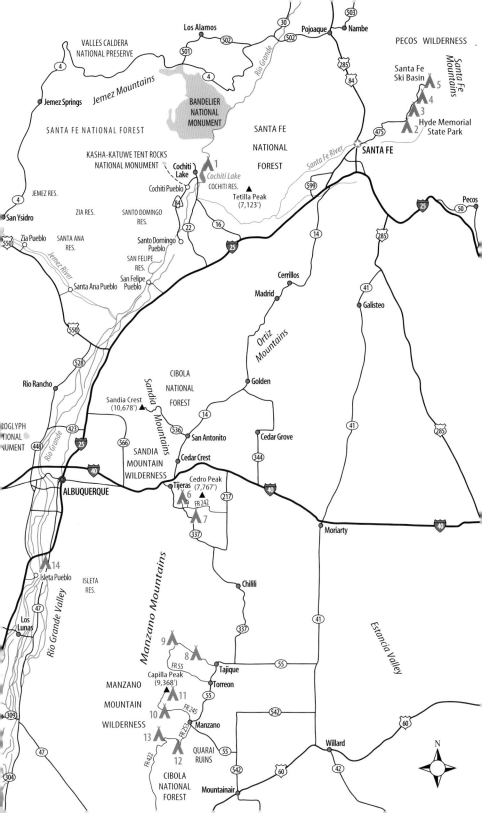

1 COCHITI LAKE

Albuquerque-Santa Fe area base camp

LOCATION: 23 miles west of Santa Fe
ELEVATION: 5,000 feet
NUMBER OF SITES: 146
RV NOTES: No maximum length; both Juniper and Cholla areas have hookups; management asks RV campers not to remain hooked up to water during their stay
FEE: Yes
SEASON: Year-round
NEAREST SUPPLY CENTER: Cochiti Lake
ACCESS ROAD: Paved
MAP: *New Mexico Road & Recreation Atlas*, p. 42, A5
DIRECTIONS: From Exit 264 on I-25, about 12 miles southwest of Santa Fe, go northwest on NM 16 toward Cochiti Lake. Drive for about 11.5 miles, past the dam; the main entrance to the recreation area will be on your right.

SCENERY: ★★★★
RVs: ★★★
TENTS: ★★★★
SHADE: ★★★
PRIVACY: ★★★
FACILITIES: ★★★★★
CAMPGROUND ACTIVITIES: ★★★★★
AREA ACTIVITIES: ★★★★★
WHEELCHAIR ACCESSIBILITY: ★★★★★

Adjacent to the Cochiti Pueblo, Cochiti Lake Recreation Area is both a resort-style campground and a convenient base camp for exploring the entire central New Mexico region. The park's campgrounds flank the 1,200-acre no-wake lake, with fine views of the lake, high-desert plains and mesas, and the Jemez and Sandia Mountains. Administered by the U.S. Army

Corps of Engineers and created by one of the largest earth dams in the world, Cochiti Lake offers water-based recreation including sailing, windsurfing, canoeing, and swimming. Enjoy free public boat ramps plus a private marina with slips for rent. Fishing is accessible both in the lake above the dam and in the Rio Grande below in Al Black Recreation Area, open 24 hours a day. Mountain bikers can follow the access road through the town of Cochiti Lake and into the foothills of the Jemez Mountains.

The visitor center includes displays, pay phones, a short nature trail, and an overlook. It is wheelchair-accessible, as are the restrooms and showers, fishing in the Al Black Area, and some campsites. The group area accommodates 75–100 people, with picnic tables, grills, some shelters, and one hydrant.

KASHA-KATUWE TENT ROCKS NATIONAL MONUMENT

About halfway between Santa Fe and Albuquerque on the Cochiti Indian Reservation sits an amazing network of canyons lined with unusual geological formations called "tent rocks." The formations resemble sand that is piled in the bottom of an hourglass, hardened, then topped with a small rock on the point. Throughout the millennia, volcanoes in the area erupted, forming a deep layer of ash and rock. During the erosion process, cones developed in those places protected by water-resistant rocks. Now visitors can follow a trail that meanders through these cones into a slot canyon and up onto the mesa top, which boasts a 360-degree view of the Jemez, Sangre de Cristo, and Sandia mountain ranges. Take Exit 259 from I-25 and drive north on NM 22 to the Cochiti Lake Dam. Follow the signs to the Kasha-Katuwe Tent Rocks parking area.

Sites are almost always available, as this is a very large campground. On the west side of the lake lies the Cochiti boat ramp and marina as well as **Juniper**, which has 34 campsites, each with electric hookup, table, grill, and fire ring. Water is available throughout, along with a dump station, restrooms, and showers. **Chamisa** has 21 campsites, each with a shelter, table, grill, and fire ring. Water and vault toilets are available. **Apache Plume** is used for overflow camping and has 22 sites, each with a shelter, table, grill, and fire ring. Water is available, but there are no restrooms. In Tetilla Peak Recreation Area on the east side of the lake is **Cholla**, which has 51 campsites, each with a grill and table, including 26 with electric hookups and four with shelters. Restrooms and showers are centrally located. **Coyote**, also on the east side, has 18 sites, each with a tent pad, table, and pedestal grill. Drinking water is available.

Closed sundown to sunrise. Reservations can be made at 877-444-6777 or ReserveUSA.com. **U.S. Army Corps of Engineers Camp Office, 505-465-0307.**

Cochiti Lake is a short drive away from the amazing rock formations at Kasha-Katuwe Tent Rocks National Monument (see p. 35)

2 BLACK CANYON
Black Canyon Trailhead and the Santa Fe National Forest

LOCATION: 7.5 miles northeast of Santa Fe
ELEVATION: 8,300 feet
NUMBER OF SITES: 46
RV NOTES: No maximum length
FEE: Yes
SEASON: May–October
NEAREST SUPPLY CENTER: Santa Fe
ACCESS ROAD: Paved
MAP: *New Mexico Road & Recreation Atlas,*
p. 43, A7

SCENERY: ★★★	
RVs: ★★	
TENTS: ★★★	
SHADE: ★★★★	
PRIVACY: ★★★	
FACILITIES: ★★★	
CAMPGROUND ACTIVITIES: ★★	
AREA ACTIVITIES: ★★★★★	
WHEELCHAIR ACCESSIBILITY: ★★	

DIRECTIONS: From the Santa Fe Plaza area, follow signs for the ski basin on NM 475. The entrance to the Black Canyon Campground is about 7 miles up the highway on the right.

A cool, forested campground, Black Canyon can serve as a convenient base camp for exploring the Santa Fe National Forest above and the city of Santa Fe below. Hardy winter athletes stay here in the off-season. The Black Canyon Trail, good for campers with children, starts from the campground.

Basic with picnic tables and fire rings, sites can be difficult to get on holidays and when there are major festivals in Santa Fe. Since a recent renovation, all sites are ADA compliant. The park has vault toilets, and drinking water is available. The designated group area consists of a double campsite with a central fire pit.

Gate closed sundown to sunrise. Reservations at 877-444-6777. **Española Ranger District,** 505-753-7331.

Loretto Chapel, Santa Fe

3 HYDE MEMORIAL STATE PARK

Santa Fe area base camp

LOCATION: 8 miles northeast of Santa Fe

ELEVATION: 8,830 feet

NUMBER OF SITES: 50

RV NOTES: 55 feet maximum; the RV area is open year-round; the dump station is south of the main campground, just before the visitor center

FEE: Yes

SEASON: Year-round, though a section of the campground closes during winter

NEAREST SUPPLY CENTER: Santa Fe

ACCESS ROAD: Paved

MAP: *New Mexico Road & Recreation Atlas*, p. 43, A7

DIRECTIONS: From the Santa Fe Plaza area, follow signs for the ski basin on NM 475. The entrance to Hyde is about 8 miles up the highway on the right.

Situated in the Sangre de Cristo Mountains along the road to the Santa Fe ski area, Hyde can serve as an excellent base camp for hiking and mountain biking excursions into the Santa Fe National Forest or for trips to the historic Plaza below. Most sites sit below tall pines, and in autumn the RV spots in the reservation area overlook a grove of golden aspens in the canyon.

SCENERY:	★★★
RVs:	★★★
TENTS:	★★★★
SHADE:	★★★★
PRIVACY:	★★★
FACILITIES:	★★★★
CAMPGROUND ACTIVITIES:	★★★
AREA ACTIVITIES:	★★★★★
WHEELCHAIR ACCESSIBILITY:	★★★

Winter brings opportunities for sledding, skating, and cross-country skiing. Fans of works constructed by the Civilian Conservation Corps (CCC) will enjoy the historic lodge on the grounds.

Sites begin filling up for the weekend on Thursday nights, though they are usually available most weekdays. For the RV sites, reservations are recommended. Almost any festival weekend is busy.

Wheelchair-accessible facilities include the visitor center, parking, restrooms, and some campsites. Drinking water and pay phones are available. The group area consists of three large pavilions with grills, tables, and fire

rings, one including a fireplace. A volleyball court is also available for groups. Just beyond the visitor center on the right, the main campground offers sites with tables, fire rings, and some shelters. Also here are restrooms, two of the three group shelters, a tent-only area, an ice-skating pond, and a sledding area. The RV area, beyond the main campground entrance on the left, has paved driveways and seven electric hookups. The third group area sits just south of the visitor center.

Closed 11 p.m.–8 a.m. Reservations at 877-664-7787 or www.icampnm.com. **Park Manager, 505-983-7175.**

4 BIG TESUQUE

Streamside aspen grove and Pecos Trailhead

SCENERY: ★★★★
RVs: NR
TENTS: ★★
SHADE: ★★★★
PRIVACY: ★★★★
FACILITIES: ★★★
CAMPGROUND ACTIVITIES: ★★
AREA ACTIVITIES: ★★★★★
WHEELCHAIR ACCESSIBILITY: ★★

LOCATION: 11 miles northeast of Santa Fe
ELEVATION: 9,600 feet
NUMBER OF SITES: 7
RV NOTES: All sites are walk-ins
FEE: No
SEASON: Year-round, but may be snow-covered in winter; sites maintained May–October
NEAREST SUPPLY CENTER: Santa Fe
ACCESS ROAD: Paved
MAP: *New Mexico Road & Recreation Atlas*, p. 43, A7

DIRECTIONS: From the Santa Fe Plaza area, follow signs for the ski basin on NM 475. The entrance to Hyde is about 11.5 miles up the highway on the right.

This creekside campground is enchanting. In fall, sunlight filters through azure skies and gold aspen leaves. In summer, wildflowers surround you. During winter, the silver bark of aspens contrast against fresh snow.

The sites are well-spaced along the creek to provide privacy. The Camp is a popular launch for hikes into the Pecos Wilderness, including a cross-country ski route. Photographers, note Big Tesuque is in a ravine on the west face of the mountain, so sunlight hits the stream later in the morning.

Weekends can be very busy though nights are typically quiet; overflow options exist at Black Canyon and Hyde Memorial State Park. Restrooms and one campsite are wheelchair-accessible. Sites have picnic tables and grills, but no drinking water is available.

No reservations. **Española Ranger District, 505-753-7331.**

5 ASPEN BASIN

Windsor Trailhead, Pecos Wilderness, and the Santa Fe Ski Area

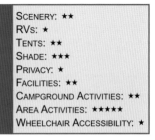

LOCATION: 15 miles northeast of Santa Fe
ELEVATION: 9,700 feet
NUMBER OF SITES: 6
RV NOTES: All of the sites are walk-ins, but there is plenty of space for any size RV in the parking lots
FEE: No
SEASON: Year-round, but may be snow-covered in winter; sites maintained May–October
NEAREST SUPPLY CENTER: Santa Fe
ACCESS ROAD: Paved
MAP: *New Mexico Road & Recreation Atlas*, p. 37, G7
DIRECTIONS: From the Santa Fe Plaza area, follow signs for the ski basin on NM 475. Drive about 15 miles to the Santa Fe Ski Area.

SCENERY:	★★
RVs:	★
TENTS:	★★
SHADE:	★★★
PRIVACY:	★
FACILITIES:	★★
CAMPGROUND ACTIVITIES:	★★
AREA ACTIVITIES:	★★★★★
WHEELCHAIR ACCESSIBILITY:	★

Aspen Basin is composed of a handful of sites near the beginning of the Windsor Trail and within the Santa Fe Ski Area parking lot in an island of trees. Although mountain bikes are not allowed into the Pecos Wilderness, bikers frequently use these campsites as a starting point for riding down to Aspen Vista, where they can reach a limited-access forest road that climbs up to a mountaintop. The view is spectacular along the way as the road climbs from aspen groves to above the treeline. This route is also popular with cross-country skiers. No drinking water is available.

No reservations. **Española Ranger District, 505-753-7331.**

HOT-AIR BALLOON FIESTA

Balloonists from around the world descend upon Albuquerque every October to participate in the Albuquerque International Balloon Fiesta. More than 700 balloonists participated in the 2002 event, according to event organizers, dazzling more than 800,000 spectators. People gather well before dawn to witness the lovely Mass Ascension, in which hundreds of colorful hot-air balloons launch one after another for hours, filling the sky with colorful spectacles including the Flight of Nations and Special Shapes, along with the traditional teardrops.

Albuquerque is located in the Rio Grande Valley, which boasts a special wind effect called The Box. This allows for a balloon to launch and head south along the river at one altitude, then change altitude and return toward the launch site.

If you plan to attend, bundle up, take lots of film, and be sure to save your appetite for some great breakfast burritos.

Visitors are dazzled by the Special Shapes Ascension.

6 CEDRO PEAK (GROUP)

Albuquerque area base camp

LOCATION: 8 miles east of Albuquerque
ELEVATION: 7,400 feet
NUMBER OF SITES: 2 group areas
RV NOTES: No maximum length; the campground has a dump station
FEE: Yes
SEASON: May–October
NEAREST SUPPLY CENTER: Tijeras
ACCESS ROAD: Fair-weather; call ahead for conditions
MAP: *New Mexico Road & Recreation Atlas*, p. 42, D5

SCENERY: ★★★
RVS: ★★
TENTS: ★★★
SHADE: ★★★
PRIVACY: ★★
FACILITIES: ★★★
CAMPGROUND ACTIVITIES: ★★
AREA ACTIVITIES: ★★★★★
WHEELCHAIR ACCESSIBILITY: ★★

DIRECTIONS: From Exit 167 on the eastern boundary of Albuquerque, drive east on I-40 for about 6.5 miles. Take Exit 175 for Cedar Crest/Tijeras and veer right toward Tijeras. Follow NM 337 south for about 5 miles and turn left onto FR 242. After about 0.6 mile, you will encounter a fork in the road; take the left fork. Stay on that road for about 1.3 miles. The campground entrance will be on your left.

This group camping facility in the northern end of the Manzano Mountain Range is also the closest campground to the Sandia Mountains and Albuquerque. The Cedro Peak Trailhead lies within the campground, offering an easy, family-friendly hike to the top of the peak. Sites are set among cedar, piñon, and live oak. The Sandia Ranger District office, a short drive away, not only houses exhibits but stands beside the ruins of the Tijeras Pueblo.

A large fire ring flanked by benches and an open playing field attract groups year after year. Two large shelters provide shade. Horses are welcome but need to stay in the parking areas. Drinking water is available.

Reservations required: **Sandia Ranger District, 505-281-3304.**

PETROGLYPH NATIONAL MONUMENT

Scattered among the many volcanic boulders that line the rim of Albuquerque's West Mesa are thousands of rock drawings known as petroglyphs. Ancestral Puebloan inhabitants and Spanish settlers scratched shapes of people, crosses, birds, cats, snakes, and a myriad of other creatures into the surface of the dark basalt rocks spewed from the surrounding volcanoes. There are more than 20,000 of these intriguing images spread across 7,232 acres within the boundaries of the monument. Trails of varying lengths guide visitors through the concentrations of petroglyphs.

West of Albuquerque, on I-40, take Exit 154 to Unser Blvd. Follow Unser north for about 3 miles. The entrance to the visitor center will be on the left.

7 DEADMAN (GROUP)

Forested seclusion

LOCATION: 8 miles southeast of Albuquerque
ELEVATION: 7,400 feet
NUMBER OF SITES: 1 group area
RV NOTES: No maximum length
FEE: Yes
SEASON: May–October
NEAREST SUPPLY CENTER: Tijeras
ACCESS ROAD: Fair-weather; call for conditions

SCENERY: ★★★
RVs: ★
TENTS: ★★★
SHADE: ★★★★
PRIVACY: ★★★★★
FACILITIES: ★★
CAMPGROUND ACTIVITIES: ★
AREA ACTIVITIES: ★★★★★
WHEELCHAIR ACCESSIBILITY: ★

MAP: *New Mexico Road & Recreation Atlas*, p. 42, D5
DIRECTIONS: From Exit 167 on the eastern boundary of Albuquerque, drive east on I-40 for about 6.5 miles. Take Exit 175 for Cedar Crest/Tijeras, then veer right toward Tijeras. Follow NM 337 south for about 8 miles. The campground entrance will be on your left.

Filled with cedar and piñon trees, Deadman offers a forested, extremely private camp experience. The campground is reserved by many groups year after year. This campground can serve as a base camp for groups who want to hike, bike, and ride horses in the Manzanos or take day trips into Albuquerque. No drinking water is available.

Reservations required: **Sandia Ranger District, 505-281-3304.**

TURQUOISE TRAIL

Consider taking the road less traveled between Santa Fe and Albuquerque: the Turquoise Trail. NM 14, also known as North 14, runs roughly parallel to I-25 but winds past the green, east side of the Sandias, the west side of the Ortiz Mountains, red-rock outcroppings, and the rolling grasslands just south of Santa Fe. In Santa Fe, NM 14 is called Cerrillos Road and terminates a few blocks from the historic Plaza. From Exit 175 off I-40 east of Albuquerque, drive north on NM 14. You pass through former mining boomtowns turned artist colonies such as Golden, Madrid, and Cerrillos. En route you can access the Crest Road (NM 536), which climbs into the Sandia Mountains in Cibola National Forest and up to the highest peak in the range, 10,678-foot Sandia Crest. In the summer, hiking, biking, and picnicking opportunities abound along this highway; in winter, cross-country skiing and romping in the Capulin Snow Play Area are popular activities.

8 TAJIQUE

A forested escape

LOCATION: 2.8 miles west of Tajique
ELEVATION: 6,960 feet
NUMBER OF SITES: 4
RV NOTES: Not recommended
FEE: No
SEASON: Year-round, but may be inaccessible because of snow
NEAREST SUPPLY CENTER: Mountainair

SCENERY: ★★
RVS: ★
TENTS: ★★
SHADE: ★★★★★
PRIVACY: ★★★
FACILITIES: ★★
CAMPGROUND ACTIVITIES: ★
AREA ACTIVITIES: ★★★
WHEELCHAIR ACCESSIBILITY: ★

ACCESS ROAD: Fair-weather; call ahead for conditions
MAP: *New Mexico Road & Recreation Atlas*, p. 42, E5
DIRECTIONS: From Tijeras, just east of Albuquerque, take NM 337 south for about 28 miles. Turn right onto NM 55, heading west for about 3 miles to the village of Tajique. Just past the cemetery, turn right onto FR 55 (Tajique-Torreon Loop Road). The entrance to the campground is about 3 miles in on the left.

Set alongside a streambed that fills with snowmelt in the spring, this little campground offers a quiet spot shaded by juniper and piñon. No drinking water is available. For mountain bikers, the 21-mile Tajique-Torreon Loop (FR 55) makes a nice day trip. If you continue to follow the road past the Tajique Campground, you will encounter a variety of trailheads, including that for the spectacular Fourth of July Trail, which originates in the Fourth of July Campground.

No reservations. **Mountainair Ranger District, 505-847-2990.**

Church of San Francisco in Golden along the Turquoise Trail (see p. 45)

9 FOURTH OF JULY

Bigtooth maples, aspens, and the Fourth of July Trailhead

LOCATION: 7 miles northwest of Tajique

ELEVATION: 7,600 feet

NUMBER OF SITES: 24

RV NOTES: Not recommended for large RVs; small pop-up types are fine

FEE: No

SEASON: May–October

NEAREST SUPPLY CENTER: Mountainair

ACCESS ROAD: Fair-weather; call ahead for conditions

MAP: *New Mexico Road & Recreation Atlas*, p. 42, E5

DIRECTIONS: From Tijeras, just east of Albuquerque, take NM 337 south for about 28 miles. Turn right onto NM 55 headed west for about 3 miles to the village of Tajique. Just past the cemetery, turn right onto FR 55, also called the Tajique-Torreon Loop Road. The entrance to the campground is about 7 miles in on the right.

Recently renovated, the Fourth of July Campground provides a cool mountain retreat in the Manzanos. The Fourth of July Trail begins at the campground and links with the Cerro Blanco Trail, which ultimately connects to the Crest Trail. The path wanders through the largest stand of bigtooth maple in New Mexico and past alligator juniper, ponderosa pine, and even aspen trees at the higher elevations.

SCENERY:	★★★
RVs:	★
TENTS:	★★★
SHADE:	★★★★
PRIVACY:	★★★
FACILITIES:	★★★
CAMPGROUND ACTIVITIES:	★★★
AREA ACTIVITIES:	★★★
WHEELCHAIR ACCESSIBILITY:	★★

In fall the mountains provide a spectacular array of colors, from the reds of the bigtooth maples to the gold of the aspens. Since these trees stand on the range's eastern face, photographers should plan to shoot before the sun drops over the crest in the afternoon. The forest roads in the area are great mountain-biking routes, but note that bikes and motorized vehicles are not allowed in the Manzano Wilderness.

There are two camping loops with 24 total sites (usually available) and three wheelchair-accessible vault toilets. Each site has a picnic table, fire grates, and level, if small, tent areas. No drinking water is available. No reservations. **Mountainair Ranger District, 505-847-2990.**

10 NEW CANYON

Cool forest retreat and New Canyon Trailhead

LOCATION: 5 miles northwest of Manzano

ELEVATION: 7,760 feet

NUMBER OF SITES: 10, plus 2 primitive sites marked by tables along the road before the actual campground

RV NOTES: 30 feet maximum length, but all sites are walk-ins

FEE: No

SEASON: Year-round, but may be inaccessible because of snow

NEAREST SUPPLY CENTER: Mountainair

ACCESS ROAD: Fair-weather; call ahead for conditions

MAP: *New Mexico Road & Recreation Atlas*, p. 42, E5

DIRECTIONS: From Tijeras, just east of Albuquerque, take NM 337 south for 28 miles. Turn right onto NM 55, heading southwest for 12 miles to the town of Manzano. Turn right onto FR 245. Drive 11 miles; the campground entrance will be on your right.

SCENERY: ★★★	
RVs: ★	
TENTS: ★★★	
SHADE: ★★★★	
PRIVACY: ★★★	
FACILITIES: ★★★	
CAMPGROUND ACTIVITIES: ★★	
AREA ACTIVITIES: ★★★★	
WHEELCHAIR ACCESSIBILITY: ★★	

Nestled under towering pines, New Canyon was originally constructed by the CCC and still boasts distinctive stone fire pits with grills. Most sites fill on summer weekends. No drinking water is available.

The New Canyon Trail starts from the campground and links up with the Crest and Osha Peak Trails. A 4x4 drive or arduous mountain-bike ride up to Capilla Peak is worth the trip for the view—and additional trailheads. The Quarai Ruins of Salinas Pueblo Missions National Monument are about 14 miles away.

No reservations. **Mountainair Ranger District, 505-847-2990.**

SCENIC DRIVE: THE MANZANOS

This drive takes you past old Spanish villages, including Chilili, Tajique, Torreon, and Manzano on NM 337 and NM 55. Each is part of a community land grant that was given to settlers in the 1800s by Spanish colonial governors. These grants provided small plots of land on which individuals could build a house and farm, while giving a large tract to the community as a whole, often consisting of thousands of acres. In many cases, descendents of the original families still occupy the land. Some of the communities have posted signs asking that no photographs be taken. Please respect their wishes.

Begin at Tijeras, about 17 miles east of Albuquerque via I-40 and Historic US 66, then head south on NM 337. NM 55 picks up where NM 337 ends, continuing west then south to Mountainair at US 60, some 54 miles from Tijeras. When you reach Mountainair, which held its centennial celebration in 2003, take a break in the dining room of the historic Shaffer Hotel. Its ornate, Native American–inspired ceiling, fixtures, fireplaces, and folk art will amaze you. Located right on NM 55, the hotel façade is decorated with swastikas, which was a Native American symbol prior to the Third Reich. Mountainair is also home to the headquarters for the Salinas Pueblo Missions National Monument.

11 CAPILLA

*360-degree mountaintop views, the Crest Trail,
and raptor watching*

SCENERY: ★★★★★
RVs: NR
TENTS: ★★★
SHADE: ★★★★
PRIVACY: ★★★
FACILITIES: ★★★
CAMPGROUND ACTIVITIES: ★★★
AREA ACTIVITIES: ★
WHEELCHAIR ACCESSIBILITY: ★★★

LOCATION: 14 miles northwest of Manzano
ELEVATION: 9,300 feet
NUMBER OF SITES: 8; no overflow area
RV NOTES: Not recommended
FEE: Yes
SEASON: June–October
NEAREST SUPPLY CENTER: Mountainair
ACCESS ROAD: Primitive, 4x4-accessible only, and unsuitable for drivers with a fear of heights

MAP: *New Mexico Road & Recreation Atlas*, p. 42, F5
DIRECTIONS: From Tijeras, just east of Albuquerque, take NM 337 south for 28 miles. Turn right onto NM 55 headed west for 12 miles to the town of Manzano. Turn right onto FR 245. Drive 14 miles; the campground entrance will be on your right.

The view from Capilla Campground is simply spectacular. Many of the campsites look down on the Estancia valley, more than 3,000 feet below. Walk back to the campground entrance, and the Rio Grande valley rolls out some 4,300 feet below. Visitors are welcome to hike up to the Capilla Peak Lookout tower to enjoy 360-degree views of the surrounding valleys and peaks. If you go, be prepared for significant temperature drops, weather changes, and windy conditions on top of the 9,368-foot mountain. Across the road from the campground lies the Manzano Wilderness and access to the Crest Trail. Be advised that no bikes or motorized vehicles are allowed within designated wilderness areas.

Photographers can capture dramatic vistas or document the myriad wildflowers that bloom all summer here. Since the Manzano Mountains loom above a high-desert environment, you have the advantage of seeing through amazingly clear air. This is Big Sky Country.

Most sites are occupied during summer weekends. The sites are well spaced, providing a good degree of privacy. Plenty of trees and Adirondack shelters provide decent shade, and tent campers should take advantage of the shelters against strong, year-round winds. After a recent renovation, every site is wheelchair-accessible and fitted with grills, picnic tables, and new vault toilets. Some sites have rebuilt shelters based on the original CCC designs. No drinking water is available.

No reservations. **Mountainair Ranger District, 505-847-2990.**

HawkWatch

*Ever wanted to see eagles, hawks, and kestrels up close? HawkWatch International pro-*vides that chance at two research stations in New Mexico, one in the Manzano Mountains and one in the Sandias. Dedicated to studying, banding, and counting migrating raptors across the West, HawkWatch also provides environmental education and interpretation to visitors. The Manzano site at Capilla Peak operates Aug. 15–Nov. 5 and the Sandia site Feb. 24–May 5, weather permitting (visit www.hawkwatch.org).

To reach Capilla Peak, take I-40 east from Albuquerque to Exit 175. At Tijeras go straight at the stoplight onto NM 337. Drive south about 28 miles, then turn right onto NM 55 west about 12 miles to Manzano. Turn right onto FR 245 and drive about 9 miles to the Capilla Peak Campground entrance. Park about 200 yards before Fire Tower Road and hike west across the meadow to an unmarked trail that follows the ridge northwest to the observation site.

To reach the Sandia site take I-40 to the Carnuel exit. Go east on NM 333 (old US 66) about 1.8 miles and turn left into Monticello. Follow the paved road and turn left onto Allegre. Take the second right and follow the street to a trailhead parking lot. Hike the Three Gun Spring Trail through the boundary fence. Continue until you see a sign for the HawkWatch Trail. The total distance is 1.5 miles—and 1,000 feet of elevation gain.

12 MANZANO MOUNTAINS STATE PARK

Salinas Pueblo Missions and Manzanos base camp

SCENERY: ★★★
RVs: ★★★★
TENTS: ★★★★★
SHADE: ★★★
PRIVACY: ★★
FACILITIES: ★★★★
CAMPGROUND ACTIVITIES: ★★★
AREA ACTIVITIES: ★★★★
WHEELCHAIR ACCESSIBILITY: ★★★

LOCATION: 4 miles south of Manzano
ELEVATION: 7,600 feet
NUMBER OF SITES: 37; overflow areas available
RV NOTES: No maximum length; there are 8 electric sites, and the dump station is at the entrance to the loop road
FEE: Yes
SEASON: April–October, including Easter weekend if it falls in March

NEAREST SUPPLY CENTER: Mountainair
ACCESS ROAD: Paved
MAP: *New Mexico Road & Recreation Atlas*, p. 42, F5
DIRECTIONS: From Tijeras, just east of Albuquerque, take NM 337 south for about 28 miles. Turn right onto NM 55, heading west for about 12 miles to the town of Manzano. Turn right onto FR 253 and travel for about 2.6 miles. You will see the park entrance in front of you.

Set in the shade of juniper and piñon trees, this popular park offers a comfortable base camp for exploring the Manzano Mountains as well as the Salinas Pueblo Missions National Monument. The closest ruins, Quarai, lie only 1.8 miles from the campground. The trailheads for Box Canyon and Red Canyon are less than 6 miles away. Within the park lie multiple short trails. The small visitor center offers information about local wildlife, geology, and historical and cultural attractions. A checklist for raptor watching is usually available from the visitor center. Fishing is often possible in a small lake near the center of the town of Manzano.

The camp is laid out in a main loop, with a separate section in the southwest corner for group camping. Each campsite has a pad, picnic table, and grill, and some have shelters. Sites on the right side of the loop road are a bit more private than those in the center. If all spots are filled, there is an overflow area. Water spigots are scattered throughout the campground. The gated group section has 20 campsites and a large shelter, with four fixed tables, large grills, and a water hydrant. The area can accommodate up to 150 people.

Wheelchair-accessible areas include the picnic sites, one newly refurbished campsite, the group camping area, and restrooms, which also have running water.

Reservations are recommended: 877-664-7787 or www.icampnm.com. **Park Ranger Station, 505-847-2820.**

SALINAS PUEBLO MISSIONS NATIONAL MONUMENT

In the 17th century, Spanish missionaries settled at the southern end of the Manzano Mountains for two reasons: to convert nearby pueblo inhabitants to Christianity and to take advantage of the local salt lakes. By the 1670s, both the Native Americans and the Spanish had abandoned the area, leaving the spectacular ruins of their massive mission churches. The national monument is spread out over three sites: Quarai, Abó, and Gran Quivira, radiating north, west, and south, respectively, of the town of Mountainair and park headquarters. Each of the ruin sites has a visitor center. The Quarai site is the closest to the Manzano-region campgrounds. To get to Quarai from Tijeras, just east of Albuquerque, take NM 337 south for about 28 miles. Turn

Ruins of the early 17th-century church Nuestra Señora de La Purisima Concepción de Cuarac, at Quarai

right onto NM 55 headed west for about 12 miles to the town of Manzano. The entrance to the park is a few miles farther, on the right.

13 RED CANYON

Trailheads and horseback riding through forested canyons

LOCATION: 5 miles southwest of Manzano
ELEVATION: 7,700 feet
NUMBER OF SITES: 50; no overflow area
RV NOTES: 40 feet maximum length
FEE: Yes
SEASON: April–November
NEAREST SUPPLY CENTER: Mountainair
ACCESS ROAD: Fair-weather; call ahead for conditions
MAP: *New Mexico Road & Recreation Atlas*, p. 42, F5

SCENERY: ★★★	
RVS: ★★	
TENTS: ★★★	
SHADE: ★★★★★	
PRIVACY: ★★★	
FACILITIES: ★★★	
CAMPGROUND ACTIVITIES: ★★	
AREA ACTIVITIES: ★★★	
WHEELCHAIR ACCESSIBILITY: ★★	

DIRECTIONS: From Tijeras, just east of Albuquerque, take NM 337 south for about 28 miles. Turn right onto NM 55, heading west for about 12 miles to the town of Manzano. Turn right onto FR 253 and travel for about 5 miles to the campground entrance, on the right.

Red Canyon provides access into Manzano Wilderness via the Red Canyon, Spruce Spring, and Box Canyon Trails, either on foot or horseback. Be advised that bikes and motorized vehicles are not permitted in the wilderness. Red Canyon is also a good base camp for exploring the Salinas Pueblo Missions National Monument.

Equipped with picnic tables and grills, campsites are usually available, and the vault toilets are wheelchair-accessible. The upper camp area is set up around horse corrals for equestrian camping. A group area consists of a cluster of campsites around a central gathering place with pedestal grills and a pit fire ring. No drinking water is available.

No reservations. **Mountainair Ranger District, 505-847-2990.**

14 ISLETA LAKES
Fishing and golf

LOCATION: 11.8 miles south from the intersection of I-40 and I-25 in Albuquerque
ELEVATION: 5,000 feet
NUMBER OF SITES: 40
RV NOTES: No maximum length; sites have gravel pads and hookups for water and electric; there is a central dump station
FEE: Yes
SEASON: Year-round
NEAREST SUPPLY CENTER: Albuquerque
ACCESS ROAD: Paved to campground, then dirt
MAP: *New Mexico Road & Recreation Atlas*, p. 42, E4
DIRECTIONS: From Exit 215 on I-25, go south on NM 47. The entrance to the Isleta Lakes Recreation Area will be on your right.

SCENERY: ★★
RVS: ★★★★
TENTS: ★★★
SHADE: ★★
PRIVACY: ★★
FACILITIES: ★★★★★
CAMPGROUND ACTIVITIES: ★★★
AREA ACTIVITIES: ★★★★★
WHEELCHAIR ACCESSIBILITY: ★★★

Located on the Isleta Reservation, this campground is large and conveniently situated for exploring Albuquerque. If you plan to visit Acoma, Laguna, or other points west along I-40 with Isleta as your starting point, try driving south on I-25 to Los Lunas and take the scenic NM 6 heading northwest. You'll pass through a landscape full of mesas and drive parallel to one of the busiest rail lines in the Southwest.

Fishing in the small lakes is a popular activity. Sites are scattered under cottonwoods and in open, graveled areas. The campground also has a store and showers, and drinking water is available. Isleta Pueblo's golf course and casino are a short drive away.

No reservations. **Isleta Lakes Recreation Area, 505-877-0370.**

Claret cup cactus

SOUTHERN SANGRE DE CRISTOS

North of Santa Fe, the Sangre de Cristo Mountains dominate the landscape. On the west side of the southern Sangres lie many Rio Grande pueblos and old Spanish towns, like Las Trampas and Truchas, that define the scenic High Road to Taos (see p. 63). To the east, the mighty mountains soften into rolling plains, land that the Santa Fe Trail once crossed. The legendary Pecos River begins high in these peaks, cutting a deep canyon as it flows past the Pecos National Historical Park. Hiking and equestrian adventures await in the Pecos Wilderness. Campgrounds are found along virtually every road penetrating the mountains.

Nambe Falls Recreation Area includes views of the Sangre de Cristo Range

Area Campgrounds

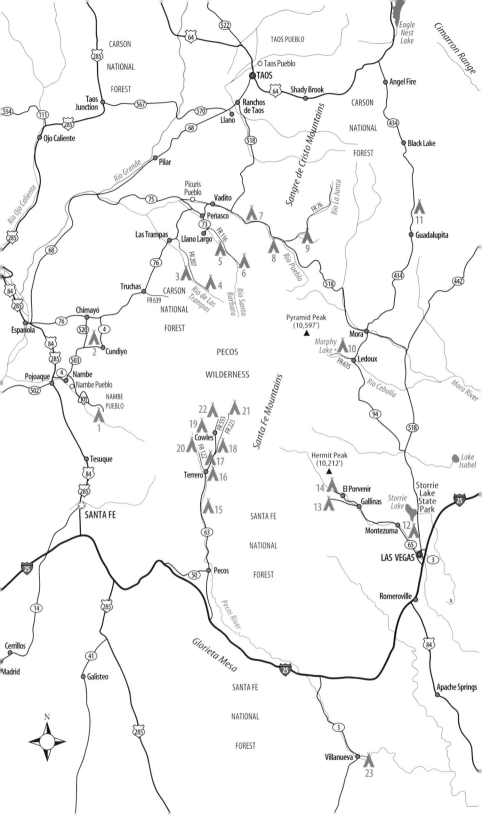

1 NAMBE FALLS RECREATION AREA

Sacred waters and mountain views

LOCATION: 5 miles southeast of Nambe
ELEVATION: 6,500 feet
NUMBER OF SITES: Dispersed
RV NOTES: Small- to medium-sized RVs can fit in the camping areas just beyond the entrance
FEE: Yes
SEASON: April–September
NEAREST SUPPLY CENTER: Pojoaque
ACCESS ROAD: Maintained gravel
MAP: *New Mexico Road & Recreation Atlas*, p. 37, G7
DIRECTIONS: From US 84/285, travel east on NM 4 for 2.6 miles. Bear right (southeast) onto Reservation Road 101 for about 5 miles to the recreation area.

SCENERY:	★★★★
RVs:	★
TENTS:	★★
SHADE:	★★★
PRIVACY:	★★★★
FACILITIES:	★
CAMPGROUND ACTIVITIES:	★★
AREA ACTIVITIES:	★★★★
WHEELCHAIR ACCESSIBILITY:	★

Set in the western foothills of the Sangre de Cristos, Nambe Pueblo invites visitors to hike and fish for rainbow and cutthroat trout in their beautiful lake. The campsites are scattered among piñon and juniper trees around the lake's edge. Visitors are also welcome to see the tribe's herd of buffalo.

Some sites are primitive, with just a fire ring, while others have picnic tables. No drinking water is available.

Closed sundown to sunrise. No reservations. **Nambe Falls, 505-455-2304.**

2 Santa Cruz Lake Recreation Area
Lake fishing and historic villages

Location: 2.5 miles north of Cundiyo
Elevation: 6,400 feet
Number of Sites: 58
RV Notes: No maximum length, but the access road has sharp turns
Fee: Yes
Season: Year-round, but may be inaccessible because of snow
Nearest Supply Center: Pojoaque
Access Road: Paved; not for those with a fear of heights
Map: *New Mexico Road & Recreation Atlas*, p. 37, F7
Directions: From US 285/84 in Pojoaque, take NM 4 east toward Nambe. In Nambe, NM 4 becomes NM 503. Follow NM 503 for about 11 miles. The entrance to the recreation area will be on your left.

Scenery:	★★★★★
RVs:	★★
Tents:	★★★
Shade:	★★★★
Privacy:	★★
Facilities:	★★★★
Campground Activities:	★★
Area Activities:	★★★
Wheelchair Accessibility:	★★

Driving to Santa Cruz Lake Recreation Area, you will pass through the Nambe Indian Reservation, rugged canyons, verdant valleys, and towns that have existed since the original Spanish settlers. One of the nearby villages, Chimayó, is home to the Santuário de Chimayó, a small church famous for producing miracles.

Seeing Santa Cruz Lake for the first time is a bit of a surprise. It sits at the bottom of a gorge bordered by Sangre de Cristo foothills on one side and a sheer granite wall on the other. The clear blue water is a haven for anglers and families looking for a cool getaway.

Campers can choose from lakeside camping in the North Lake area or go with the spectacular vistas of the Overlook area, perched hundreds of feet above the lake with a clear view of the Sangre de Cristos and the water. Photographers, note that the granite wall opposite the North Lake campground gets morning sun, while the Sangres are lit by afternoon sun.

Summer weekends can be very busy. **North Lake** is a loop offering sites with shelters, tables, grills, and fire rings; drinking water is available. If North Lake is full, try **Overlook**, which also has sites with tables, grills, and fire rings; some sites have shelters. Restrooms are wheelchair-accessible. Reservations not required. **BLM Taos Office, 505-758-8851.**

3 TRAMPAS DIAMANTE

Forested sites near stream fishing

LOCATION: 5.75 miles southeast of Las Trampas
ELEVATION: 8,700 feet
NUMBER OF SITES: 5
RV NOTES: 16 feet maximum length
FEE: No
SEASON: Year-round, but may be inaccessible because of snow
NEAREST SUPPLY CENTER: Peñasco
ACCESS ROAD: Fair-weather; call ahead for conditions
MAP: *New Mexico Road & Recreation Atlas*, p. 37, E8
DIRECTIONS: From Peñasco, take NM 76 south for about 5 miles. Turn left onto FR 207. Drive 5.75 miles and the campground will be on the right.

SCENERY: ★★★	
RVs: ★	
TENTS: ★★	
SHADE: ★★★	
PRIVACY: ★★★	
FACILITIES: ★	
CAMPGROUND ACTIVITIES: ★★	
AREA ACTIVITIES: ★★★	
WHEELCHAIR ACCESSIBILITY: ★	

Popular as a fishing spot, this simple campground sits adjacent to the Rio de las Trampas in a broad, forested ravine just below the forest road.

The Trampas Trailhead sits a few miles farther up the road. The historic Spanish towns of Truchas, Las Trampas, and Chimayó are a short drive away.

Sites have picnic tables and fire rings. There is one toilet but no drinking water.

No reservations. **Camino Real Ranger District, 505-587-2255.**

4 TRAMPAS TRAILHEAD

Pecos Wilderness access

LOCATION: 8 miles southeast of Las Trampas
ELEVATION: 9,000 feet
NUMBER OF SITES: 4
RV NOTES: 16 feet maximum length, but RVs may have difficulty moving in the parking area during summer peak times
FEE: No
SEASON: Year-round, but may be inaccessible because of snow
NEAREST SUPPLY CENTER: Peñasco
ACCESS ROAD: Fair-weather; call ahead for conditions
MAP: *New Mexico Road & Recreation Atlas*, p. 37, F8
DIRECTIONS: From Peñasco, take NM 76 south for about 5 miles. Turn left onto FR 207 and drive about 8 miles; the campground is at the end of the road.

SCENERY: ★★★
RVs: ★
TENTS: ★★
SHADE: ★★★★
PRIVACY: ★
FACILITIES: ★
CAMPGROUND ACTIVITIES: ★★
AREA ACTIVITIES: ★★
WHEELCHAIR ACCESSIBILITY: ★

The campground is at a very popular trailhead for accessing the Pecos Wilderness. The sites show heavy use and occasional abuse but are well shaded below large pines. Visitors are welcome to fish in the adjacent Rio de las Trampas. On summer weekends, hikers' vehicles can crowd the area. Trampas Diamante is an overflow option.

Campsites include some picnic tables and fire rings. There are toilets but no drinking water.

No reservations. **Camino Real Ranger District, 505-587-2255.**

Aspens in the Pecos Wilderness

5 HODGES

Verdant pastures and primitive camping

SCENERY: ★★★★
RVs: ★
TENTS: ★★
SHADE: ★★★
PRIVACY: ★★★★★
FACILITIES: ★
CAMPGROUND ACTIVITIES: ★★
AREA ACTIVITIES: ★★★
WHEELCHAIR ACCESSIBILITY: ★

LOCATION: 3.2 miles southeast of Llano Largo
ELEVATION: 8,200 feet
NUMBER OF SITES: Dispersed

RV NOTES: 22 feet maximum length
FEE: No
SEASON: Year-round, but may be inaccessible because of snow
NEAREST SUPPLY CENTER: Peñasco
ACCESS ROAD: Fair-weather; call ahead for conditions
MAP: *New Mexico Road & Recreation Atlas*, p. 37, E8
DIRECTIONS: From Peñasco, take NM 73 south for about 1.5 miles. Turn left onto FR 116 and travel about 3.5 miles. At the fork in the road, go right, cross over the cattle guard, and turn right again. Hodges Campground will be down a dirt road on the right.

Hodges offers a primitive camping experience in the lush, green valley of the Rio Santa Barbara, nestled in the foothills along the Sangre de Cristos' west face. The campground is popular with anglers and large groups that want to be able to spread out but still have privacy. To get to the campground's one toilet from the campground entrance, continue straight on the access road rather than turning right and crossing the little bridge. To find a site, look for the scattered fire rings. There is no drinking water.

No reservations. **Camino Real Ranger District, 505-587-2255.**

SCENIC DRIVE: THE HIGH ROAD TO TAOS

This drive takes you back in time to New Mexico's Spanish colonial period and through present-day Native American pueblo communities. From Pojoaque Pueblo on US 84/285, head east on NM 503 through the Nambe Pueblo and follow the road north as it winds through an almost Martian landscape of gulleys and spires eroded out of red and beige rock.

Turn left onto NM 520 leading to the Santuário de Chimayó, a little mission church famous for its miraculous healing dirt. Keep following NM 520 through green valleys until you can turn right onto NM 76, heading east.

At Truchas, you may want to veer off of NM 76 for a detour through the center of town and up into the mountains as far as your vehicle will take you on FR 639, a road that becomes progressively rougher. You will see historic adobe architecture, artist studios, and ranches as the road winds up into the Sangre de Cristos.

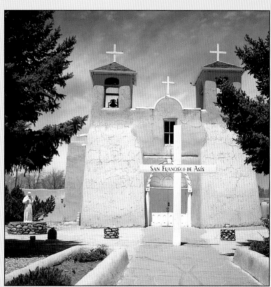

San Francisco de Asis Church, Ranchos de Taos

Once you are back at the junction with NM 76, continue north into the Carson National Forest. The village of Las Trampas has a beautiful mission church with a plaza that has barely changed in the last century. The road meanders through pine forests until the landscape opens up into the lush valley of the Rio Santa Barbara, the heart of the Picuris Pueblo. The Picuris artisans are world-renowned for their mica pottery. Head east on NM 75 until you reach NM 518, then head north. You will find a number of pullouts suitable for gazing upon the 13,000-foot peaks that rise above Taos. The High Road ends in Ranchos de Taos, home of the San Francisco de Asis Mission Church, perhaps the most painted and photographed church in the state.

6 SANTA BARBARA

Aspens and popular Pecos Wilderness Trailhead

LOCATION: 5.7 miles southeast of Llano Largo
ELEVATION: 8,900 feet
NUMBER OF SITES: 20
RV NOTES: 32 feet maximum length
FEE: Yes
SEASON: May–October
NEAREST SUPPLY CENTER: Peñasco
ACCESS ROAD: Fair-weather; call ahead for conditions
MAP: *New Mexico Road & Recreation Atlas*, p. 37, E8
DIRECTIONS: From Peñasco, take NM 73 south for about 1.5 miles. Turn left onto FR 116 and travel about 6 miles. The campground is at the end of the road.

SCENERY: ★★★★
RVs: ★★
TENTS: ★★★
SHADE: ★★★★
PRIVACY: ★★★
FACILITIES: ★★★
CAMPGROUND ACTIVITIES: ★★
AREA ACTIVITIES: ★★
WHEELCHAIR ACCESSIBILITY: ★★★

Newly renovated, Santa Barbara is a popular site for accessing the northern end of the Pecos Wilderness on foot or horseback via Trail #24 along the Middle Fork of the Rio Santa Barbara. Anglers also enjoy the fishing here.

Campsites are usually available, but parking may be difficult on summer weekends and holidays, since this is popular trailhead for backpackers. The campground has drinking water, toilets, picnic tables, grills, and horse corrals. One campsite and a vault toilet are wheelchair-accessible. There are two group areas: the larger has five picnic tables with two grills, and the smaller has three tables and one grill.

Reservations not accepted. **Camino Real Ranger District, 505-587-2255.**

7 COMALES

Roadside camping and special trout waters

LOCATION: 5.6 miles southeast of Vadito
ELEVATION: 7,900 feet
NUMBER OF SITES: 13
RV NOTES: 22 feet maximum length; campground roads are rough
FEE: Yes
SEASON: Year-round, but may be snow-covered in winter
NEAREST SUPPLY CENTER: Peñasco
ACCESS ROAD: Paved to campground
MAP: *New Mexico Road & Recreation Atlas*, p. 37, E8
DIRECTIONS: From Vadito, travel 5.6 miles southeast on NM 518. The campground is on the left.

SCENERY: ★★★
RVs: ★
TENTS: ★★
SHADE: ★
PRIVACY: ★★
FACILITIES: ★★
CAMPGROUND ACTIVITIES: ★★
AREA ACTIVITIES: ★★★
WHEELCHAIR ACCESSIBILITY: ★

Set alongside the special trout waters of the Rio Pueblo in front of a dramatic rock wall, this is an easy-to-access fishing spot. The dirt roads through this campground are rough and the area well-used. Several of the sites overlook the river below. Access the nearby Cañon Tio Maes Trail #5 and Comales Canyon Trail #22.

The accommodations are primitive, offering tables, fire rings, and a toilet but no drinking water.

No reservations. **Camino Real Ranger District, 505-587-2255.**

FISHING NEW MEXICO

New Mexico is a major destination for anglers. Like most states, New Mexico has rules guiding all fishing activities. Anyone over the age of 12 needs a valid fishing license for all locations; in addition, different bodies of water have different regulations. Designated Special Trout Waters, such as the 1-mile stretch at Comales Campground, require the use of single, barbless hooks and have strict bag-limit and lure rules. Official Youth, Seniors, and Handicapped Waters, such as one of the ponds at Cowles, dot the landscape. Detailed rules also govern activities in winter trout and summer catfish waters such as Oasis State Park and Carrizozo Lake. The New Mexico Department of Game and Fish website at www.gmfsh.state.nm.us has complete rules and regulations, or call 800-862-9310.

Also note that Indian reservations have their own respective fishing regulations distinct from the state's, so call the appropriate tribal office before setting out to fish at those campgrounds and recreation areas.

8 AGUA PIEDRA

Trails and trout fishing in a forested canyon

LOCATION: 10.25 miles southeast of Vadito
ELEVATION: 8,400 feet
NUMBER OF SITES: 40
RV NOTES: 32 feet maximum length, but there are no RV facilities
FEE: Yes
SEASON: May–October
NEAREST SUPPLY CENTER: Peñasco
ACCESS ROAD: Paved
MAP: *New Mexico Road & Recreation Atlas*, p. 37, E8
DIRECTIONS: From Vadito, travel 10.25 miles southeast on NM 518. The campground is on the right.

SCENERY: ★★★
RVs: ★★
TENTS: ★★★★
SHADE: ★★★
PRIVACY: ★★★
FACILITIES: ★★★★
CAMPGROUND ACTIVITIES: ★★★
AREA ACTIVITIES: ★★★
WHEELCHAIR ACCESSIBILITY: ★★

Sitting on the hillsides above the trout-filled waters of the Rio Pueblo, Agua Piedra offers universal-access fishing. Venture into the Carson National Forest on horseback or foot via the Agua Piedra/Serpent Lake Trail #19 and Cordova Canyon Trail #17. Horse corrals are available nearby.

Campsites, which are usually obtainable, have picnic tables and fire rings. There is drinking water. Four of the campsites, plus the toilets and fishing access, are wheelchair-accessible. A group area for day use is also at hand.

Reservations not accepted. **Camino Real Ranger District, 505-587-2255.**

9 LA JUNTA CANYON

Riverside camping in a forested canyon

SCENERY: ★★★★
RVS: ★★
TENTS: ★★★★
SHADE: ★★★
PRIVACY: ★★★
FACILITIES: ★★★★
CAMPGROUND ACTIVITIES: ★★★
AREA ACTIVITIES: ★★★
WHEELCHAIR ACCESSIBILITY: ★

LOCATION: 22 miles south of Ranchos de Taos
ELEVATION: 9,000 feet

NUMBER OF SITES: 20

RV NOTES: RVs up to 30 feet can access sites in the Duran area; RVs up to 16 feet can fit at Upper La Junta but are not recommended

FEE: Yes

SEASON: Year-round, but may be inaccessible because of snow

NEAREST SUPPLY CENTER: Peñasco

ACCESS ROAD: Dirt; maintained year-round

MAP: *New Mexico Road & Recreation Atlas*, p. 37 (E,8)

DIRECTIONS: From Ranchos de Taos, travel south on NM 518 and southeast on NM 518 for 22 miles and turn north (left) onto FR 76. The Duran campsites are scattered along the right side of the road. The Upper La Junta campground is 6.2 miles down FR 76.

Generally quiet and rustic, the campsites line the banks of Duran Creek and Rito de la Presa in a forested canyon. The **Duran** area sites offer large, private spaces for camping; most sites provide picnic tables and fire rings. Many sites also adjoin meadows perfect for group activities—but watch out for cow pies. The trailheads for La Cueva Lake Trail #8 and the Duran/Policarpio Trail #13 are in the campground. **Upper La Junta** spaces are closer together but still provide a good degree of privacy, along with picnic tables and fire rings.

Summer weekends are the busiest times, and the area is a favorite for ATVers. There are four toilets stationed throughout the canyon. Drinking water is available at a pump about 3 miles into the canyon. No wheelchair-accessible facilities are available.

Reservations for Duran at 877-444-6777 or ReserveUSA.com. **Camino Real Ranger District, 505-587-2255.**

10 MORPHY LAKE STATE PARK
A little lake with a mountain-peak view

LOCATION: 2.7 miles northwest of Ledoux
ELEVATION: 7,900 feet
NUMBER OF SITES: 20
RV NOTES: 20 feet maximum length; rough, narrow access road can be muddy
FEE: Yes
SEASON: Year-round, but may be inaccessible because of snow
NEAREST SUPPLY CENTER: Mora
ACCESS ROAD: Rough, fair-weather; call ahead for conditions
MAP: *New Mexico Road & Recreation Atlas,* p. 37, F9
DIRECTIONS: From Mora, drive 7 miles south on NM 94. Turn right onto FR 635 and travel about 4 miles to the park entrance.

SCENERY: ★★★★★
RVs: ★★
TENTS: ★★★★
SHADE: ★★★★
PRIVACY: ★★★
FACILITIES: ★★★★
CAMPGROUND ACTIVITIES: ★
AREA ACTIVITIES: ★★★
WHEELCHAIR ACCESSIBILITY: ★★

Morphy Lake is a hidden jewel in the foothills of the Sangre de Cristos. Fish for trout while gazing on Pyramid Peak in the distance (photographers, note that it gets morning sun). The park is a bit tough to get to given the condition of the access road, but it is worth the drive, passing old villages with picturesque adobe structures. A high-clearance, 4x4 vehicle is best. Summer weekends and holidays are very busy.

The campsites wrap around the lake. All developed sites have picnic tables and grills, and some have shelters. No drinking water is available. There are wheelchair-accessible vault toilets and a boat ramp for launching small, no-wake boats. Primitive, tent-only sites lie under the pines to the left as you enter the campground.

Reservations at 877-664-7787 or www.icampnm.com. **Park Manager, 505-387-2328.**

11 COYOTE CREEK STATE PARK

Fishing, creekside strolls, and birdwatching

LOCATION: 2.6 miles north of Guadalupita
ELEVATION: 7,800 feet
NUMBER OF SITES: 47
RV NOTES: 38 feet maximum length; the dump station lies to the right before the visitor center, down the road and across the creek
FEE: Yes
SEASON: May–October
NEAREST SUPPLY CENTER: Mora
ACCESS ROAD: Paved to campground
MAP: *New Mexico Road & Recreation Atlas*, p. 37, E10
DIRECTIONS: From Mora, drive north for 17 miles on NM 434 to the campground.

SCENERY: ★★★★
RVs: ★★★★★
TENTS: ★★★★
SHADE: ★★★
PRIVACY: ★★★
FACILITIES: ★★★★★
CAMPGROUND ACTIVITIES: ★★★
AREA ACTIVITIES: ★★
WHEELCHAIR ACCESSIBILITY: ★★★★

Streamside in the eastern Sangre de Cristo foothills, Coyote Creek Campground provides beautiful sites with decent privacy. Wander 1.5 miles of nature trails and keep an eye out for beavers, birds, and coyotes. Fish in one of the most densely stocked waters in New Mexico. The campground is an RV- and family-camping favorite. Reservations are recommended for hookup sites.

The visitor center, which also houses the showers, is just inside the gate. The 17 electric hookup sites are in a loop just past the visitor center. There is a group shelter and an RV dump station, along with restrooms, showers, drinking water, a pay phone, and a playground. Facilities are all wheelchair-accessible, including an interpretive trail.

Reservations at 877-664-7787 or www.icampnm.com. **Park Manager**, 505-387-2328.

12 STORRIE LAKE STATE PARK

Windsurfing, fishing, and a Wild West town

LOCATION: 4 miles north of Las Vegas
ELEVATION: 6,600 feet
NUMBER OF SITES: 45
RV NOTES: 40 feet maximum length; the hookup sites have pull-thrus
FEE: Yes
SEASON: Year-round
NEAREST SUPPLY CENTER: Las Vegas
ACCESS ROAD: Paved
MAP: *New Mexico Road & Recreation Atlas*, p. 37, H10
DIRECTIONS: From Exit 345 on I-25 in Las Vegas, head north on NM 518. Travel for 4 miles to the park.

SCENERY: ★★★	
RVs: ★★★★	
TENTS: ★★★	
SHADE: ★★★	
PRIVACY: ★★★	
FACILITIES: ★★★★★	
CAMPGROUND ACTIVITIES: ★★★	
AREA ACTIVITIES: ★★★★	
WHEELCHAIR ACCESSIBILITY: ★★★★★	

Windsurf or sail on blue waters that meld into the rolling grasslands outside Las Vegas, New Mexico. The foothills of the Sangre de Cristos serve as the backdrop for this lovely park. Fish along the quiet shoreline or from a boat in the no-wake lake. Storrie Lake State Park is a nice place to relax. Or use it as a base camp for exploring the Pecos Wilderness or the once infamous Wild West town of Las Vegas—stopping point for the likes of Wyatt Earp, Doc Holliday, and Billy the Kid, as well as for travelers crossing the Santa Fe Trail. This campground is also a comfortable stopover for travelers on I-25.

The campground stretches along the edge of the lake. Holiday weekends are usually very busy. All facilities are wheelchair-accessible, including the group area, boat ramp, fishing access, and an interpretive trail. All sites have tables and grills. Drinking water, phones, and a playground are also available. The sites with water and electric hookups are in a loop to the left of the campground entrance. To the right of the entrance are sites with no hookups, although many have shelters. Primitive camping is available around the edge of the lake past the hookup loop.

Hours are 6 a.m.–sunset from April to September, and 7 a.m.–sunset from October to March.

Reservations at 877-664-7787 or www.icampnm.com. **Park Manager, 505-425-7278.**

13 E.V. Long
Streamside camping

Location: 4.2 miles northwest of Gallinas
Elevation: 7,400 feet
Number of Sites: 21
RV Notes: Small RVs only
Fee: Yes
Season: May–November
Nearest Supply Center: Las Vegas
Access Road: Paved; not for those with a fear of heights
Map: *New Mexico Road & Recreation Atlas*, p. 37, G9

Scenery: ★★★	
RVs: ★	
Tents: ★★★	
Shade: ★★★★	
Privacy: ★★★★	
Facilities: ★★	
Campground Activities: ★★	
Area Activities: ★★	
Wheelchair Accessibility: ★	

Directions: From Exit 343 on I-25 in Las Vegas, drive north on NM 65 toward Montezuma and the Armand Hammer United World College. After 1.8 miles, you come to the junction with NM 3. Keep going straight on NM 65 for 12.2 miles. Veer left at the fork in the road and you will see the entrance to E.V. Long on the right.

A small streamside campground, E.V. Long offers angling and access to trailheads close by that lead into the Pecos Wilderness, including the trail to Hermit Peak, which begins in nearby El Porvenir Campground. Sites at E.V. Long are well-spaced, and most are separated by stands of trees. A few open areas are large enough to accommodate larger groups. The drive to the campground takes you through the historical town of Las Vegas, past Montezuma Castle (today part of the Armand Hammer United World College of the American West), and up a narrow, winding road through old Spanish ranching villages. Drinking water is available.

No reservations. **Pecos Ranger Station, 505-757-6121.**

14 EL PORVENIR

Trailhead to Hermit Peak

LOCATION: 5.5 miles northwest of Gallinas
ELEVATION: 7,500 feet
NUMBER OF SITES: 13
RV NOTES: Small RVs only
FEE: Yes
SEASON: May–November 15
NEAREST SUPPLY CENTER: Las Vegas
ACCESS ROAD: Paved
MAP: *New Mexico Road & Recreation Atlas,* p. 37, G9

SCENERY: ★★★	
RVs: ★	
TENTS: ★★★	
SHADE: ★★★★★	
PRIVACY: ★★★★	
FACILITIES: ★	
CAMPGROUND ACTIVITIES: ★★	
AREA ACTIVITIES: ★★	
WHEELCHAIR ACCESSIBILITY: ★	

DIRECTIONS: From Exit 343 on I-25 in Las Vegas, drive north on NM 65 toward Montezuma and the Armand Hammer United World College. After 1.8 miles, you come to the junction with NM 3. Keep going straight on NM 65 for 12.2 miles. Veer right at the fork in the road and drive 2.5 miles to the campground.

This small loop of campsites sits high up in forests along the edge of the Pecos Wilderness. The setting is rustic and well-shaded below tall pines. Drinking water is available, and sites sport picnic tables and grills. The campground has one pit toilet. Trail #223, just outside the campground entrance, leads to Hermit Peak, named for a missionary who lived in a cave near the mountaintop.

No reservations. **Pecos Ranger Station, 505-757-6121.**

15 FIELD TRACT

Secluded fishing and Pecos base camp

LOCATION: 9 miles north of Pecos
ELEVATION: 7,400 feet
NUMBER OF SITES: 14
RV NOTES: No maximum length
FEE: Yes
SEASON: May–November 15
NEAREST SUPPLY CENTER: Pecos
ACCESS ROAD: Paved

SCENERY: ★★★	
RVs: ★★	
TENTS: ★★★	
SHADE: ★★★★	
PRIVACY: ★★★	
FACILITIES: ★★★	
CAMPGROUND ACTIVITIES: ★★	
AREA ACTIVITIES: ★★★★★	
WHEELCHAIR ACCESSIBILITY: ★★★	

MAP: *New Mexico Road & Recreation Atlas,*
p. 37, H8
DIRECTIONS: From Pecos, drive north 9 miles on NM 63. The campground
will be on the right.

Field Tract offers comfortable access to the excellent fishing in the Pecos River. Tree-ringed sites, a few with Adirondack shelters, wrap around a small glade. Drinking water is available. The river is separated from the campground by a narrow band of brush and trees, providing secluded fishing opportunities.

This is also a nice base camp for exploring the nearby Pecos National Historical Park, the historic town of Pecos, and the Glorieta Pass Civil War Battlefield, as well as hikes along the variety of area trails that head into the Pecos Wilderness.

No reservations. **Pecos Ranger Station, 505-757-6121**.

16 BERT CLANCY WILDLIFE AREA

Fishing in the Pecos

LOCATION: 13.3 miles north of Pecos
ELEVATION: 7,600 feet
NUMBER OF SITES: Dispersed
RV NOTES: No maximum length
FEE: No
SEASON: Year-round, but may be snow-covered in winter
NEAREST SUPPLY CENTER: Pecos
ACCESS ROAD: Rough, fair-weather; call ahead for conditions
MAP: *New Mexico Road & Recreation Atlas*, p. 37, G8
DIRECTIONS: From Pecos, drive north on NM 63 for about 13.3 miles to a fork in the road with a bridge, and turn right. The entrance to the area is just past the bridge.

SCENERY: ★★
RVs: ★
TENTS: ★★
SHADE: ★
PRIVACY: ★
FACILITIES: ★★★
CAMPGROUND ACTIVITIES: ★★
AREA ACTIVITIES: ★★★
WHEELCHAIR ACCESSIBILITY: ★

This is a well-used spot for large groups to enjoy fishing in the Pecos River. The facilities are primitive, but campers are able to spread out along the river's edge. There are a handful of picnic tables and vault toilets. No drinking water is available, but a country store, complete with horses for hire, lies right across the river.

No reservations. **Department of Game and Fish, NE Area, 505-445-2311.**

17 LINKS TRACT

Secluded primitive group area

LOCATION: 15.8 miles north of Pecos
ELEVATION: 8,600 feet
NUMBER OF SITES: Dispersed
RV NOTES: No maximum length
FEE: No
SEASON: Year-round, but may be inaccessible because of snow
NEAREST SUPPLY CENTER: Pecos
ACCESS ROAD: Rough, fair-weather; call ahead for conditions; the road north of Terrero is not for those with a fear of heights
MAP: *New Mexico Road & Recreation Atlas*, p. 37, G8
DIRECTIONS: From Pecos, drive north on NM 63 for about 14.5 miles. Turn right at the sign for the campground, which may be still labeled "Davis Willow," about 1.3 miles up the forest road.

SCENERY: ★★★★	
RVs: ★	
TENTS: ★★	
SHADE: ★★	
PRIVACY: ★★★★	
FACILITIES: ★	
CAMPGROUND ACTIVITIES: ★	
AREA ACTIVITIES: ★★★★	
WHEELCHAIR ACCESSIBILITY: ★	

Links Tract is a primitive camping environment offering wonderful views of the surrounding mountains and plenty of space for large or small groups looking for privacy. There is one pit toilet. No drinking water is available.

No reservations. **Pecos Ranger Station, 505-757-6121**.

18 MORA

Two rivers run through it

SCENERY: ★★★
RVs: ★
TENTS: ★★
SHADE: ★★★★
PRIVACY: ★
FACILITIES: ★
CAMPGROUND ACTIVITIES: ★★
AREA ACTIVITIES: ★★★★★
WHEELCHAIR ACCESSIBILITY: ★

LOCATION: 16.5 miles north of Pecos
ELEVATION: 7,900 feet
NUMBER OF SITES: Dispersed
RV NOTES: No maximum length
FEE: No
SEASON: Year-round, but may be inaccessible because of snow
NEAREST SUPPLY CENTER: Pecos
ACCESS ROAD: Paved; the road beyond Terrero is not for those with a fear of heights
MAP: *New Mexico Road & Recreation Atlas*, p. 37, G8
DIRECTIONS: From Pecos, drive north on NM 63 for about 16.5 miles.

An extremely popular campground for fishing enthusiasts, Mora sits where the Pecos and Mora rivers converge. The campground is divided by NM 63. The sites along the Pecos, single file between the river and the road, are set farther apart than those across the road adjacent to the Mora River. The campground and the areas just to the north and south show very heavy use with large, well-trampled dirt expanses. Please be sure to camp *only* in designated sites, which are those with picnic tables. There is a pit toilet. No drinking water is available.

No reservations. **Pecos Ranger Station, 505-757-6121.**

19 COWLES

Creekside camping with Adirondack shelters

LOCATION: 19.5 miles north of Pecos
ELEVATION: 8,200 feet
NUMBER OF SITES: 6
RV NOTES: All sites are walk-ins
FEE: Yes
SEASON: May–November
NEAREST SUPPLY CENTER: Pecos
ACCESS ROAD: Paved; the road beyond
Terrero is not for those with a fear of heights
MAP: *New Mexico Road & Recreation Atlas*, p. 37, G8
DIRECTIONS: Drive 19.5 miles north from Pecos on NM 63, then turn left at
the bridge. You'll see the Adirondack shelters in front of you on the left.

SCENERY: ★★★★
RVs: NR
TENTS: ★★★★★
SHADE: ★★★★★
PRIVACY: ★★★
FACILITIES: ★★★
CAMPGROUND ACTIVITIES: ★★
AREA ACTIVITIES: ★★★★★
WHEELCHAIR ACCESSIBILITY: ★

Laid out next to a small meadow and a babbling brook, Cowles is a nice
campground for accessing nearby trailheads and getting in a little fishing in
the ponds a few hundred yards away. From the ponds, enjoy the marvelous
view up the river toward the high peaks of the Pecos Wilderness. There are
six walk-in sites with Adirondack shelters, picnic tables, and grills. A toilet
is in the camp but no drinking water is available. Expect to arrive on Thursday
if you want a site on a summer weekend.

No reservations. **Pecos Ranger Station, 505-757-6121.**

20 HOLY GHOST

Pecos Wilderness Trailhead and creekside camping

LOCATION: 15.6 miles north of Pecos
ELEVATION: 8,400 feet
NUMBER OF SITES: 25
RV NOTES: 32 feet maximum length
FEE: Yes
SEASON: May–November 15
NEAREST SUPPLY CENTER: Pecos
ACCESS ROAD: Dirt; call ahead for conditions; the road beyond Terrero is not for those with a fear of heights

SCENERY: ★★★★	
RVs: ★	
TENTS: ★★★	
SHADE: ★★★	
PRIVACY: ★★★	
FACILITIES: ★	
CAMPGROUND ACTIVITIES: ★★	
AREA ACTIVITIES: ★★★★★	
WHEELCHAIR ACCESSIBILITY: ★	

MAP: *New Mexico Road & Recreation Atlas*, p. 37, G8
DIRECTIONS: From Pecos, drive north on NM 63 for about 13.3 miles to a fork in the road with a bridge. Turn left onto FR 122 along Holy Ghost Creek, and travel 2.3 miles to the campground, past the cluster of houses to the end of the road.

Holy Ghost is a popular, scenic campground and drop-off point for hiking into the Pecos Wilderness and fishing in Holy Ghost Creek. The area lies in a meadow surrounded by dense forest. Sites are spaced along the creek, offering a degree of privacy and the lull of running water. The camp has picnic tables, fire rings, and toilets. Drinking water is available.

Reservations for groups at 877-444-6777. **Pecos Ranger Station, 505-757-6121.**

21 IRON GATE

4x4 access to the edge of the Pecos Wilderness

LOCATION: 23 miles north of Pecos
ELEVATION: 9,400 feet
NUMBER OF SITES: 6
RV NOTES: Not recommended
FEE: Yes
SEASON: May–November 15
NEAREST SUPPLY CENTER: Pecos
ACCESS ROAD: Very rough, fair-weather; high-clearance, 4x4 vehicles recommended; not for those with a fear of heights
MAP: *New Mexico Road & Recreation Atlas*, p. 37, G8
DIRECTIONS: From Pecos drive north on NM 63 for about 20 miles, then turn right onto FR 223. Follow FR 223 for about 3 miles to the campground.

SCENERY: ★★★★
RVs: NR
TENTS: ★★★
SHADE: ★★★★
PRIVACY: ★★★
FACILITIES: ★★
CAMPGROUND ACTIVITIES: ★
AREA ACTIVITIES: ★★★
WHEELCHAIR ACCESSIBILITY: ★

Home to a popular trailhead, hikers and horseback riders use Iron Gate as their starting point for adventures in the Pecos Wilderness. Half of the fun of Iron Gate is the drive in: the rough, dirt road winds past remote ranches and summer homes, offering marvelous vistas of the Pecos Mountains with their beautiful stands of aspens. But, unless you have a high-clearance 4x4 that can take on all roads, call the Pecos Ranger Station before committing to the drive.

The six developed sites can be full most summer weekends. Horse corrals are available, but there is no drinking water here.

No reservations. **Pecos Ranger Station, 505-757-6121.**

22 JACK'S CREEK

Trailheads and Pecos Wilderness splendor

LOCATION: 22 miles north of Pecos
ELEVATION: 8,400 feet
NUMBER OF SITES: 46, plus 2 group areas
RV NOTES: No maximum length, but there are no hookups or dump station
FEE: Yes
SEASON: May–October
NEAREST SUPPLY CENTER: Pecos
ACCESS ROAD: Paved; not for those with a fear of heights

SCENERY: ★★★★★
RVs: ★★
TENTS: ★★★
SHADE: ★★★
PRIVACY: ★★★★
FACILITIES: ★★★
CAMPGROUND ACTIVITIES: ★★★
AREA ACTIVITIES: ★★★★★
WHEELCHAIR ACCESSIBILITY: ★★★

MAP: *New Mexico Road & Recreation Atlas*, p. 37, G8
DIRECTIONS: From Pecos, drive about 18.5 miles north on NM 63 to Cowles. FR 555 branches off to the right; follow it for 3.5 miles to the campground.

If mountain views are what you're after, then Jack's Creek is your destination. Set high in the Sangre de Cristos next to the Pecos Wilderness, the campground contains multiple trailheads as well as a very large equestrian camping area complete with horse corrals and sites large enough to accommodate large trailers and multiple vehicles. Recently renovated, the facilities are in nice condition and well-spaced to provide sufficient privacy. Sites ring large, grassy areas. Holiday weekends are very busy.

The two group areas provide paved parking, tables, fire rings, grills, and water, and accommodate 30–40 people each. Group Area B is wheelchair-accessible, as are the restrooms and some campsites.

The equestrian area, immediately to your right as you enter the campground, comes complete with adjacent horse corrals as well as toilets, fire rings, and picnic tables. To access the individual-sites area, take the road straight in front of you as you enter the campground. Sites have fire rings, grills, and tables. Drinking water is available.

Reservations for groups at 877-444-6777 or ReserveUSA.com. **Pecos Ranger Station, 505-757-6121.**

23 Villanueva State Park
Coronado's trail and canyon fishing

LOCATION: 1 mile east of Villanueva
ELEVATION: 5,600 feet
NUMBER OF SITES: 34
RV NOTES: 40 feet maximum length; there are 12 electric sites, a dump station, and centrally located water along the riverside sites
FEE: Yes
SEASON: Year-round
NEAREST SUPPLY CENTER: Pecos or Las Vegas
ACCESS ROAD: Paved
MAP: *New Mexico Road & Recreation Atlas*, p. 43, C9
Directions: From Las Vegas, take I-25 south for 23 miles to Exit 323. Go south for 15 miles on NM 3. In the town of Villanueva, look for the park's sign. The access road veers off to the left.

SCENERY: ★★★★★
RVS: ★★★★
TENTS: ★★★
SHADE: ★★★
PRIVACY: ★★★
FACILITIES: ★★★★★
CAMPGROUND ACTIVITIES: ★★★
AREA ACTIVITIES: ★★
WHEELCHAIR ACCESSIBILITY: ★★★

History abounds in beautiful, and very popluar, Villanueva State Park. Once a rest stop along the trail Francisco Vasquez de Coronado followed in 1540 as he explored the land that was to become New Mexico, the park and the nearby town of Villanueva provide a glimpse into the state's colonial past. Also within the grounds are ruins of prehistoric Native American structures. The campground is divided into two primary sections: the sites along the Pecos River, perfect for RVs and hardcore anglers, and El Cerro Upper Campground, also called the Overlook, ideal for tent camping and those looking for privacy and stunning views of the red cliff walls that line

the river. The park includes a visitor center as well as a variety of short hiking trails. Interpretive talks take place throughout the year; call ahead for details. The visitor center, picnic areas, restrooms, showers, playground, and, in fair weather, riverbank fishing are all wheelchair-accessible.

Riverside sites have electric hookups and are near showers, a playground, and a dump station. El Cerro Upper Campground is mainly for tent camping; since the access road is very steep and rocky, RVs are not recommended. Each site has a table, grill, and fire ring; some have shelters. The group shelter accommodates 75 people and has six large tables, a patio area with two large grills, and a water fountain; reservations are required.

Drinking water is available, but bring your own firewood and fishing licenses. Call ahead for fire restrictions in midsummer. Holiday and summer weekends can be very busy.

Open 7 a.m.–9 p.m. in summer; 7 a.m.–7 p.m. in winter. Reservations at 877-664-7787 or www.icampnm.com. **Park Manager, 505-421-2957.**

THE ENCHANTED CIRCLE

The Enchanted Circle describes the magical, mountainous region ringed by roads that begin and end in Taos. Contained within are New Mexico's tallest peak at 13,161 feet, Mount Wheeler, and several other mountains in this part of the Sangre de Cristo Range that top 12,000 feet. To the west, the Rio Grande Gorge splits the earth as much as 800 feet deep in places. Whitewater enthusiasts come to challenge the river in the Taos Box segment of the Rio Grande. A little farther west beyond the gorge are the extreme southern end of the San Juan Mountains and the Cruces Basin Wilderness. Just north of the Circle is the lush Valle Vidal area, an excellent location for spotting elk, black bears, and other large, wild creatures. To the east of the Circle, the Santa Fe Trail once passed through the Wild West town of Cimarron. The Taos Ski Valley takes visitors deep into the mountains and provides access to a multitude of trail-heads for paths crisscrossing the Wheeler Peak Wilderness and the Columbine-Hondo Wilderness Study Area. Visitors are welcome in the world-renowned Taos Pueblo, nestled below Pueblo Peak.

Red River Gorge at Wild Rivers Recreation Area

Area Campgrounds

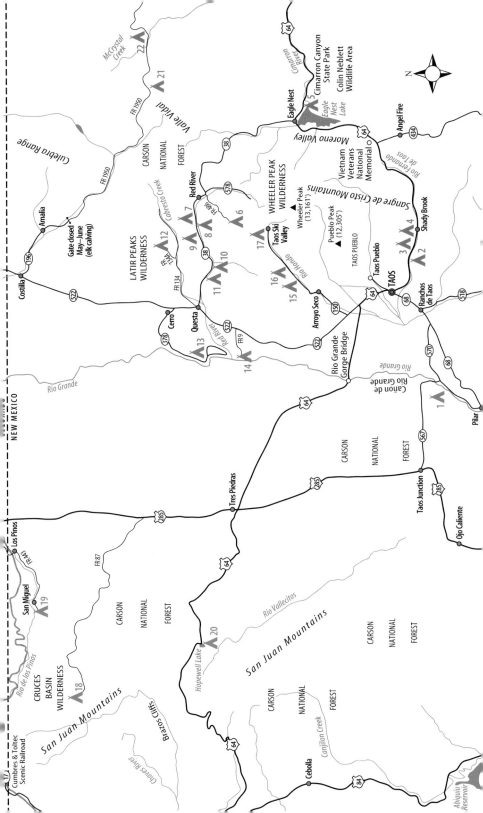

1 ORILLA VERDE RECREATION AREA

Canyon views, whitewater, and fishing

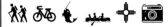

LOCATION: 1.5 miles north of Pilar
ELEVATION: 6,000 feet
NUMBER OF SITES: 37 plus 2 group
RV NOTES: No maximum length; the renovated Pilar area, just inside the recreation area, has the electric sites
FEE: Yes
SEASON: Year-round, but may be inaccessible because of snow
NEAREST SUPPLY CENTER: Ranchos de Taos
ACCESS ROAD: Fair-weather; call ahead for conditions
MAP: *New Mexico Road & Recreation Atlas*, p. 37, D7
DIRECTIONS: From Pilar on NM 68, head north on NM 570 for 2.5 miles to the park.

SCENERY:	★★★★★
RVs:	★★
TENTS:	★★★
SHADE:	★★★
PRIVACY:	★★★★
FACILITIES:	★★★
CAMPGROUND ACTIVITIES:	★★★★
AREA ACTIVITIES:	★★★★★
WHEELCHAIR ACCESSIBILITY:	★★★

The Wild and Scenic Rio Grande cuts through the Orilla Verde Recreation Area in spectacular fashion. Running through a gorge up to 800 feet deep, the river attracts rafters and kayakers craving whitewater runs, and the north end of this park is a popular put-in. Fly fishermen flock to Orilla Verde as well, taking advantage of waters teeming with native brown trout, German brown trout, rainbow trout, and northern pike. Because of the variety of

The Enchanted Circle 87

ecosystems that exist between the river bottom and the plains above, the gorge is home to a vast array of creatures: raptors, songbirds, waterfowl, beavers, cougars, ringtails, and mule deer. Near the entrance to the recreation area, on NM 68 at Pilar, is the Rio Grande Gorge visitor center. Campsites, which are usually available, vary from secluded riverside spots to a larger campground set on an outcrop above the river. Visitors can hike the 2.5-mile round-trip La Vista Verde Trail past archaeological sites. The park road lends itself to mountain biking.

RIO GRANDE GORGE BRIDGE

Built in 1965, the Rio Grande Gorge Bridge crosses the Wild and Scenic Rio Grande flowing at an average of 650 feet below, 800 feet at its deepest. It is the second highest suspension bridge in the nation and spans about 500 feet in length. View the canyon below, the Sangre de Cristo Mountains towering above Taos, and the rolling plains above the river. If you have a fear of heights, you may not want to visit, let alone walk out onto, the observation decks. To reach the bridge from Taos, drive north and west for about 12 miles on US 64.

Orilla Verde Recreation Area visitors can take a roundabout route to their destination from the west for a final view of the gorge, south of the bridge, that makes crossing miles and miles of high-desert scrub worthwhile. (Acrophobics will probably want to skip this route, too.) From Tres Piedras, take US 285 south for 20.5 miles and turn left onto NM 567. From Ojo Caliente, drive north on US 285 for 10.8 miles, then turn right onto NM 567.

Parts of the recreation area were renovated in 2003. **Pilar** is now geared toward RVs, with 10 electric and water hookups. **Rio Bravo** has nine tent-pad sites with small shelters, fire rings, and tables, as well as showers and a group shelter accommodating 30. **Arroyo Hondo** sits in a sandy riverbank area providing primitive sites, a vault toilet, and some shelters. **Lone Juniper** is another primitive area with five sites and a vault toilet; a boat ramp is being added. **Petaca** is primitive as well, with five or six sites, two vault toilets, and running water. **Taos Junction** has developed individual sites, primitive sites, a 50-person shelter, flush toilets, and hydrants.

Rio Pueblo is a very primitive, pack-in/pack-out area. To get there, follow the main campground road to the bridge. Cross the bridge, take the primitive road to the right, and follow the road to the Horseshoe Overlook. Look for the fire rings.

Reservations available for group sites at 505-758-8851. **Rio Grande Gorge Visitor Center, 505-751-4899.**

2 LAS PETACAS
Shady fishing spot

LOCATION: 4.2 miles southeast of Taos
ELEVATION: 7,400 feet
NUMBER OF SITES: 8
RV NOTES: Campers up to 16 feet can fit
FEE: Yes
SEASON: May–October
NEAREST SUPPLY CENTER: Taos
ACCESS ROAD: Paved
MAP: *New Mexico Road & Recreation Atlas*, p. 37, D8
DIRECTIONS: From NM 68 in Taos, take US 64 east for 4.2 miles to the campground.

SCENERY:	★★
RVS:	★
TENTS:	★★★
SHADE:	★★★★
PRIVACY:	★★
FACILITIES:	★★
CAMPGROUND ACTIVITIES:	★★
AREA ACTIVITIES:	★★★★★
WHEELCHAIR ACCESSIBILITY:	★

As the closest campground to Taos Plaza, Las Petacas can be a convenient overnight stop while exploring Taos and the Enchanted Circle. There is access to the Rio Fernando de Taos for fishing, and numerous trailheads are within a short drive. Sites are fairly well shaded but are within sight and earshot of US 64. Las Petacas's proximity to town can also be one of its drawbacks, since the campground can often be a popular evening spot for non-campers. No drinking water is available.

No reservations. **Camino Real Ranger District, 505-587-2255.**

3 La Sombra

Shady fishing spot

Location: 7 miles southeast of Taos
Elevation: 7,800 feet
Number of Sites: 12
RV Notes: Campers up to 16 feet can fit
Fee: Yes
Season: May–October
Nearest Supply Center: Taos
Access Road: Paved
Map: *New Mexico Road & Recreation Atlas,*
p. 37, D9
Directions: From NM 68 in Taos, take US 64
east for 7 miles to the campground.

Scenery: ★★
RVs: ★
Tents: ★★★
Shade: ★★★★
Privacy: ★★
Facilities: ★★
Campground Activities: ★★
Area Activities: ★★★★★
Wheelchair Accessibility: ★

La Sombra lies almost midway through Taos Canyon, also known as Fernandez Canyon. Nearby is the hamlet of Shady Brook, which is made up of a cluster of galleries and a motel. Several trails in Carson National Forest are within a few miles of the campground. Campers are welcome to fish in the Rio Fernando de Taos, which flows through the camp. The sites run parallel to US 64, only a few hundred feet away. La Sombra could be a convenient place to stop overnight while touring the Enchanted Circle. No drinking water is available.

No reservations. **Camino Real Ranger District, 505-587-2255.**

Scenic Drive: Enchanted Circle Scenic Byway

The Enchanted Circle describes a series of routes that begin and end in Taos, wrapping 84 miles around the northern end of New Mexico's southern Sangre de Cristos. If you begin the journey heading east out of Taos, US 64 takes you along the Rio Fernando de Taos through the Fernandez Canyon (also called Taos Canyon), climbing switchbacks up into ponderosa pine forests and over 9,101-foot Palo Flechado Pass. Just beyond the pass, the landscape opens up, revealing the vast meadows below Angel Fire; the beautiful, white Vietnam Veterans National Memorial is perched on a hillside to the left. Turn north on NM 38 at Eagle Nest and pass through the quaint little hamlet and beside its scenic lake. Continue on through the Moreno Valley, with views of Mount Wheeler and some of New Mexico's other tallest peaks touching the sky to the south. The next town you reach, the resort town of Red River, has a Wild West feel to it. Nearby is the junction with FR 486, which climbs to the stunning Goose Lake (see p. 94). Paralleling the flowing Red River out of the town, you will begin to descend, passing the Questa Molybdenum Mine. At Questa, you'll head south on NM 522, coming out of the canyons and high mountains and skirting the foothills of the Sangre de Cristos' west face. The plant life progressively reduces in stature, changing from predominantly piñon, juniper, and cedar forests to chamisa and rabbitbrush rangelands rolling out to the west as far as the eye can see. At the next stoplight, follow the signs for US 64 east back into Taos, winding past fields and public-access points of the famous Taos Pueblo. (If you visit the Taos Pueblo, note that visitor and camera fees help support the local economy.) The highway becomes the Taos main street, Paseo del Pueblo Norte, which will take you back to the historic Plaza.

4 CAPULIN
Waterfall trail and fishing

SCENERY: ★★
RVs: ★
TENTS: ★★★
SHADE: ★★★★
PRIVACY: ★★
FACILITIES: ★★
CAMPGROUND ACTIVITIES: ★★
AREA ACTIVITIES: ★★★★★
WHEELCHAIR ACCESSIBILITY: ★

LOCATION: 8 miles southeast of Taos
ELEVATION: 8,000 feet
NUMBER OF SITES: 12
RV NOTES: Campers up to 16 feet can fit
FEE: Yes
SEASON: May–October
NEAREST SUPPLY CENTER: Taos
ACCESS ROAD: Paved
MAP: *New Mexico Road & Recreation Atlas*, p. 37, D9
DIRECTIONS: From NM 68 in Taos, take US 64 east for 8 miles.

Only 8 miles from town, Capulin can be a convenient spot to stay for the night when exploring Taos and the Enchanted Circle. The campground stretches out between the Rio Fernando de Taos and US 64, with the highway dominating the soundscape. The trailhead to Ice Cave Waterfall starts in the camp, but don't expect a huge natural wonder at the trail's end. According to a forest ranger, the small waterfall turns into an ice column in the winter, but there's no real cave to speak of. Like Las Petacas, Capulin is occasionally an evening hangout for non-campers. There are picnic tables and grills but no drinking water. A couple of sites offer a fair amount of grassy space, enough to comfortably throw a ball or let the kids run.

No reservations. **Camino Real Ranger District, 505-587-2255.**

5 CIMARRON CANYON STATE PARK

Jagged cliffs, a running river, and lots of wildlife

LOCATION: 3 miles southeast of Eagle Nest

ELEVATION: 8,000 feet

NUMBER OF SITES: 88

RV NOTES: 35 feet maximum length; no dump station or other RV facilities are available

FEE: Yes

SEASON: Year-round, but may be inaccessible because of snow

NEAREST SUPPLY CENTER: Eagle Nest

ACCESS ROAD: Paved

MAP: *New Mexico Road & Recreation Atlas*, p. 37, C10

DIRECTIONS: From the junction of US 64 and NM 38, take US 64 3 miles east to the park.

Jagged, granite cliffs called The Palisades tower above the quick-flowing waters of the Cimarron River. Narrow marshes serve as home and watering hole to beavers, deer, elk, black bears, turkeys, and other wildlife. The river and a cluster of small lakes are well-stocked with brown and rainbow trout. Choose from four different hiking

SCENERY: ★★★★★
RVS: ★★★
TENTS: ★★★
SHADE: ★★★
PRIVACY: ★★★
FACILITIES: ★★★★
CAMPGROUND ACTIVITIES: ★★★★
AREA ACTIVITIES: ★★★★★
WHEELCHAIR ACCESSIBILITY: ★★★★

trails that originate in the park. Photograph the dramatic granite of the cliffs, running roughly east-west in the narrow canyon, around midday to capture adequate light. Bicycle from the park into the beautiful Moreno Valley. Visit the stirring Vietnam Veterans National Memorial near Angel Fire. Wander through historic Cimarron, once a major stop on the Santa Fe Trail. Bring horses and ride into the Colin Neblett Wildlife Area, the state's largest. Cimarron State Park is an outdoor enthusiast's dream.

Sites are usually available but vary in amenities; parking, picnic areas, and some campsites are wheelchair-accessible. **Tolby Creek** has paved driveways, tables, grills, and water hydrants; tents can be pitched in all sites. **Blackjack Tent Area** offers nicely secluded, dispersed campsites set in the woods along the river, with fire rings and picnic tables. **Maverick** is a very popular, tightly spaced area. Sites have picnic tables and fire rings with grills. Choose a lakefront spot only if you are willing to have people pass close to your site to go fishing. RV-friendly **Ponderosa** is a large, paved parking area ringed by sites. All of the camp areas except for Blackjack have drinking water and running water in the bathrooms.

Reservations at 877-664-7787 or www.icampnm.com. **Park Manager,** **505-377-6271.**

VIETNAM VETERANS NATIONAL MEMORIAL

Above Angel Fire gleams a white structure, keeping watch over the green valley below. From one angle, the building seems to resemble a dove in flight and from another seems to be a sail in the wind. However you look at it, it is a powerful monument. Built by a father to commemorate the life of the son he lost in

Vietnam, the memorial includes a chapel and visitor center. From Taos, take US 64 east toward Angel Fire for about 22 miles. The memorial is perched on a hill on the left.

6 GOOSE LAKE

4x4 adventure, hiking, and bighorn sheep

LOCATION: 9 miles southwest of Red River
ELEVATION: 11,600 feet
NUMBER OF SITES: Dispersed
RV NOTES: Do not attempt to drive an RV on FR 486
FEE: No
SEASON: June–September
NEAREST SUPPLY CENTER:
Red River
ACCESS ROAD: Very rough, fair-weather, and *only* accessible by high-clearance 4x4s
MAP: *New Mexico Road & Recreation Atlas*, p. 37, C9
DIRECTIONS: From the junction of NM 38 and NM 578, take NM 578 south for about 0.6 mile. Turn right onto FR 486 and travel 7 miles to the lake.

SCENERY: ★★★★★
RVs: NR
TENTS: ★
SHADE: ★★★★★
PRIVACY: ★★★★★
FACILITIES: ★
CAMPGROUND ACTIVITIES: ★★★
AREA ACTIVITIES: ★
WHEELCHAIR ACCESSIBILITY: ★

If you want to experience camping where the treeline ends and the tundra begins, *and* do it without backpacking in, Goose Lake provides the perfect opportunity. The little, crystal-clear lake lies at the base of a steep, rocky cliff wall, home to bighorn sheep; most of the year the cliff top is frosted with snow. To get a sheep's-eye view of the Sangres' tallest peaks, including 13,161-foot Mount Wheeler and 12,163-foot Fraser Mountain, walk the edge of the lake to the left and across Goose Lake Creek until you see a trail zigzagging up the cliff. Climb up that path to the top of the ridge, and I guarantee that both the view and the hike will take your breath away.

Ruins of a mining camp near Goose Lake

The campsites, all walk-ins, lie under tall pines a short distance from the lake. From the end of the road, which also serves as the parking area, walk past the outhouse and you will see scattered fire rings and well-packed spots where you can camp. No drinking water is available. Do not camp at the lake's edge.

A note about the access road: *Do not attempt to take anything less than a heavy-duty high-clearance vehicle* up the white-knuckle miles on FR 486 to Goose Lake. Even with the best of vehicles, the odds are that you will scrape bottom at least once. If you can handle the drive, the view will more than repay your efforts.

No reservations. **Questa Ranger District**, 505-586-0520.

A herd of elk above Goose Lake

A Visit to Goose Lake

Once on a late June evening I had a choice: drive up to Goose Lake and make sure I was in camp for sunrise, or choose another campground in the Red River area. Normally I would not have hesitated, but this campground was a little different. Just to get onto FR 486 leading to the lake, I had to ford a creek more than a foot deep. Storm clouds were gathering overhead, and the sun was setting. I took a deep breath, looked at Chaos, and said, "What's the worst that can happen?" I plunged into the creek.

The road surface on the other side was basically scree, with an occasional boulder peeking through the surface. In many cases the road edge was a sheer drop-off. Four-wheel low was the gear of choice. Since it was so late in the day, I only had to pass one Jeep tour group and, thankfully, the encounter occurred at an atypically wide spot. After I'd driven for almost an hour, a light rain began falling from the rapidly darkening sky. That's when I heard the thunk. My heart skipped a beat. I stopped the truck and slowly stepped out into the drizzle. A quick inspection found no holes, dents, or other sustained damage. I suspected a tire might be losing air, though—and changing a tire on this road could be tragic.

I wiped my face with the falling rain and figured I'd see how far I was from my destination and whether I'd be car-camping in the middle of a forest road. To my complete surprise, only a few hundred feet farther, hidden behind tall pines, lay the sublime Goose Lake itself, nestled at the base of a towering cliff face crowned by snowbanks. The tree line essentially ended at the lake's surface. My spirits revived; I drove the short distance to the campsite and hunkered down for the night, anxiously awaiting the morning.

In the predawn glow, I awoke to the sound of rocks falling down the cliff above the lake. Bighorn sheep were traversing the wall and dislodging rocks as they progressed.

To my great relief, my tire had not flattened overnight. Now I could explore this mountaintop oasis with my mind at ease.

The water was perfectly clear and reflected the cliffs above as the sun gradually illuminated the wall. Tundra shrubs, flowers, and grasses carpeted the ground adjacent to the lake. A trail zigzagged up a gentler section of the slope, which I felt compelled to climb. Hiking was tough given the oxygen-thin air at 12,000 feet, but a spectacular landscape emerged as the sun and I progressed higher. Toward the top the trail leveled out amid tiny tundra flowers and delicate mosses. The path became less distinguishable, marked only by cairns. Following the little stone piles, I was in awe of the landscape unfolding before me: mountaintop meadows complete with a herd of elk, and a view of the entire southern Sangre de Cristo Range. I just sat down and reveled in Mother Nature's splendor.

7 Junebug

Town of Red River and fishing

LOCATION: 1.5 miles west of Red River
ELEVATION: 8,600 feet
NUMBER OF SITES: 20
RV NOTES: 22 feet maximum length
FEE: Yes
SEASON: May–October
NEAREST SUPPLY CENTER: Red River
ACCESS ROAD: Paved
MAP: *New Mexico Road & Recreation Atlas*, p. 37, C9
DIRECTIONS: From Red River, travel 1.5 miles west on NM 38 to the campground.

SCENERY: ★★★
RVS: ★★
TENTS: ★★★
SHADE: ★★★
PRIVACY: ★★
FACILITIES: ★★★
CAMPGROUND ACTIVITIES: ★★★
AREA ACTIVITIES: ★★★★★
WHEELCHAIR ACCESSIBILITY: ★★★★★

Along with Fawn Lakes, Junebug is perhaps the most popular campground in the Red River resort area. Just outside the ski town of Red River, Junebug offers fishing in the river and easy access to activities and shopping. Arrive early to get a space, or try nearby campgrounds.

Facilities include tables, fire rings, and toilets. The parking pads are gravel. There are no hookups or dump station, but drinking water is available.

No reservations. **Questa Ranger District,** 505-586-0520.

8 ELEPHANT ROCK

Wheelchair-accessible fishing and trails

LOCATION: 2.2 miles west of Red River
ELEVATION: 8,600 feet
NUMBER OF SITES: 20
RV NOTES: 22 feet maximum length
FEE: Yes
SEASON: May–October
NEAREST SUPPLY CENTER: Red River
ACCESS ROAD: Paved
MAP: *New Mexico Road & Recreation Atlas*, p. 37, C9
DIRECTIONS: From Red River, travel 2.2 miles west on NM 38 to the campground.

SCENERY:	★★★
RVs:	★★
TENTS:	★★★
SHADE:	★★★
PRIVACY:	★★★★
FACILITIES:	★★★
CAMPGROUND ACTIVITIES:	★★★
AREA ACTIVITIES:	★★★★★
WHEELCHAIR ACCESSIBILITY:	★★★★★

Set along the Red River, Elephant Rock offers plenty of wheelchair-accessible amenities, including campsites, restrooms, trails, and proximity to the popular Fawn Lakes fishing area, which lies just across the highway. Campsites have tables and fire rings, and parking pads are gravel. Sites are attractively perched along a gently sloping hillside, and many have barriers that afford privacy. There are no hookups or dump station, but drinking water is available.

No reservations. **Questa Ranger District, 505-586-0520.**

9 Fawn Lakes

Wheelchair-accessible camping and trails

LOCATION: 3.2 miles west of Red River
ELEVATION: 8,450 feet
NUMBER OF SITES: 20
RV NOTES: 22 feet maximum length
FEE: Yes
SEASON: May–October
NEAREST SUPPLY CENTER: Red River
ACCESS ROAD: Paved
MAP: *New Mexico Road & Recreation Atlas*, p. 37, C9
DIRECTIONS: From Red River, travel 3.2 miles west on NM 38.

SCENERY: ★★★★
RVs: ★★
TENTS: ★★★
SHADE: ★★★
PRIVACY: ★★
FACILITIES: ★★★
CAMPGROUND ACTIVITIES: ★★★
AREA ACTIVITIES: ★★★★★
WHEELCHAIR ACCESSIBILITY: ★★★★★

This very popular riverside campground lures anglers from far and wide. Additionally, Fawn Lakes has many wheelchair-accessible facilities, including campsites, restrooms, trails, and the fishing area. Arrive early to get a space, or try nearby campgrounds. A short gravel path takes you from the campground to the lakes. Around the lake are pads that jut out into the water, with plenty of space for a chair and gear.

Campsites have tables and fire rings. The parking pads are gravel. There are no hookups or dump stations, but drinking water is available.

No reservations. **Questa Ranger District, 505-586-0520.**

10 COLUMBINE

Columbine-Twining National Recreation Trail and mining

LOCATION: 5 miles east of Questa
ELEVATION: 7,900 feet
NUMBER OF SITES: 20
RV NOTES: 22 feet maximum length
FEE: Yes
SEASON: May–October
NEAREST SUPPLY CENTER: Questa
ACCESS ROAD: Paved
MAP: *New Mexico Road & Recreation Atlas*,
p. 37, C8
DIRECTIONS: From Questa, travel 5 miles east on NM 38 to the campground.

SCENERY: ★★★
RVs: ★★
TENTS: ★★★
SHADE: ★★★
PRIVACY: ★★
FACILITIES: ★★★
CAMPGROUND ACTIVITIES: ★★
AREA ACTIVITIES: ★★★★★
WHEELCHAIR ACCESSIBILITY: ★★★

This campground accesses the Columbine-Twining National Recreation Trail, which enters the Wheeler Peak Wilderness and skirts the Columbine-Hondo Wilderness Study Area. Pick up the trailhead at the far end of the main loop, which runs clockwise through the camp.

Even though there are no real RV amenities except for nice gravel parking pads, Columbine is popular with RVers. Just to the left as you enter the campground, the RV section overlooks a dramatic rock wall but is quite close to NM 38. Tent sites are nestled among cottonwoods and pines; Columbine Creek winds through the campground. Just to the north of the campground along NM 38 is the Questa Molybdenum Mine.

The campground offers tables, fire rings, and toilets. The parking pads are gravel. There are no hookups or dump station, but drinking water is available.

No reservations. **Questa Ranger District, 505-586-0520**.

11 GOAT HILL

Primitive roadside accommodations

LOCATION: 3.5 miles east of Questa
ELEVATION: 7,500 feet
NUMBER OF SITES: 20
RV NOTES: 22 feet maximum length
FEE: Yes
SEASON: May–October
NEAREST SUPPLY CENTER: Questa
ACCESS ROAD: Paved
MAP: *New Mexico Road & Recreation Atlas*, p. 37, C8
DIRECTIONS: From Questa, travel 3.5 miles east on NM 38 to the campground.

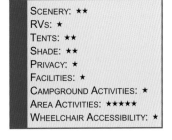

SCENERY: ★★
RVs: ★
TENTS: ★★
SHADE: ★★
PRIVACY: ★
FACILITIES: ★
CAMPGROUND ACTIVITIES: ★
AREA ACTIVITIES: ★★★★★
WHEELCHAIR ACCESSIBILITY: ★

Located just outside of Questa, Goat Hill is a bare-bones camping option. Providing only fire rings, a few picnic tables, and a toilet, the campground does offer the easiest of fishing access to the Red River, which flows right beside the campsites. The parking area and most of the campground surface is bare dirt. Drinking water is available.

No reservations. **Questa Ranger District, 505-586-0520.**

12 CABRESTO LAKE

Fishing, hiking, and a great 4x4 road

LOCATION: 7.6 miles northeast of Questa
ELEVATION: 9,200 feet
NUMBER OF SITES: 9
RV NOTES: Not recommended
FEE: No
SEASON: May–October
NEAREST SUPPLY CENTER: Questa
ACCESS ROAD: Very rough; accessible by high-clearance 4x4 only

MAP: *New Mexico Road & Recreation Atlas*, p. 37, B8
DIRECTIONS: Drive 5 miles northeast of Questa on FR 134, then continue 2 miles north on FR 134A to the campground.

SCENERY: ★★★★★
RVs: NR
TENTS: ★★
SHADE: ★★★★
PRIVACY: ★★★★
FACILITIES: ★
CAMPGROUND ACTIVITIES: ★★★
AREA ACTIVITIES: ★★★
WHEELCHAIR ACCESSIBILITY: ★

After driving 2 miles up one of the rockiest passable roads in the state, the little turquoise lake at the top is a beautiful surprise. Set in a high-mountain valley, the lake is surrounded by pine forests laced with aspens. The alpine Latir Peaks Wilderness surrounds you. Fork Lake Trail #82 begins in the camp. Fishing and nonmotorized boating are also draws. Taking a mountain bike down the forest road would also qualify as an adventure.

The facilities are primitive—just picnic tables, fire rings, and a toilet—but the sites are well-spaced. No drinking water is available.

No reservations. **Questa Ranger District, 505-586-0520.**

13 WILD RIVERS RECREATION AREA

Two canyons, whitewater, and hiking

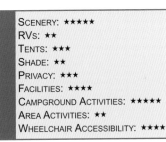

LOCATION: 8 miles west of Questa
ELEVATION: 7,460 feet
NUMBER OF SITES: 21 rim-area;
12 river's-edge, hike-in only
RV NOTES: 28 feet maximum length;
El Aguaje and Big Arsenic fit RVs best,
but there are no RV facilities
FEE: Yes
SEASON: Year-round, but may be
inaccessible because of snow
NEAREST SUPPLY CENTER: Questa
ACCESS ROAD: Fair-weather; call ahead for conditions
MAP: *New Mexico Road & Recreation Atlas*, p. 37, B8
DIRECTIONS: From Cerro just north of Questa on NM 522, take
NM 378 west. Travel for 10.8 miles to the park entrance.

SCENERY: ★★★★★
RVs: ★★
TENTS: ★★★
SHADE: ★★
PRIVACY: ★★★
FACILITIES: ★★★★
CAMPGROUND ACTIVITIES: ★★★★★
AREA ACTIVITIES: ★★
WHEELCHAIR ACCESSIBILITY: ★★★★

As you drive across a grassy plain with the mighty Sangre de Cristos in your rearview mirror, you come around a small hill and discover that a great chasm lies before you. The Wild Rivers Recreation Area sits on a narrow peninsula created by the confluence of the Rio Grande and the Red River

flowing 650 feet below. The area's name refers to the Wild and Scenic Rivers designation for 60 miles of the free-running Rio Grande from the Colorado border through the canyon, and for the lower 4 miles of the Red River. The campgrounds are perched along the edge of these great, breathtaking gorges.

Choose from hikes of varying lengths and degrees of difficulty to access the rivers below, or just stroll the paths that crisscross the flat park area. Raft the whitewater, or fish for northern pike, native brown trout, and German brown trout—assuming you're prepared to descend into the canyon and then climb out again. Bike or in-line skate on the paved, 4.5-mile loop road. Explore the exhibits and attend summer interpretive programs at the visitor center.

You might also come eye to eye with soaring red-tail hawks or photograph mule deer and prairie dogs. Photographers have options at all times of the day. In the late morning the Red River canyon bottom, because it runs northeast-southwest, gets light a little sooner than does the Rio Grande. The Sangre de Cristos lie to the east of the park and receive the light of the setting sun.

Wild Rivers has five developed campgrounds—**Big Arsenic Springs**, **Little Arsenic Springs**, **Montoso**, **La Junta**, and El Aguaje—each with tables, grills, drinking water, and restroom facilities. Sites are usually available. Twenty-one of the sheltered sites are scattered among the campgrounds on the mesa top. Twelve more sheltered campgrounds are along the river's edge, requiring you to pick a trail and hike down to access them. Wheelchair-accessible facilities include some sites, restrooms, trails, and the visitor center. The group shelter at La Junta fits 50 and the group shelter at El Aguaje fits up to 30.

Reservations for group areas at 505-758-8851. **Visitor Center, 505-770-1600.**

A view of the Rio Grande Gorge

14 CEBOLLA MESA

Gorge's edge camping

LOCATION: 8 miles southwest of Questa
ELEVATION: 7,200 feet
NUMBER OF SITES: 5
RV NOTES: 32 feet maximum length
FEE: No
SEASON: Year-round, but may be inaccessible because of snow
NEAREST SUPPLY CENTER: Questa
ACCESS ROAD: Fair-weather; call ahead for conditions
MAP: *New Mexico Road & Recreation Atlas*, p. 37, C8
DIRECTIONS: Take NM 522, 4.9 miles south from Questa to FR 9. Turn right (west) and drive 3.4 miles to campground.

SCENERY: ★★★★
RVs: ★
TENTS: ★★
SHADE: ★
PRIVACY: ★★★
FACILITIES: ★★
CAMPGROUND ACTIVITIES: ★★
AREA ACTIVITIES: ★
WHEELCHAIR ACCESSIBILITY: ★★

This Forest Service campground just south of the confluence of the free-running Rio Grande and Red River is in close proximity to the campgrounds of the BLM-administered Wild Rivers Recreation Area. Like those campgrounds, Cebolla Mesa is in a spectacular setting, but it's advisable to bring your own shade. Campsites are steps away from the rim of the Rio Grande Gorge; the river flows by some 650 feet or more below. Visitors can hike the mile-long Rio Grande Wild and Scenic River Trail #102 down to the water's edge at the bottom of the gorge. Anglers go to fish for northern pike, native brown trout, and German brown trout. Although the trail switchbacks as it descends, still make sure you can climb back up if you head down to fish.

No drinking water or facilities are available, so pack it in and pack it out.

No reservations. **Questa Ranger District, 505-586-0520.**

Blue yucca

15 LOWER HONDO

Taos Ski Valley camping and fishing

LOCATION: 11.7 miles north of Taos
ELEVATION: 7,850 feet
NUMBER OF SITES: 4
RV NOTES: 22 feet maximum length
FEE: No
SEASON: Year-round, but may be snow-covered in winter
NEAREST SUPPLY CENTER: Arroyo Seco
ACCESS ROAD: Paved

SCENERY: ★★	
RVS: ★	
TENTS: ★★	
SHADE: ★★★★	
PRIVACY: ★★★	
FACILITIES: ★	
CAMPGROUND ACTIVITIES: ★★	
AREA ACTIVITIES: ★★★★★	
WHEELCHAIR ACCESSIBILITY: ★	

MAP: *New Mexico Road & Recreation Atlas*, p. 37, C8
DIRECTIONS: From Taos Plaza, travel north 3 miles on US 64, then veer right onto NM 522 for another mile. Turn right onto NM 150 and drive north for 7.7 miles, passing through Arroyo Seco on the way, to the campground.

Lower Hondo is a convenient base camp for exploring Taos and Taos Ski Valley, fishing in the Rio Hondo, and accessing nearby trailheads that lead into the Wheeler Peak Wilderness and the Columbine-Hondo Wilderness Study Area. Sites are nestled below tall pines along the river's edge, which provide a bit of a barrier between the road and the campsites. No drinking water is available.

No reservations. **Questa Ranger District, 505-586-0520.**

SCENIC DRIVE: TAOS SKI VALLEY

This route takes you into the heart of the northern end of the southern Sangre de Cristos, right to the foot of New Mexico's tallest peak, Mount Wheeler (elevation 13,161 feet). The short journey passes through the quaint town of Arroyo Seco and ends at the resort, a cluster of hotels and restaurants that make up the town called Taos Ski Valley, at the base of the ski slopes. If you happen to reach the end during an early evening monsoon shower in late July or August, look up toward Mount Wheeler. You just may see a rainbow that will create a picture-perfect scene (see p. 109). (see p. 109) *From Taos Plaza, head north for 3 miles on US 64, then veer right onto NM 522 for another mile. Turn right onto NM 150 and follow the road through Arroyo Seco up into the valley about 15 miles to the end.*

16 CUCHILLO DE MEDIO

Taos Ski Valley camping and fishing

LOCATION: 13 miles north of Taos
ELEVATION: 8,050 feet
NUMBER OF SITES: 3
RV NOTES: 22 feet maximum length
FEE: No
SEASON: May–October
NEAREST SUPPLY CENTER: Arroyo Seco
ACCESS ROAD: Paved
MAP: *New Mexico Road & Recreation Atlas,* p. 37, C8

SCENERY: ★★
RVs: ★
TENTS: ★★
SHADE: ★★★★★
PRIVACY: ★★★★
FACILITIES: ★
CAMPGROUND ACTIVITIES: ★★
AREA ACTIVITIES: ★★★★★
WHEELCHAIR ACCESSIBILITY: ★

DIRECTIONS: From Taos Plaza, head north on US 64 for 3 miles, then veer right onto NM 522 for another mile. Turn right onto NM 150 and drive north for 9 miles, passing through Arroyo Seco, to the campground.

Like Lower Hondo, Cuchillo de Medio has sites, well-shaded under tall pines, scattered along the fishable Rio Hondo. Cuchillo's handful of walk-in sites allow campers to pitch their tents a bit farther from the road, allowing the rushing river to better drown out traffic noise. A number of trailheads leading into the Wheeler Peak Wilderness and the Columbine-Hondo Wilderness Study Area are nearby. Cuchillo can also be a nice base camp while exploring Taos. No drinking water is available.

No reservations. **Questa Ranger District, 505-586-0520.**

A view of the Columbine-Hondo Wilderness Study Area with Mount Wheeler in the distance

17 TWINING

Hiking heaven at the top of the ski valley

LOCATION: 19 miles north of Taos
ELEVATION: 9,400 feet
NUMBER OF SITES: 4; overflow available
RV NOTES: The parking area can fit any size RV, but the campsites are walk-ins
FEE: No
SEASON: Year-round, but may be snow-covered in winter
NEAREST SUPPLY CENTER: Arroyo Seco
ACCESS ROAD: Paved

SCENERY: ★★★★
RVS: ★
TENTS: ★★★
SHADE: ★★★★★
PRIVACY: ★★★
FACILITIES: ★
CAMPGROUND ACTIVITIES: ★★★
AREA ACTIVITIES: ★★★★★
WHEELCHAIR ACCESSIBILITY: ★

MAP: *New Mexico Road & Recreation Atlas*, p. 37, C9
DIRECTIONS: From Taos Plaza, head north on US 64 for 3 miles, then veer right onto NM 522 for another mile. Turn right onto NM 150 and drive north for 15 miles, through Arroyo Seco, to the campground.

The closest campground to Taos Ski Valley, Twining puts campers on the edge of hiking heaven. Lying below 13,161-foot Mount Wheeler, the highest point in the state, the campground is a terminus of the Columbine-Twining National Recreation Trail through the Wheeler Peak Wilderness and Columbine-Hondo Wilderness Study Area. In addition, you can access numerous trailheads: Wheeler Peak Trail #90, Williams Lake Trail #62, Bull of the Woods Pasture Road Trail #90, and Long Canyon Trail #63. Campers can also fish the Rio Hondo. The view to the south overlooks buildings and parking lots, but if you can look beyond the manmade, New Mexico's tallest peaks loom beyond. Photographers can shoot Mount Wheeler best in the evening sun.

Summer weekends and holidays are very popular. The campground provides grills, picnic tables, and toilets. No drinking water is available.

Reservations not accepted. **Questa Ranger District, 505-586-0520.**

18 LAGUNITAS

Fishing lakes and the Cruces Basin Wilderness

LOCATION: 25.5 miles southwest of San Antonio, Colorado
ELEVATION: 10,400 feet
NUMBER OF SITES: 12
RV NOTES: RVs not recommended
FEE: No
SEASON: May–October
NEAREST SUPPLY CENTER: Taos
ACCESS ROAD: Very primitive, fair-weather; high clearance 4x4 recommended

SCENERY: ★★★★★	
RVS: NR	
TENTS: ★★	
SHADE: ★★★★	
PRIVACY: ★★★★	
FACILITIES: ★	
CAMPGROUND ACTIVITIES: ★★★★	
AREA ACTIVITIES: ★★★★	
WHEELCHAIR ACCESSIBILITY: ★★★	

MAP: *New Mexico Road & Recreation Atlas*, p. 36, B5
DIRECTIONS: From Tres Piedras, go north on US 285 10 miles, turn left (west) on FR 87, and drive about 28 miles to the campground. Follow the signs to the upper area.

Nestled on the edge of the remote Las Cruces Basin Wilderness, Lagunitas' two small lakes are surrounded by rolling grasslands and aspen groves, which provide a great setting for secluded fishing. The campground is ringed by tall pines, and is convenient for trips into the wilderness on foot or horseback. The drive to the camp is also spectacular, passing solitary ranches and skirting the edges of deep valleys. You might see elk, deer, coyotes, or black bears. Hiking is fantastic, but bring your topo maps and compass—there are no designated trails through the wilderness. Mountain biking is also popular on the forest roads outside of the wilderness. Remember that bikes and motorized vehicles are not allowed in the wilderness area itself. Vault toilets have recently been installed. No drinking water is available.

Reservations not accepted. **Tres Piedras Ranger District**, 505-758-8678.

19 RIO DE LOS PINOS RECREATION AREA
Fishing and river beauty

LOCATION: 9.5 miles southwest of San Antonio, Colorado

ELEVATION: 8,550 feet

NUMBER OF SITES: 4 plus dispersed

RV NOTES: 28 feet maximum length

FEE: No

SEASON: May–September

NEAREST SUPPLY CENTER: Taos

ACCESS ROAD: Fair-weather; call ahead for conditions

MAP: *New Mexico Road & Recreation Atlas*, p. 36, A6

DIRECTIONS: From Tres Piedras, travel north on US 285 for 32 miles to San Antonio, Colorado. Turn left onto FR 443 heading southwest and travel for 15 miles to the recreation area, passing through the villages of Ortiz, Colorado, and Los Pinos and San Miguel on the New Mexico side.

SCENERY:	★★★★
RVs:	★
TENTS:	★★
SHADE:	★★★★★
PRIVACY:	★★★
FACILITIES:	★
CAMPGROUND ACTIVITIES:	★★
AREA ACTIVITIES:	★★
WHEELCHAIR ACCESSIBILITY:	★

The Rio de Los Pinos is a fishing paradise. The clear-running river flows past a handful of developed sites and plenty of dispersed camping spots. Wildlife teems below and above the river; you might see deer, coyotes, and a variety of birds during your visit. The relatively flat, well groomed dirt roads are perfect for leisurely bike rides.

A few sites have picnic tables, but most are primitive with just a fire ring. Vault toilets are available, but no drinking water is.

No reservations. **State Game and Fish Department**, 800-862-9310.

20 HOPEWELL LAKE

The heart of Carson National Forest

LOCATION: 19.1 miles west of Tres Piedras
ELEVATION: 9,750 feet
NUMBER OF SITES: 39
RV NOTES: No maximum but no facilities
FEE: Yes
SEASON: Year-round; may be snow-covered in winter
NEAREST SUPPLY CENTER: Taos
ACCESS ROAD: Paved
MAP: *New Mexico Road & Recreation Atlas*, p. 36, C6
DIRECTIONS: From Tres Piedras, drive 19.1 miles west on US 64.

SCENERY: ★★★★
RVs: ★★
TENTS: ★★★★★
SHADE: ★★
PRIVACY: ★★★
FACILITIES: ★★★
CAMPGROUND ACTIVITIES: ★★★
AREA ACTIVITIES: ★★★★★
WHEELCHAIR ACCESSIBILITY: ★★★

Constructed in 2002 and set high in the San Juan Mountains west of Taos, Hopewell Lake Campground actually lies on a forested hill above the lake without lake views. Sites shaded by pines and aspens are scattered along the edge of large meadows. After you turn onto the main access road, the first left leads down to the lakeside day-use area. Pass that turnoff to enter the campground. The area is full of trails, many of which are open for year-round exploration on foot or horseback. The lake is a popular fishing and no-wake boating location. No swimming is allowed in the lake.

Sites have tent pads, grills, and fire rings. Parking pads are level, packed gravel. Vault toilets and hydrants are centrally located. Vault toilets and campsite tables are wheelchair-accessible. Primitive tent camping is also available on the shore opposite the developed campground. Corrals and watering troughs are available for horses. Most summer weekends are very busy.

No reservations. **Tres Piedras Ranger District, 505-758-8678.**

21 CIMARRON

Pine forests, aspen groves, and wildlife

LOCATION: 23 miles southeast of Amalia
ELEVATION: 9,300 feet
NUMBER OF SITES: 32
RV NOTES: 22 feet maximum length
FEE: Yes
SEASON: May–November
NEAREST SUPPLY CENTER: Questa or Cimarron
ACCESS ROAD: Maintained gravel

SCENERY: ★★★★
RVs: ★★
TENTS: ★★★
SHADE: ★★★
PRIVACY: ★★★★
FACILITIES: ★★★
CAMPGROUND ACTIVITIES: ★★★
AREA ACTIVITIES: ★★★
WHEELCHAIR ACCESSIBILITY: ★★

MAP: *New Mexico Road & Recreation Atlas*, p. 37, B10
DIRECTIONS: From Costilla, travel east on NM 196 past Amalia to the junction with FR 1950. Take FR 1950 about 27.5 miles to FR 1910 and bear right into the camp. During elk calving season (May–June) the approach is via US 64 east of Cimarron onto FR 1950 through Cerrososo Canyon.

Set among tall pines high up in the Valle Verde section of the Carson National Forest, Cimarron Campground offers private sites, many with great views of mountains and aspens. Cimarron is popular both for equestrian activities and for hiking. Anglers can fish in the beautiful Shuree Ponds (above), accessed by a short drive to the west on FR 1950 or by a mile-long hike. The Ponds lie in a grassy valley ringed by aspens. The drive to the campground traverses spectacular canyon and high country.

Sites are usually available, though Cimarron is very busy during hunting season. Tables and fire rings are in each site, and some sites have horse facilities. The camp has vault toilets and drinking water. Some campsites are also wheelchair-accessible.

No reservations. **Questa Ranger District, 505-586-0520.**

22 McCrystal Creek

Pioneer cabin, meadow and mountain views

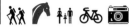

Location: 30 miles southeast of Amalia
Elevation: 8,100 feet
Number of Sites: 60
RV Notes: No maximum length, but there are no RV facilities
Fee: Yes
Season: May–October
Nearest Supply Center: Questa or Cimarron
Access Road: Maintained gravel

Scenery:	★★★★★
RVs:	★★
Tents:	★★★
Shade:	★★★★
Privacy:	★★
Facilities:	★★★★
Campground Activities:	★★★
Area Activities:	★★★
Wheelchair Accessibility:	★★★

Map: *New Mexico Road & Recreation Atlas*, p. 37, B10

Directions: From Costilla, travel east on NM 196 past Amalia to the junction with FR 1950. Take FR 1950 about 30 miles to FR 1910 and bear right into the camp. During elk calving season (May–June) the approach is via US 64 east of Cimarron onto FR 1950 through Cerrososo Canyon.

The view from McCrystal Creek is stunning. Located high in the Valle Vidal region of the Carson National Forest, the campground overlooks an idyllic pasture, complete with running brook and 9,000-foot peaks in the distance. The drive to McCrystal Creek is rewarding from either approach. From the west, wind through the canyon of Costilla Creek, then climb up into aspen country. From the east, you pass through rangeland in Cerrososo Canyon as you gain elevation. Fishing at nearby Shuree Ponds, hiking, and horseback riding are the main attractions here, as well as hunting in season. There are plenty of forest roads for mountain biking. A self-guided trail to a pioneer cabin starts at the campground entrance.

Sites, which are usually available, are well-spaced and have tables and fire rings with grills. Six campsites are available for horse campers. Toilets, some campsites, and the interpretive trail are wheelchair-accessible. Drinking water is available.

Reservations not required. **Questa Ranger District, 505-586-0520.**

THE JEMEZ

Northwest of Albuquerque, the Jemez (pronounced *HAY-mus*) Mountains encircle a massive volcanic crater called the Valles Caldera. The vast, lush valleys within and surrounding the crater are now a national preserve and home to herds of elk. The approach into the Jemez from the southwest takes visitors through the Jemez Pueblo and a canyon lined with dramatic red cliffs. The town of Jemez Springs beckons guests to soak in the public baths, fed by the hot springs prevalent throughout the Jemez. The San Pedro Parks Wilderness spreads out over the northwest corner of the range. Bandelier National Monument, famous for its Ancestral Puebloan cliff dwellings, lies to the southeast.

Jemez River near Vista Linda Campground

Los Alamos introduced the world to the Jemez without trying, as word spread after World War II about the home of the first atomic bomb. The Pueblos of San Juan, Santa Clara, Pojoaque, San Ildefonso, Cochiti, Santo Domingo, and San Felipe line the Rio Grande in the eastern foothills of the Jemez. Santa Ana, Zia, and Jemez Pueblos line the Jemez River, which feeds into the Rio Grande from the west.

Area Campgrounds

1 Paliza

CCC camp and mountain biking

> SCENERY: ★★★
> RVS: ★★
> TENTS: ★★★★
> SHADE: ★★★★★
> PRIVACY: ★★★
> FACILITIES: ★★★
> CAMPGROUND ACTIVITIES: ★★
> AREA ACTIVITIES: ★★★★★
> WHEELCHAIR ACCESSIBILITY: ★★★

LOCATION: 5 miles northeast of Ponderosa via FR 10
ELEVATION: 6,850 feet
NUMBER OF SITES: 25, plus 2 group
RV NOTES: 32 feet maximum length
FEE: Yes
SEASON: May–October

NEAREST SUPPLY CENTER: Jemez Springs
ACCESS ROAD: Fair-weather; call ahead for conditions
MAP: *New Mexico Road & Recreation Atlas*, p. 36, G4
DIRECTIONS: From San Ysidro, drive 6 miles north on NM 4. Turn right onto NM 290, which becomes FR 10, and travel for 8.5 miles to the campground.

Paliza occupies an area shaded by pines not far from the Jemez Pueblo. This family campground was once a Civilian Conservation Corps camp, and their distinctive Adirondack shelters are still in use today. Recent renovations have added to the campground picnic tables, fire rings, and toilets, and several sites were made into doubles with three tables and parking space for two trailers. Parking pads were also enlarged to better accommodate RVs. Drinking water is available.

You'll encounter **Paliza Group** just before the family area. Look for the little sign on the access road. Each of two loops has a covered pavilion. The larger area has a stage and more room for RVs. The smaller loop offers walk-in tent camping. Other group amenities include water, a volleyball court, and horseshoe pits. The group sites are by reservation only.

The access road (FR 266) continues past the campground all the way to the Kasha-Katuwe Tent Rocks (see p. 35). This route is accessible only by mountain bike or 4x4. Call the ranger station for details.

Reservations for groups at 877-444-6777. **Jemez Ranger District, 505-829-3535.**

2 VISTA LINDA

Rock cliffs, fishing, and Jemez Springs

LOCATION: North of San Ysidro
ELEVATION: 6,000 feet
NUMBER OF SITES: 13
RV NOTES: 28 feet maximum length
FEE: Yes
SEASON: Year-round
NEAREST SUPPLY CENTER: Jemez Springs
ACCESS ROAD: Paved
MAP: *New Mexico Road & Recreation Atlas,*
p. 36, G4

SCENERY: ★★★★★
RVs: ★★★
TENTS: ★★★★
SHADE: ★★
PRIVACY: ★★★
FACILITIES: ★★★
CAMPGROUND ACTIVITIES: ★★
AREA ACTIVITIES: ★★★★★
WHEELCHAIR ACCESSIBILITY: ★★★★

DIRECTIONS: From San Ysidro, drive north 13 miles on NM 4;
the campground entrance is on the left.

As its name suggests, Vista Linda truly has a beautiful view. The campground lies alongside the Jemez River and below bright red cliffs. Although the highway is visible from most campsites, the setting is still spectacular. You can fish for rainbow trout, brown trout, Rio Grande chub, and Rio Grande sucker. The campground is wheelchair-friendly; campsites and facilities, including fishing pads, are accessible. Drinking water is available.

The Jemez Pueblo's Walatowa visitor center, the Jemez State Monument, and the Soda Dam are only a short drive away. The Jemez Valley is full of hot springs, including those feeding the public baths in the village of Jemez Springs, and many are accessible by taking a short hike, such as those lining the trails above Battleship Rock. Be aware that clothing is optional.

Gate closed 10 p.m.–6 a.m. No reservations. **Jemez Ranger District, 505-829-3535.**

3 SAN ANTONIO

Hot Springs and creekside camping

LOCATION: Just north of La Cueva
ELEVATION: 7,700 feet
NUMBER OF SITES: 30
RV NOTES: 35 feet maximum length
FEE: Yes
SEASON: May–October
NEAREST SUPPLY CENTER: La Cueva
ACCESS ROAD: Paved
MAP: *New Mexico Road & Recreation Atlas,*
p. 36, F4

SCENERY: ★★★
RVS: ★★★
TENTS: ★★★
SHADE: ★★
PRIVACY: ★★★
FACILITIES: ★★★
CAMPGROUND ACTIVITIES: ★★★
AREA ACTIVITIES: ★★★★★
WHEELCHAIR ACCESSIBILITY: ★★★

DIRECTIONS: From Jemez Springs, drive about 8 miles north on
NM 4 to NM 126. At La Cueva, continue 1.5 miles north on NM 126
to the campground.

This very popular campground lies in a meadow under ponderosa pines
along the San Antonio Creek, where anglers can fish for trout. Visitors can
also soak in the nearby San Antonio Hot Springs, about 4 miles north on
FR 376. It is a short drive to the ruins at Jemez State Monument, to Jemez
Springs, or to the spectacular meadows around the ancient volcanic crater
at Valles Caldera National Preserve. On the north and south ends of the camp
are walk-in sites. Drinking water is available. The amenities are aging, but
the campground is usually full all summer.

Gate closed 10 p.m.–6 a.m. Reservations at 877-444-6777. **Jemez
Ranger District, 505-829-3535.**

4 FENTON LAKE STATE PARK

Hiking, canoeing, and David Bowie

LOCATION: 9.6 miles west of La Cueva
ELEVATION: 7,700 feet
NUMBER OF SITES: 30
RV NOTES: 40 feet maximum; the nearest dump station is at Trails End in La Cueva
FEE: Yes
SEASON: Year-round, but may be snow-covered in winter
NEAREST SUPPLY CENTER: La Cueva
ACCESS ROAD: Paved to the last 0.5 mile
MAP: *New Mexico Road & Recreation Atlas*, p. 36, G4
DIRECTIONS: From La Cueva, follow NM 126 west for 9.6 miles.

SCENERY: ★★★★
RVS: ★★★
TENTS: ★★★
SHADE: ★★★★
PRIVACY: ★★★
FACILITIES: ★★★★
CAMPGROUND ACTIVITIES: ★★★★
AREA ACTIVITIES: ★★★★★
WHEELCHAIR ACCESSIBILITY: ★★★★★

A lush high-country oasis, Fenton Lake provides a cool retreat in summer and a cross-country skiing playground in winter. Cruise the cool water in a boat or fish for trout from the shore. Hike through glades along the river or

enjoy various nearby trails that traverse the Jemez. Observe a wide range of wildlife that visit the marshy area. And why David Bowie? The 1976 Nicholas Roeg cult movie, *The Man Who Fell to Earth*, starring Bowie, was filmed here.

Most warm-season weekends and holidays, starting with Easter, are busy. Parking, picnic areas, two campsites, restrooms, fishing piers, and the group day-use area are all wheelchair-accessible. Pay phones are available.

Several small loops and well-spaced sites along the canyon bottom of the Rio Cebolla comprise this campground. Drinking water is

available. The five sites with RV electric and water hookup lie near the park entrance. Near the end of the road in the grassy area by the river, the sites are a bit more primitive. The group campground is about a mile into the campground and has its own gate. This primitive area can accommodate 40–45 people and has its own vault toilet, tables, and fire rings. Call 505-829-3630 for group reservations.

Gate hours: summer, 6 a.m.–9 p.m.; winter, 7 a.m.–7 p.m. Reservations at 877-664-7787 or www.icampnm.com. **Park Manager, 505-829-3630**.

VALLES CALDERA NATIONAL PRESERVE

Forming the heart of the Jemez Mountains is the Valles Caldera, an extinct volcanic crater that is now a nature preserve. At dawn and dusk, elk can often be seen grazing in the vast, open fields of grass covering the valley floor. From late fall through late spring, the Valles Caldera is a giant, blinding sea of snow, crisscrossed by a variety of animal tracks. Anyone can view the area from observation points along NM 4. However, to keep the area as pristine as possible while providing for both wildlife viewing and solitude, special access rules have been enacted by the Valles Caldera Trust, which administers the preserve. Recreation and hunting regulations continue to evolve. For the latest information, visit www.vallescaldera.gov.

5 REDONDO

Relaxation among the pines

LOCATION: 2.1 miles southeast of La Cueva
ELEVATION: 8,100 feet
NUMBER OF SITES: 60
RV NOTES: 45 feet maximum length
FEE: Yes
SEASON: May–October
NEAREST SUPPLY CENTER: La Cueva
ACCESS ROAD: Paved
MAP: *New Mexico Road & Recreation Atlas,* p. 36, G4
DIRECTIONS: From La Cueva, drive 2.1 miles southeast on NM 4 to the campground entrance on the left.

SCENERY: ★★★
RVs: ★★
TENTS: ★★★
SHADE: ★★★★
PRIVACY: ★★★★
FACILITIES: ★★★
CAMPGROUND ACTIVITIES: ★★
AREA ACTIVITIES: ★★★★★
WHEELCHAIR ACCESSIBILITY: ★★

As a park ranger commented, this is the kind of campground where you pitch a tent and kick back with your favorite book. The sites are well-spaced, and the camp provides vault toilets, picnic tables, and fire rings with grills. Drinking water is available. A short hike across the street takes visitors to the San Diego Overlook. Access to the East Fork of the Jemez River is about 3 miles away. Nearby logging roads are good for strolling and mountain biking in the summer and for cross-country skiing in the winter.

Gate closed 10 p.m.–6 a.m. Reservations can be made at 877-664-7787 or www.icampnm.com. **Jemez Ranger District, 505-829-3535**.

SCENIC DRIVE: JEMEZ MOUNTAIN TRAIL

While visiting the Jemez, you can pick up this looping national scenic byway from US 550 near San Ysidro. Drive northeast on NM 4; attractions along the way include the Jemez Pueblo and the Walatowa Visitor Center, stunning red cliffs in the canyon, the town of Jemez Springs and hot springs for which it is named, Soda Dam, and Battleship Rock. At La Cueva, you have two route options. The northern route follows NM 126 to Cuba and then loops south on US 550 back to San Ysidro, passing by Fenton Lake State Park, Seven Springs Fish Hatchery, remote canyons and ranches, and amazing hidden places. The eastern route follows NM 4, taking you along the southern edge of the dramatic Valles Caldera (see opposite) and terminating at the famous canyons of Bandelier National Monument.

6 JEMEZ FALLS

Waterfalls, hot springs and fishing

LOCATION: 5.5 miles southeast of La Cueva
ELEVATION: 8,000 feet
NUMBER OF SITES: 47
RV NOTES: 45 feet maximum length; parking pads are paved
FEE: Yes
SEASON: May–October
NEAREST SUPPLY CENTER: La Cueva
ACCESS ROAD: Paved
MAP: *New Mexico Road & Recreation Atlas*, p. 36, G4
DIRECTIONS: From La Cueva, drive 5.4 miles southeast on NM 4 to the campground entrance, on the right.

SCENERY: ★★★	
RVs: ★★	
TENTS: ★★★	
SHADE: ★★★	
PRIVACY: ★★★	
FACILITIES: ★★★	
CAMPGROUND ACTIVITIES: ★★★	
AREA ACTIVITIES: ★★★★★	
WHEELCHAIR ACCESSIBILITY: ★★★	

Jemez Falls is set in a pine forest with access to the popular waterfall 0.5 mile down a trail from the campground. Campers come to fish in the Jemez River and hike Trail #137 to McCauley Springs and Battleship Rock. The campground has a wheelchair-accessible outdoor amphitheater where interpretive talks are held in the summer. Vault toilets and some campsites are also ADA compliant.

Sites have tables and fire rings with grills. Toilets and drinking water are available. Most summer weekends find Jemez Falls full; nearby Redondo is a good overflow area.

Gate closed 10 p.m.–6 a.m. No reservations. **Jemez Ranger District, 505-829-3535.**

7 BANDELIER NATIONAL MONUMENT
Cliff dwellings and storied canyons

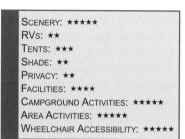

LOCATION: 8.2 miles southwest of White Rock
ELEVATION: 6,600 feet
NUMBER OF SITES: 94
RV NOTES: 40 feet maximum length; Juniper Campground has a dump station but no hookups
FEE: Yes
SEASON: Year-round, but may be inaccessible because of snow
NEAREST SUPPLY CENTER: White Rock
ACCESS ROAD: Paved
MAP: *New Mexico Road & Recreation Atlas*, p. 36, G5
DIRECTIONS: From US 84/285 in Pojoaque, travel west on NM 502 for about 11.5 miles to the junction with NM 4. Veer left onto NM 4 and drive 12.5 miles to the entrance to Bandelier.

SCENERY:	★★★★★
RVs:	★★
TENTS:	★★★
SHADE:	★★
PRIVACY:	★★
FACILITIES:	★★★★
CAMPGROUND ACTIVITIES:	★★★★★
AREA ACTIVITIES:	★★★★★
WHEELCHAIR ACCESSIBILITY:	★★★★★

To hike or drive from **Juniper Campground** into the canyons below is to travel back in time. Bandelier National Monument is an amazing collection of Ancestral Puebloan ruins, along with petroglyphs carved into volcanic rock. The campground is a short drive or a decent hike to the visitor center in Frijoles Canyon, the Loop Trail, and the heart of Bandelier. The trail winds through ruins dating from the 12th to the 16th centuries. Visitors are welcome to climb into small caves that were once homes and scale a ladder up to the amazing "Ceremonial Cave," recently renamed the Alcove House, which contains a reconstructed kiva. Longer trails

into the Bandelier and Dome Wilderness Areas, of varying degrees of difficulty, provide access to more remote ruins and clusters of petroglyphs.

The visitor center tells the history of the area and introduces the wildlife that now call the canyon home. The center also has phones, a bookstore, a gift shop, and a café. Valles Caldera National Preserve, Los Alamos, and the Puye Cliff Dwellings on the Santa Clara Pueblo are all a short drive away. Photographers can make images of the southwest-facing ruins in Frijoles Canyon optimally in the afternoon.

Juniper Campground occupies the mesa above Frijoles Canyon. Sites, which are usually available, have paved parking, grills, picnic tables—and enough space for up to three tents. The area is somewhat shaded by piñon, juniper, and ponderosa pine. The restrooms have flush toilets but no showers. Drinking water is available. Restrooms, as well as some parking spaces in Loop B, are wheelchair-accessible. Call ahead to make sure the loop is open. **Ponderosa Group** lies 6 miles west of the Bandelier entrance. It has two sites that can accommodate 10–50 people each. The area is for tents only and has pit toilets, grills, and picnic tables. Reservations required, 505-672-3861, ext. 534.

Note: Dogs are allowed in the campground but not on any trails.

No reservations. **Frijoles Canyon Visitor Center, 505-672-3861**.

A cliff dwelling at Bandelier National Monument

8 RESUMIDERO

San Pedro Parks Wilderness trailhead

LOCATION: 15.5 miles southeast of Gallina
ELEVATION: 9,200 feet
NUMBER OF SITES: Dispersed
RV NOTES: RVs not recommended
FEE: No
SEASON: Year-round, but may be snow-covered in winter
NEAREST SUPPLY CENTER: Cuba
ACCESS ROAD: Fair-weather; call ahead for conditions
MAP: *New Mexico Road & Recreation Atlas*, p. 36, E3

SCENERY: ★★★
RVs: NR
TENTS: ★★
SHADE: ★★★
PRIVACY: ★★★★
FACILITIES: ★
CAMPGROUND ACTIVITIES: ★★
AREA ACTIVITIES: ★★
WHEELCHAIR ACCESSIBILITY: ★

DIRECTIONS: From Gallina, travel 5.5 miles east on NM 96. Turn south (right) onto FR 429 and travel 4.5 miles to the junction with FR 172. Go straight; the road changes to FR 103. Drive on FR 103 for 4.1 miles, then turn right onto FR 93 and drive 2.5 miles to the campground.

Located at the edge of the San Pedro Parks Wilderness, Resumidero offers a base camp for hiking excursions. The Vega Redondo Trailhead, which links to other trails in the wilderness, starts from the campground. Lush meadows, or parks, distinguish San Pedro Parks, which is crisscrossed by flowing streams. This primitive area has a few fire rings, picnic tables, and an outhouse. No drinking water is available.

No reservations. **Coyote Ranger District, 505-638-5526.**

9 RIO PUERCO

Fishing and streamside camping

LOCATION: 14 miles southeast of Gallina
ELEVATION: 8,200 feet
NUMBER OF SITES: 4
RV NOTES: RVs not recommended
FEE: No
SEASON: May–October
NEAREST SUPPLY CENTER: Cuba
ACCESS ROAD: Fair-weather; call ahead for conditions

SCENERY: ★★★
RVs: NR
TENTS: ★★
SHADE: ★★★★★
PRIVACY: ★★★
FACILITIES: ★
CAMPGROUND ACTIVITIES: ★★
AREA ACTIVITIES: ★★★
WHEELCHAIR ACCESSIBILITY: ★

MAP: *New Mexico Road & Recreation Atlas*, p. 36, F4
DIRECTIONS: From Gallina, travel 5.5 miles east on NM 96. Turn south (right) onto FR 429 and travel 4.5 miles to the junction with FR 172. Go straight; the road changes to FR 103. Drive on FR 103 for 4.5 miles to the campground.

A remote little campground, Rio Puerco is a nice streamside fishing spot set alongside a forest road. The area is heavily used during hunting season. No drinking water is available.

No reservations. **Coyote Ranger District, 505-638-5526.**

10 RIO DE LAS VACAS

Fishing and hunting base camp

LOCATION: 11.6 miles east of Cuba
ELEVATION: 8,250 feet
NUMBER OF SITES: 16
RV NOTES: 28 feet maximum length
FEE: Yes
SEASON: May–October
NEAREST SUPPLY CENTER: Cuba
ACCESS ROAD: Fair-weather; call ahead for conditions

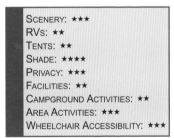

SCENERY: ★★★
RVs: ★★
TENTS: ★★
SHADE: ★★★★
PRIVACY: ★★★
FACILITIES: ★★
CAMPGROUND ACTIVITIES: ★★
AREA ACTIVITIES: ★★★
WHEELCHAIR ACCESSIBILITY: ★★★

MAP: *New Mexico Road & Recreation Atlas*, p. 36, F3
DIRECTIONS: From Cuba, drive 12.1 miles east on NM 126 to the campground.

Set in a pine forest on the edge of a meadow, this recently renovated area is popular for fishing and as a base camp during hunting season. Less than 5 miles away lie trailheads into the San Pedro Parks Wilderness, a landscape dominated by large, open meadows crisscrossed by streams and ringed by aspens and pines. The sites have picnic tables and grills, and all facilities, including vault toilets, are now wheelchair-accessible. Drinking water is available.

No reservations. **Cuba Ranger District, 505-289-3264.**

11 CLEAR CREEK

Updated streamside camping and meadow views

LOCATION: 10.4 miles east of Cuba
ELEVATION: 8,500 feet
NUMBER OF SITES: 13
RV NOTES: 30 feet maximum length
FEE: Yes
SEASON: May–October
NEAREST SUPPLY CENTER: Cuba
ACCESS ROAD: Fair-weather; call ahead for conditions

SCENERY: ★★★
RVs: ★★
TENTS: ★★
SHADE: ★★★★
PRIVACY: ★★★
FACILITIES: ★★
CAMPGROUND ACTIVITIES: ★★
AREA ACTIVITIES: ★★★
WHEELCHAIR ACCESSIBILITY: ★★★

MAP: *New Mexico Road & Recreation Atlas*, p. 36 (F,3)
DIRECTIONS: From Cuba, drive 10.4 miles east on NM 126 to the campground.

Lying near the Rio de Las Vacas Campground, Clear Creek also has a pine forest setting beside a meadow. Fishing and the hunting season keep the area popular. This is also the closest campground to FR 70, which accesses the short trail to San Gregorio Lake, a popular trout fishing spot. The lake lies within the San Pedro Parks Wilderness, an area of high-mountain meadows intersected by streams and encircled by aspens and pine forests.

Sites have picnic tables and grills, and all facilities, including vault toilets, are now wheelchair-accessible. The renovated group area has a pavilion, separate bathroom, group grill, and group fire ring, and accommodates up to 50 people. No drinking water is available. Reservations for groups only. **Cuba Ranger District, 505-289-3264.**

RIO CHAMA BASIN

The Rio Chama and southern end of the San Juan Mountains shape the landscape of north-central New Mexico. The Chama feeds a number of manmade lakes as it flows south, eventually funneling through the red-rock cliffs and canyons that shaped the art of Georgia O'Keeffe. Almost 25 miles of the Rio Chama, downstream from El Vado Dam through the Chama River Canyon Wilderness, is a designated National Wild and Scenic River. High-mountain meadows host wildflowers that explode with color in the summer. The renowned narrow-gauge Cumbres & Toltec Scenic Railroad begins its 64-mile journey to Antonito, Colorado, in the village of Chama, which lies at the foot of 10,015-foot Cumbres Pass. The Jicarilla Apache call this region home and invite anglers and lovers of the outdoors to enjoy their many lakes, lush pastures, and beautiful surroundings.

Striped cliffs near Abiquiu

Area Campgrounds

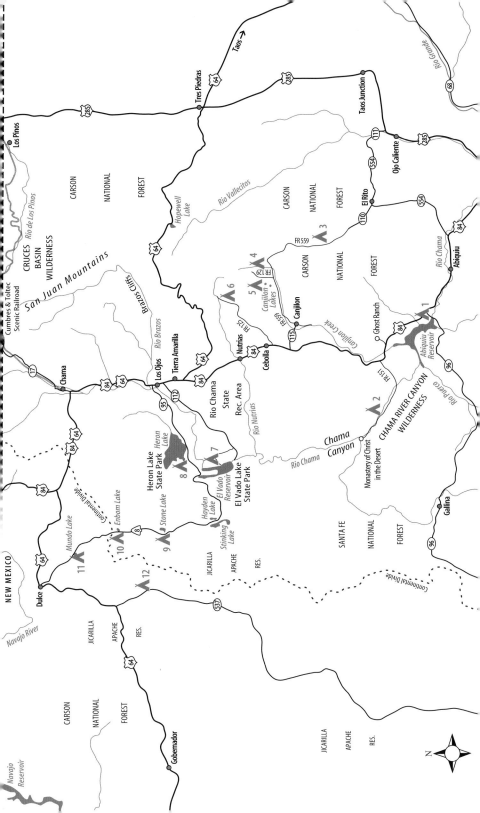

1 RIANA AT ABIQUIU RESERVOIR

Georgia O'Keeffe's haunts, vermilion cliffs, and fishing

LOCATION: 7.8 miles northwest of Abiquiu
ELEVATION: 6,450 feet
NUMBER OF SITES: 54
RV NOTES: No maximum length; sites 1–15 have water and electrical hookups
FEE: Yes; per camping unit, not site
SEASON: Year-round
NEAREST SUPPLY CENTER: Abiquiu
ACCESS ROAD: Paved

SCENERY: ★★★★★
RVS: ★★★★★
TENTS: ★★★★
SHADE: ★★
PRIVACY: ★★
FACILITIES: ★★★★★
CAMPGROUND ACTIVITIES: ★★★
AREA ACTIVITIES: ★★★★★
WHEELCHAIR ACCESSIBILITY: ★★★★

MAP: *New Mexico Road & Recreation Atlas*, p. 36, E5
DIRECTIONS: From Abiquiu, drive 7 miles northwest on US 84, then turn left onto NM 96. The campground is at the bottom of the hill.

Riana lies in a countryside of undulating red cliffs and spires made famous by the artist Georgia O'Keeffe. On the southwestern shore of 4,000-acre Abiquiu Lake, the campground offers deluxe amenities and makes a great base camp for exploring north central New Mexico. O'Keeffe's historic Ghost Ranch home is nearby, and Bandelier National Monument, Los Alamos, Taos, and Santa Fe are all within 60 miles. The Jemez Mountains provide ample hiking opportunities. The Rio Chama offers rafting in the spring and early summer. Below the dam in beautiful Chama Canyon, as well as in the lake, anglers catch a variety of fish. Photographers can capture the cliff face by the lake in the morning sun and, from the junction of NM 96 and US 84, the cliffs of Ghost Ranch in the afternoon.

Puerco has water and electrical hookups. **Chama** and **Pedernal** have spaces that accommodate RVs and tents but no hookups. Parking is 50–300 yards from walk-up campsites in the **Tent Area** (sites 40–54); sites 16–39 are ideal for car campers. All campers have access to the showers, dump station, and playground. No off-road vehicles are allowed. Boaters can call for the latest water conditions at 505-685-4371.

The overnight group area (maximum 40) features a large pavilion shelter with five tables, three grills, two 20-amp outlets, water, nearby toilets, and ample parking. Showers and a playground are also available. The visitor center, comfort stations, showers, picnic sites, and some campsites are wheelchair-accessible.

Holiday weekends usually fill the campground. Overflow camping is available for a small fee.

Gate closed 8 p.m.–8 a.m. Reservations for campsites at 877-444-6777 or ReserveUSA.com; for group shelter at 505-685-4371. **U.S. Army Corps of Engineers Camp Office, 505-685-4371.**

2 RIO CHAMA

Whitewater, striped cliffs, and a monastery

SCENERY: ★★★★★
RVs: NR
TENTS: ★★★
SHADE: ★
PRIVACY: ★★★★★
FACILITIES: ★
CAMPGROUND ACTIVITIES: ★★★★★
AREA ACTIVITIES: ★★★★★
WHEELCHAIR ACCESSIBILITY: ★★

LOCATION: 22 miles northwest of Abiquiu

ELEVATION: 6,300 feet

NUMBER OF SITES: 10, plus 1 group site and 2 dispersed sites

RV NOTES: RVs are not recommended because of the difficult access road

FEE: No

SEASON: May–September

NEAREST SUPPLY CENTER: Abiquiu

ACCESS ROAD: Fair-weather; call ahead for conditions; not for those with a fear of heights

MAP: *New Mexico Road & Recreation Atlas*, p. 36, D4

DIRECTIONS: From Abiquiu, drive northwest on US 84 for about 15 miles, past the Ghost Ranch Living Museum. Turn west (left) onto FR 151, and travel about 12 miles to the campground. If you prefer primitive camping, try the Whirlpool dispersed area, the first camp you will see; use only the two designated sites.

The approach to the Rio Chama is as spectacular as the campground's setting. Forest Road 151 into Chama Canyon passes striped cliffs that look like shades of sherbet. The road gradually descends to just above the fast-flowing river in the Chama River Canyon Wilderness. All around, rugged rock walls form waves of red. Wildlife, including eagles and mountain lions, call the canyon home. Although the campsites are surrounded by trees, every site is only a few feet away from a glorious view. This stretch of the river is popular for rafting, from gentle floating to Class III rapids. The Monastery of Christ in the Desert lies at the end of the road, and visitors are welcome to visit the gift shop or celebrate Mass with the Benedictines and their guests.

The campground is simple, with picnic tables and fire rings at each site. Vault toilets are wheelchair-accessible. The group area accommodates up to 50 people. No drinking water is available.

No reservations. **Coyote Ranger District, 505-638-5526.**

3 EL RITO

Hiking and fishing

LOCATION: 5.5 miles northwest
of El Rito
ELEVATION: 7,600 feet
NUMBER OF SITES: 11
RV NOTES: No maximum length
FEE: No
SEASON: April–October
NEAREST SUPPLY CENTER:
Ojo Caliente

SCENERY: ★★★
RVs: ★
TENTS: ★★
SHADE: ★★★
PRIVACY: ★★★★
FACILITIES: ★★
CAMPGROUND ACTIVITIES: ★★
AREA ACTIVITIES: ★★
WHEELCHAIR ACCESSIBILITY: ★

ACCESS ROAD: Fair-weather; call ahead for conditions
MAP: *New Mexico Road & Recreation Atlas*, p. 36, D5
DIRECTIONS: From El Rito, drive northwest 5.5 miles on NM 110, which
becomes FR 559. The campground will stretch out on the right.

El Rito is a primitive camping area beside a creek, offering fishing and
hiking options in Carson National Forest. The camp has picnic tables and
fire rings along with an outhouse. No drinking water is available.

Reservations are required for large groups. **El Rito Ranger District,
505-581-4554**.

High-mountain meadows between El Rito and Canjilon Creek

Rain in the Canyon

Rain does not always make for the best camping memories, but it did once on a trip to the Wild and Scenic Rio Chama. On a Saturday evening in April, I rolled into camp in Chama Canyon just before sunset under clear skies. I had hoped to awaken to catch the first rays of sunlight illuminating the variegated vermilion cliffs that tower above the Rio Chama. But at dawn I awoke to the soft patter of rain bouncing off my tent. Resisting the urge to snuggle deeper into my mummy sack, I donned raingear and trudged the soggy trail down to the river's edge.

The landscape I had seen the night before now appeared vivid and new. The turquoise sky had morphed into a bubbling mass of gray clouds, while the reedlike plants along the river's edge took on an almost fluorescent shade of green. The towering canyon cliffs, normally pastel shades of pink and yellow, looked more like strawberry shortcake with darkened red stripes wedged between dark beige layers.

Predawn activities of local critters were evident all along the sandy bank. Prints from little raccoon paws, deer hooves, and bird feet commingled along the water's edge before the steadily falling rain erased these traces in the soft mud. Soon the clouds began to part, the azure sky came out from hiding, and the sun lit up a section of cliffs. I watched the storm roll through the canyon and sunlight dapple the stunning canyon walls.

Rain in New Mexico is rare and fleeting. If you get the chance, take a moment and witness an already magical landscape transform before your eyes.

4 Canjilon Creek

Aspens, wildflowers, and a little creek

SCENERY: ★★★★
RVs: NR
TENTS: ★
SHADE: ★★★
PRIVACY: ★★★★★
FACILITIES: ★
CAMPGROUND ACTIVITIES: ★★
AREA ACTIVITIES: ★★
WHEELCHAIR ACCESSIBILITY: ★

LOCATION: 9 miles northeast of Canjilon

ELEVATION: 9,350 feet

NUMBER OF SITES: Dispersed

RV NOTES: RVs are not recommended

FEE: No

SEASON: Year-round, but snow-covered in winter

NEAREST SUPPLY CENTER: Tierra Amarilla

ACCESS ROAD: The roads from Canjilon to the campground are fair-weather; call ahead for conditions

MAP: *New Mexico Road & Recreation Atlas*, p. 36, C5

DIRECTIONS: From Tierra Amarilla, drive south on US 84 for about 15 miles, then go left (east) on NM 115 for 3.3 miles to Canjilon. Turn left onto FR 559, travel about 9 miles to the campground sign, then go left again onto FR 129 to the campground.

Canjilon Creek is nestled in high-mountain meadows that fill with wildflowers in summer. The creekside campground is shaded by aspens. Amenities are very primitive—a handful of picnic tables and not much more—but the wild, grassy environment makes up for it. Visitors can fish at the nearby Canjilon Lakes. No drinking water is available.

No reservations. **Canjilon Ranger District, 505-684-2489.**

5 CANJILON LAKES
Mountaintop fishing

SCENERY: ★★★★
RVS: ★★★
TENTS: ★★★
SHADE: ★★★★★
PRIVACY: ★★★
FACILITIES: ★★★
CAMPGROUND ACTIVITIES: ★★★
AREA ACTIVITIES: ★★
WHEELCHAIR ACCESSIBILITY: ★★★★

LOCATION: 10.8 miles northeast of Canjilon
ELEVATION: 9,900 feet
NUMBER OF SITES: 52
RV NOTES: 22 feet maximum length; parking pads are paved; RVs fit best in the back of Middle Canjilon Lakes Campground
FEE: Yes
SEASON: May–September
NEAREST SUPPLY CENTER: Tierra Amarilla
ACCESS ROAD: Fair-weather; call ahead for conditions

MAP: *New Mexico Road & Recreation Atlas*, p. 36, C5
DIRECTIONS: From Tierra Amarilla, drive south on US 84 for about 15 miles, then go left (east) on NM 115 for 3.3 miles to Canjilon. Turn left onto FR 559, travel about 9 miles to the campground sign, then go left again onto FR 129 about 3.3 miles to the campground.

Scenic 4x4 Drive: El Rito to Canjilon

This is a gorgeous drive through deep forests and mountain meadows in Carson National Forest, if you have a high-clearance four-wheel drive. From El Rito on NM 554, drive northwest on NM 110, which becomes FR 559. Stay on FR 559 as it winds through the mountains and meets up with a right-hand turn onto NM 115, which returns you to US 84. The distance is some 27 miles, but take a couple hours to enjoy the ride.

Six small ponds are the centerpiece of this lovely camp area. The drive up to Canjilon Lakes takes visitors through verdant meadows split by flowing streams in spring and ultimately through aspen groves in the higher elevations. The little lakes are a popular fishing spot for locals. No-wake boating is welcome.

Lower Canjilon Lakes is a loop and offers sites with tables, fire rings, and toilets. The **Middle Canjilon Lakes** area also has tables, fire rings, and toilets. Toilets and some campsites are wheelchair-accessible, and one of the lower lakes has an accessible fishing ramp. No drinking water is available. Holiday weekends, especially the Fourth of July and Labor Day, are very busy here.

No reservations. **Canjilon Ranger District, 505-684-2489**.

6 TROUT LAKES

Secluded fishing

LOCATION: 11.5 miles northeast of Cebolla
ELEVATION: 9,300 feet
NUMBER OF SITES: 12
RV NOTES: RVs not recommended
FEE: No
SEASON: Year-round, but snow-covered in winter
NEAREST SUPPLY CENTER: Tierra Amarilla
ACCESS ROAD: Fair-weather; call ahead for conditions

SCENERY: ★★★	
RVs: NR	
TENTS: ★★	
SHADE: ★★★★★	
PRIVACY: ★★★★★	
FACILITIES: ★	
CAMPGROUND ACTIVITIES: ★★	
AREA ACTIVITIES: ★	
WHEELCHAIR ACCESSIBILITY: ★	

MAP: *New Mexico Road & Recreation Atlas*, p. 36, C5
DIRECTIONS: From Tierra Amarilla, drive south on US 84 for about 13.3 miles. Turn left onto FR 125 and travel about 11.5 miles to the end of the road and the campground.

Trout Lakes offers very secluded fishing. The access road provides some fine views of the Rio Chama Valley and the Brazos Cliffs. The primitive campsites overlook a couple of stocked ponds. Surrounded by tall pines, sites have picnic tables and fire rings. There are a few outhouses. No drinking water is available.

No reservations. **Canjilon Ranger District, 505-684-2489.**

The Cumbres & Toltec Scenic Railroad in Chama is a great seasonal day trip from Trout Lakes

7 EL VADO LAKE STATE PARK

Raptors, fishing, and cliff views

LOCATION: 16.1 miles southwest of Tierra Amarilla

ELEVATION: 7,000 feet

NUMBER OF SITES: 80

RV NOTES: No maximum length

FEE: Yes

SEASON: Year-round, but may be inaccessible because of snow

NEAREST SUPPLY CENTER: Tierra Amarilla

ACCESS ROAD: Paved

MAP: *New Mexico Road & Recreation Atlas*, p. 36, C4

DIRECTIONS: From Tierra Amarilla, drive 17 miles southwest on NM 112 to the park entrance.

SCENERY:	★★★★
RVs:	★★★★
TENTS:	★★★★
SHADE:	★★★
PRIVACY:	★★
FACILITIES:	★★★★★
CAMPGROUND ACTIVITIES:	★★★★
AREA ACTIVITIES:	★★★★
WHEELCHAIR ACCESSIBILITY:	★★★

El Vado is a lovely little getaway spot. The campground areas lie on the east side of the lake; the west side lies below dramatic cliffs that catch the morning sun. The area is home to elk, deer, black bears, coyotes, and wintering bald eagles and hawks. The lake is perfect for waterskiing and other motorized aquatic sports. At certain times of the year, water is released from the lake. Whitewater rafters gather at these times to camp and run the rapids below the dam. (Call BLM for details, 505-758-8851.) The park is surrounded by the 14,000-acre Rio Chama Wildlife Area, which is criss-crossed by hikable and bikable logging trails. The Fourth of July holiday, and July weekends in general, are very popular.

Most sites at **Elk Run**, on a mesa overlooking the lake, have shelters. A dump station and restroom with showers are located near the entrance to Elk Run. Adjacent **Grassy Point** is the most developed area, with a comfort station, 19 electric and water hookup sites, plus several no-hookup sites. Most sites here also have shelters, and the playground is in this area. Just to the south on another mesa, **Piñon Beach** is a popular primitive area with fire rings and vault toilets. You can enjoy the shade trees and beach your boat right at your campsite.

The 36-by-36-foot group shelter has water and electric hookups and can accommodate 70 people and 8 to 10 vehicles. The visitor center (phones available), restrooms, showers, some sites, and the playground area are all wheelchair-accessible.

Reservations at 877-664-7787 or www.icampnm.com. **Park Manager**, 505-588-7247.

SCENIC DRIVE: TAOS TO TIERRA AMARILLA

Just follow US 64 from the Taos Plaza to Tierra Amarilla, and high-country beauty will unfold before you. Plan to make at least a few rewarding stops along the way: at the Rio Grande Gorge Bridge, Hopewell Lake, and the Brazos Cliffs Overlook. Mother Nature puts on a splendid show in every season, showcasing wildflowers in summer, golden aspens in fall, snow-blanketed meadows in winter, and lush green fields in spring. The drive is approximately 72 miles. Be aware that US 64 can frequently be closed in winter, so call ahead for conditions, 800-432-4269.

High-mountain meadows, remote ranches, and aspen groves decorate the sides of US 64 in Carson National Forest northwest of Taos

8 HERON LAKE STATE PARK

A massive outdoor playground

LOCATION: 8.5 miles west of Tierra Amarilla

ELEVATION: 7,200 feet

NUMBER OF SITES: 250

RV NOTES: No maximum length; hookup sites are in Willow Creek and Blanco; dump stations are at Willow Creek and Island View; RVs not recommended for Brushy Point or Island View areas because of tight turns on access roads

FEE: Yes

SEASON: Year-round

NEAREST SUPPLY CENTER: Tierra Amarilla

ACCESS ROAD: Paved

MAP: *New Mexico Road & Recreation Atlas*, p. 36, C4

DIRECTIONS: From Tierra Amarilla, drive north on US 84 for 2.7 miles. Turn left onto NM 95 and drive for about 6 miles to the park entrance.

SCENERY: ★★★★★	
RVs: ★★★★	
TENTS: ★★★★	
SHADE: ★★★	
PRIVACY: ★★★★	
FACILITIES: ★★★★	
CAMPGROUND ACTIVITIES: ★★★★★	
AREA ACTIVITIES: ★★★★★	
WHEELCHAIR ACCESSIBILITY: ★★★★★	

At Heron Lake, you could camp for seven days and sleep each night in a different campsite in one of seven different campgrounds, each with its own distinct environment and views. The choice of activities is equally as diverse. A large, no-wake lake, Heron boasts excellent sailing and windsurfing conditions and plenty of coves for exploration via canoe. Fishing is possible year-round. Wildlife watchers might spy deer and elk or observe osprey and bald eagles that nest here in the winter. Learn about the area in the visitor center and participate in interpretive programs such as stargazing and campfire talks. Hike the 5.5-mile trail along the Rio Chama to El Vado Lake State Park. Cycle on the main road

A colorful sunset in the Land of Enchantment.

or mountain bike to Hayden Lake on the Jicarilla Apache Reservation. The dramatic Brazos Cliffs and the town of Chama, home of the Cumbres & Toltec Scenic Railroad, are nearby.

An ADA-compliant facility, Heron Lake's visitor center (which has pay phones), parking, picnic areas, campsites, group shelter, restrooms, showers, and fishing areas are all wheelchair-accessible.

As you drive into the park, you'll see a road on the right, before you reach the visitor center, that leads to a private marina called the New Mexico Sailing Club, where you can rent a slip. Just after the visitor center, off to the right, is the access road to the north-end boat ramp. The same road takes you to the Willow Creek and Blanco Campgrounds. Situated on a cliff above the lake, **Willow Creek** is a well-wooded area that has RV sites with electric and water hookup. If winds are predicted, the trees surrounding these sites provide a good wind buffer. All sites have picnic tables and fire rings with built-in grills. There is a dump station and three sites with electric, water, and sewer hookup. A large loop, **Blanco** contains most of the reservable sites with electric and water hookups. Vault toilets, restrooms, and showers are available. **Brushy Point** and **Island View** camp areas are nestled under piñon and cedar trees, creating private spaces. The sites closest to the water all have picnic tables and grills. Restrooms, and reservation sites, are available. Island View also has a shower facility and dump station. Sites at lakeside **Salmon Run** have picnic tables and grills but no shelters. **La Laja**, **Ponderosa**, and **Ridge Rock** are basic campgrounds adjacent to a rocky beach environment. **West Side** is a primitive area with fire rings and a vault toilet.

The group area has a 60-by-40-foot concrete pad with a canopy, electricity, tables, grills, restrooms, and parking for about 20 cars. Additionally, four sites adjacent to the shelter have electric hookups.

Reservations at 877-664-7787 or www.icampnm.com. **Park Manager**, **505-588-7470**.

9 STONE LAKE

Fishing in a pastoral setting

LOCATION: About 17 miles southeast of Dulce
ELEVATION: 7,300 feet
NUMBER OF SITES: 20
RV NOTES: No maximum length
FEE: Yes
SEASON: April–November
NEAREST SUPPLY CENTER: Dulce
ACCESS ROAD: Road is paved to the campground; in the camp, the roads are fair-weather; call ahead for conditions
MAP: *New Mexico Road & Recreation Atlas*, p. 36, B3
DIRECTIONS: From Dulce, take Reservation Road 8 southeast 17.5 miles.

SCENERY: ★★★	
RVs: ★	
TENTS: ★★	
SHADE: ★★★★	
PRIVACY: ★★★	
FACILITIES: ★	
CAMPGROUND ACTIVITIES: ★★	
AREA ACTIVITIES: ★★	
WHEELCHAIR ACCESSIBILITY: ★	

This campground adjoins a popular fishing spot on the Jicarilla Apache Indian Reservation. Note that Stone Lake is a no-bait lake. The area is very green, and campers can spread out.

The facilities at this campground are not in the best shape. Some sites have usable picnic tables, shelters, and fire rings. At other sites, the picnic table is broken or otherwise unusable. No drinking water is available.

No reservations. **Jicarilla Apache Game & Fish Dept., 505-759-3255.**

10 ENBOM LAKE

Pretty fishing lake

LOCATION: 12 miles southeast of Dulce
ELEVATION: 7,700 feet
NUMBER OF SITES: 2 plus dispersed
RV NOTES: No maximum length
FEE: No (with valid fishing license)
SEASON: Year-round, but may be inaccessible
because of snow
NEAREST SUPPLY CENTER: Dulce
ACCESS ROAD: Road is paved to the camp-
ground; In the camp, the roads are fair-weather;
call ahead for conditions
MAP: *New Mexico Road & Recreation Atlas*, p. 36, B3
DIRECTIONS: From Dulce, take Reservation Road 8 southeast 12 miles to
the campground.

SCENERY: ★★★★	
RVs: ★	
TENTS: ★	
SHADE: ★	
PRIVACY: ★★★★	
FACILITIES: ★	
CAMPGROUND ACTIVITIES: ★★	
AREA ACTIVITIES: ★★	
WHEELCHAIR ACCESSIBILITY: ★	

This is another favorite fishing hole on the Jicarilla Apache Indian
Reservation. Bring your fishing permit, as it is required to camp. Only two
sites have picnic tables; the rest are primitive sites marked by flattened
ground and a fire ring. A toilet is available, but no drinking water.
No reservations. **Jicarilla Apache Game & Fish Dept., 505-759-3255.**

11 MUNDO LAKE

Night fishing in a pretty spot

LOCATION: 6 miles southeast of Dulce
ELEVATION: 7,400 feet
NUMBER OF SITES: Dispersed
RV NOTES: No maximum length
FEE: No (with valid fishing license)
SEASON: Year-round but may be inaccessible because of snow
NEAREST SUPPLY CENTER: Dulce
ACCESS ROAD: Road is paved to the campground; in the camp, the roads are fair-weather; call ahead for conditions
MAP: *New Mexico Road & Recreation Atlas*, p. 36, B3
DIRECTIONS: From Dulce, drive about 6 miles southeast on Reservation Road 8.

SCENERY: ★★★
RVs: ★
TENTS: ★
SHADE: ★
PRIVACY: ★★★
FACILITIES: ★
CAMPGROUND ACTIVITIES: ★★
AREA ACTIVITIES: ★★
WHEELCHAIR ACCESSIBILITY: ★

This little lake is on the Jicarilla Apache Indian Reservation. Night fishing for catfish is a popular activity. Campsites are located on top of a hill over-looking the lake and have shelters, tables, and fire rings. A boat dock is located at the northwest corner of the lake. No drinking water is available.

Bring your fishing permit, as it is required to camp. No reservations. **Jicarilla Apache Game & Fish Dept., 505-759-3255.**

Many parts of New Mexico are open range, so watch for cattle on roads

12 La Jara Lake

Popular fishing lake

Location: 16 miles south of Dulce
Elevation: 7,300 feet
Number of Sites: Dispersed
RV Notes: No maximum length, but the entrance road is very rough
Fee: Yes
Season: Year-round, but may be inaccessible because of snow
Nearest Supply Center: Dulce
Access Road: Road is paved to the campground; in the camp, the roads are fair-weather; call ahead for conditions
Map: *New Mexico Road & Recreation Atlas*, p. 36, B2
Directions: From Dulce, drive south on US 64 for about 11.2 miles. Veer to the left onto NM 537 and travel about 4.5 miles to the lake.

Scenery:	★★★★
RVs:	★
Tents:	★★★
Shade:	★
Privacy:	★★★
Facilities:	★
Campground Activities:	★★
Area Activities:	★★
Wheelchair Accessibility:	★

A long, narrow lake, La Jara draws anglers to primitive campsites scattered around the lakeshore. Look for fire rings and some picnic tables. The area is popular with bears, so make sure you properly store food items. The lake is on the Jicarilla Apache Indian Reservation.

A valid fishing permit is required to camp. No reservations. **Jicarilla Apache Game & Fish Dept., 505-759-3255.**

NORTHWEST

Commonly known as the Four Corners in reference to the extreme northwestern point in the state where its border touches that of Utah, Colorado, and Arizona, this region of New Mexico is home to the Navajo Nation, the southern end of the Ute Mountain Indian Reservation, and the Zuni, Laguna, and Acoma Pueblos. The landscape shifts from the southern San Juan Mountains in the east to mesas and canyons and on to the Chuska Mountains in the west. Ship Rock, The Hogback, and other massive rocky outcroppings stand like sentinels on either side as you drive south along US 491, formerly US 666. Strange, mushroomlike outcroppings called hoodoos, created by erosion, cover the earth in the Bisti/De-Na-Zin

Fishing in Navajo Lake State Park

Wilderness. Magnificent Ancient Puebloan structures fill Chaco Culture National Historical Park as well as the Aztec Ruins National Monument and Salmon Ruins to the north.

Gallup and historic US 66 lie just to the north of the Zuni Pueblo and the Zuni Mountains. The mysterious sandstone bluff called El Morro, or Inscription Rock, has beckoned travelers for centuries, inspiring many to leave their messages and drawings. To the east of El Morro stretch the ancient lava flows of El Malpais National Monument and the West Malpais Wilderness Area. South of Mount Taylor, a mountain sacred to many Native Americans, hides Sky City, the pueblo built by the Acoma on a mesa top and continuously inhabited for almost a thousand years.

Area Campgrounds

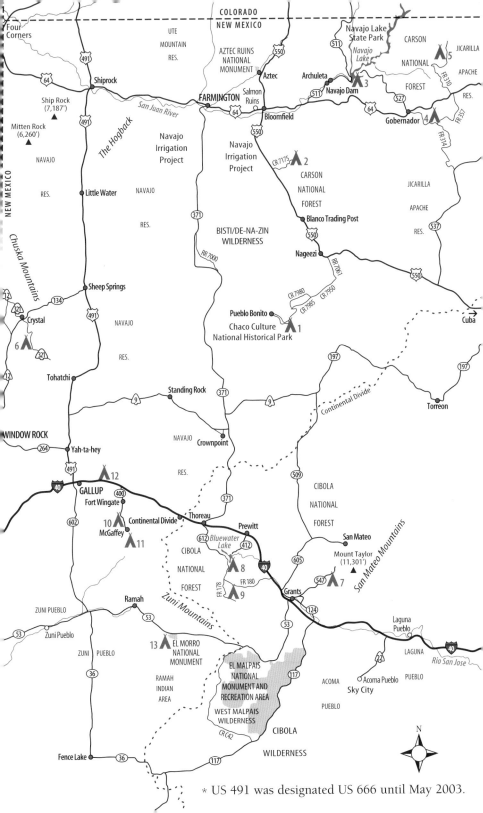

* US 491 was designated US 666 until May 2003.

1 CHACO CULTURE NATIONAL HISTORICAL PARK

Ancestral Puebloan ruins in a beautiful canyon

LOCATION: 32 miles south of Nageezi

ELEVATION: 6,200 feet

NUMBER OF SITES: 48; no overflow area

RV NOTES: 30 feet maximum length; there are no hookups, but there is a dump station, closed in winter, near the entrance to the campground

FEE: Yes

SEASON: Year-round but may be inaccessible because of snow

NEAREST SUPPLY CENTER: Cuba or Bloomfield

ACCESS ROAD: Mostly dirt. When dry, any vehicle can drive to the park. After a snow or during the rainy season in later summer, the road may be impassable except for high-clearance 4x4 vehicles. Call ahead for conditions.

MAP: *New Mexico Road & Recreation Atlas*, p. 34, F6

DIRECTIONS: From Bloomfield, travel south on US 550 for about 31 miles, past Nageezi. Turn right onto CR 7900/Reservation Road 7061 and follow the signs to Chaco. After about 5 miles on a paved road, a sign will direct you to turn right onto a dirt road (CR 7950). Follow that road and the signs for about 16 miles to the park entrance. *Note:* Many maps still show no-longer-used entrances from Nageezi or Blanco trading posts.

Camping in Chaco Canyon gives visitors a rare opportunity to experience night as the Ancestral Puebloan people must have experienced it. On account of the high altitude (6,200 feet), lack of humidity, and remote location, the number of stars visible to the naked eye increases exponentially compared to most populated areas. The silence of the night is broken

SCENERY:	★★★★★
RVS:	★★
TENTS:	★★★★
SHADE:	★
PRIVACY:	★★★★
FACILITIES:	★★★★
CAMPGROUND ACTIVITIES:	★★★★★
AREA ACTIVITIES:	★
WHEELCHAIR ACCESSIBILITY:	★★★★★

only by the cries of creatures, such as coyotes, that live in and around the canyon. During the day, visitors can explore an amazing array of spectacular ruins left by the Ancestral Puebloans, who occupied the area from A.D. 850 to 1250. Chaco is believed to have been a cultural, ceremonial, and administrative hub. Trails lead to the buildings, onto the mesas above for a bird's-eye view of Pueblo Bonito, and along cliffs decorated with petroglyphs. The park is a photographer's dream, where natural and architectural beauty blend nicely.

Administered by the National Park Service, the park is a popular destination. Gallo Campground is first-come, first-served and fills quickly, particularly during summer holidays and weekends. Try to arrive on Thursday or early Friday during peak times. Gallo is a nice place to camp off-season, but be aware it does get very cold at night during the winter.

Site #16, both campground restrooms, the visitor center (with phones and drinking water), and portions of several trails through the ruins are wheelchair-accessible. Each site has a picnic table and fire ring with a grill. Bring your own firewood. Most sites have tent pads, and some sites are separated by natural rock barriers, affording a good degree of privacy. These sites lie in the small canyon that stretches out to the left after the campground entrance. There are two campground restrooms, with running water that is not drinkable, but potable water is available at the visitor center.

Two group campsites are available, which can accommodate up to 30 people with approximately 6 tents at each. A fire pit and picnic tables are in each area. Reservations are required.

Access-road gates close at sunset. Reservations for large groups only. **Park Ranger Station, 505-786-7014.**

SCENIC DRIVE: THE NAVAJO NATION IN NEW MEXICO

Larger than the state of West Virginia and spanning portions of Arizona and Utah, the Navajo Nation sits proudly in the northwest corner of New Mexico. Starting in Gallup, US 491 (formerly US 666) rolls north past the rugged Chuska Mountains. At Yah-ta-hey, "Welcome!" in Navajo, you can take a 20-mile detour to Window Rock, the capital of the Navajo Nation across the border in Arizona.

Continuing north on US 491, you'll pass magnificent Ship Rock, Tsé Bit' A'i ("Rock with Wings"), and other monoliths with names like Mitten Rock and The Hogback. At Shiprock, head east on US 64 through Farmington, then south on NM 371. The first 10 miles or so of NM 371 surprise visitors in the spring and summer by offering a landscape that changes from beautiful beige desert to verdant green pastures, part of the Navajo Irrigation Project. Farther along, the landscape shifts again and you are surrounded by bizarre, mushroomlike rock formations, called hoodoos, in the Bisti Badlands. Detour south off of NM 371 onto Reservation Road 7000 and follow signs to an entry point into the Bisti Wilderness.

Back on NM 371, continue to Crownpoint where, on the third Friday of most months, you can attend the famous Crownpoint Navajo Rug Auction, held at Crownpoint Elementary School. At Thoreau, go west on I-40 back to Gallup. Stop on the way for curios at the town of Continental Divide, or see the stunning Red Rock State Park.

CHACO CULTURE NATIONAL HISTORICAL PARK

So you've decided to see the famous Ancestral Puebloan ruins at Chaco and set out west from Cuba on US 550, then south along county roads. As you drive the dirt roads through a rolling, high-desert landscape dotted with chamisa, rabbit brush, and the occasional scrubby piñon, you might be struck by the extreme remoteness of the place. Eventually the park entrance, and a wide, shallow canyon, come into view. The park's loop road descends into Chaco Canyon and leads to the park's main attraction, Pueblo Bonito.

It is virtually impossible to stand next to the three-story walls built a thousand years ago (Chaco flourished between A.D. 850 and 1250) and not be awestruck. The stonework is precise and sturdy, yet delicate and decorative. The log beams holding up ancient floors and roofs prompt confusion, since there is not a tree around for miles.

If you climb up through a crack in the cliff wall behind the Kin Kletso ruins, and follow the trail along the upper edge of the canyon toward Pueblo Alto, you are rewarded with a spectacular bird's-eye view of Pueblo Bonito. The circular kivas—ceremonial spaces—dominate the structure. From this site once radiated a system of straight roads connecting Pueblo Bonito with other Great Houses at Chaco and with those hundreds of miles away, near present-day Bloomfield, Crownpoint, and Pueblo Pintado.

The many marvels of Chaco continue to amaze all who see them. Beyond the ruins, three good reasons to camp at Chaco are sunrise, sunset, and starry skies in between. Try to visit in the early fall, when temperatures are in the 80s during the day and in the 40s or low 50s at night, and an abundance of wildflowers bloom after the monsoons. Always call ahead for road conditions, since all park roads are unpaved.

The National Park Service recommends accessing Chaco from the north. From Cuba, take US 550, 50 miles west to CR 7900/Reservation Road 1761, turn left, and go south for about 5 miles. At the intersection, bear right onto CR 7950 and drive about 16 unpaved miles to the park entrance. You can also access Chaco from the south starting just west of Milan off I-40 via NM 605 and NM 509, but this route is not recommended unless you have a good map and heavy-duty vehicle. Roads can wash out, and signage is sketchy.

Graceful kivas, which were ceremonial spaces, dominate the Chaco complex

2 ANGEL PEAK NATIONAL RECREATION SITE
Dramatic canyons

LOCATION: 21 miles southeast of Bloomfield
ELEVATION: 6,600 feet
NUMBER OF SITES: 7
RV NOTES: No maximum length
FEE: No
SEASON: Year-round, but may be inaccessible because of snow
NEAREST SUPPLY CENTER: Bloomfield
ACCESS ROAD: Dirt, fair-weather; call ahead for conditions
MAP: *New Mexico Road & Recreation Atlas*, p. 35, C7
DIRECTIONS: From US 64 in Bloomfield, take US 550 south for 15.2 miles to CR 7175 on the left. Drive about 6 miles to the campground.

SCENERY:	★★★★★
RVs:	★
TENTS:	★★★
SHADE:	★★
PRIVACY:	★★★★
FACILITIES:	★★
CAMPGROUND ACTIVITIES:	★★
AREA ACTIVITIES:	★
WHEELCHAIR ACCESSIBILITY:	★★

The Angel Peak area is a huge surprise the first time it is viewed. The approach on US 550 gives no indication that just to the east lies a landscape of deep canyons with spires and ridges protruding from the earth. The campground provides the basics, sites with tables and fire rings and pit toilets. No drinking water is available. Angel Peak is a convenient stopping place for Ancestral Puebloan ruins enthusiasts traveling from Chaco Culture National Historical Park to the Aztec Ruins National Monument.

No reservations. **BLM Farmington, 505-599-8900.**

3 NAVAJO LAKE STATE PARK

Fly fishing, hiking, and boating

LOCATION: 7 miles northeast of Archuleta

ELEVATION: 6,200 feet

NUMBER OF SITES: 247

RV NOTES: 50 feet maximum length in Cottonwood, 40 feet maximum in Pine and Sims; the Pine dump station is just past the visitor center; Cottonwood and Sims Mesa areas also have dump stations

FEE: Yes

SEASON: Year-round

NEAREST SUPPLY CENTER: Navajo Dam Community

ACCESS ROAD: Paved except for the rough dirt road to Cottonwood Campground; call ahead for conditions. Note that access to Sims Mesa is different from that to Pine or Cottonwood; see Directions, below

MAP: *New Mexico Road & Recreation Atlas*, p. 35, B8

DIRECTIONS: To access the main campgrounds from US 550 in Bloomfield, take US 64 east for 12.2 miles, then turn north (left) onto NM 511. Drive about 9 miles to the park. You will reach Cottonwood Campground before you come to the dam, visitor center, and main camp areas.

To reach the Sims Mesa area from US 550 in Bloomfield, take US 64 east for 38 miles, then turn north (left) onto NM 527. Drive about 17 miles to the campground.

SCENERY:	★★★★★
RVs:	★★★★
TENTS:	★★★
SHADE:	★★★
PRIVACY:	★★★
FACILITIES:	★★★★★
CAMPGROUND ACTIVITIES:	★★★★★
AREA ACTIVITIES:	★★
WHEELCHAIR ACCESSIBILITY:	★★★★★

Navajo Lake creates three distinct environments out of the rugged mesaland of northwestern New Mexico. Enjoy fly-fishing in a canyon on the world-famous San Juan River near the Cottonwood Campground below the dam. Above the dam in Pine, the park's main camp area, take advantage of boating, waterskiing, and, of course, more fishing. Experience a sandy beach and swim on the eastern shore at Sims Mesa. Trails wind through parts of the park, and kids can visit the playground. Wildlife abounds, including bald eagles in winter. For an easy day trip from base camp, visit the Aztec Ruins National Monument in the town of Aztec. The northernmost sections of the lake extend into Colorado.

Sites are usually available in all the campgrounds, but reservations are recommended for hookup sites during holidays and summer weekends. Wheelchair-accessible facilities include the visitor center, picnic areas, some campsites, the Pine playground and group shelter, restrooms, showers, and fishing facilities at Cottonwood.

Pine has four sections. The main campground offers 97 sites with just a table and grill, 34 with electric hookup, and 10 with full electric, water, and sewer hookups. Water is available from spigots. This area also has the visitor center, three pay phones, showers, an ADA campsite, a playground, a dump station, a boat ramp, and the full-service Pine Marina. The Piñon, Cedar, and Juniper loops have grills and tables but no hookups. Cedar has a shower.

Cottonwood has 47 developed sites, 25 of which have electric hookup. Hydrants, a dump station, and two ADA campsites are available. All sites have a table and grill. Sims Mesa offers 43 developed sites, 14 of which have electric hookup, plus 42 primitive sites right at the water's edge. Also here are showers, a dump station, boat ramp, full-service marina, and an ADA-compliant campsite.

Reservations at 877-664-7787 or www.icampnm.com. Park Manager, 505-632-2278.

4 CEDAR SPRING

High-country solitude

SCENERY: ★★★
RVs: NR
TENTS: ★★★★
SHADE: ★★★★★
PRIVACY: ★★★★★
FACILITIES: ★★
CAMPGROUND ACTIVITIES: ★
AREA ACTIVITIES: ★★
WHEELCHAIR ACCESSIBILITY: ★

LOCATION: 40 miles east of Bloomfield
ELEVATION: 7,300 feet
NUMBER OF SITES: 4, plus dispersed
RV NOTES: RVs not recommended
FEE: No
SEASON: Year-round but may be inaccessible because of snow
NEAREST SUPPLY CENTER: Bloomfield or Dulce
ACCESS ROAD: Very rough dirt and near-impassable if muddy; call ahead for conditions

MAP: *New Mexico Road & Recreation Atlas*, p. 35, C9
DIRECTIONS: At mile marker 106.5 along US 64, take FR 314 south until the junction with FR 357. Turn north (left) on FR 357 and travel 0.5 mile to the campground.

Located among the pines of the Carson National Forest, this campground offers a remote location and opportunities to view wild turkeys and mule deer. Sites have fire rings and picnic tables, and the camp has an outhouse. No drinking water is available.

No reservations. **Jicarilla Ranger District, 505- 632-2956.**

5 BUZZARD PARK

Pine forest solitude

LOCATION: 25 miles northeast of Gobernador
ELEVATION: 7,000 feet
NUMBER OF SITES: Dispersed
RV NOTES: RVs not recommended
FEE: No
SEASON: Year-round, but may be inaccessible because of snow
NEAREST SUPPLY CENTER: Dulce
ACCESS ROAD: Very rough dirt and near-impassable if muddy; call ahead for conditions
MAP: *New Mexico Road & Recreation Atlas*, p. 35, B9
DIRECTIONS: At mile marker 114.5 along US 64, turn north (right) onto FR 310 and travel for 15 miles to the campground.

SCENERY: ★★★	
RVs: NR	
TENTS: ★★★	
SHADE: ★★★★★	
PRIVACY: ★★★★	
FACILITIES: ★	
CAMPGROUND ACTIVITIES: ★★	
AREA ACTIVITIES: ★	
WHEELCHAIR ACCESSIBILITY: ★	

The drive to Buzzard Park is quite pretty, passing through verdant pastures and remote ranches. The major draws for this campground are the isolated location and the opportunity to see elk and wild horses. No drinking water is available.

No reservations. **Jicarilla Ranger District, 505-632-2956.**

Wildflowers abound in late spring

6 Bowl Canyon Navajo Recreation Area

Navajo Nation base camp

SCENERY: ★★★★
RVs: ★
TENTS: ★★★
SHADE: ★★
PRIVACY: ★★
FACILITIES: ★★★★★
CAMPGROUND ACTIVITIES: ★★★
AREA ACTIVITIES: ★★★★★
WHEELCHAIR ACCESSIBILITY: ★★★

LOCATION: 7.5 miles south of Crystal

ELEVATION: 7,700 feet

NUMBER OF SITES: 16

RV NOTES: Sites have parking spaces that can fit most RVs, but the access road can be very rough; call for conditions

FEE: Yes

SEASON: April–October

NEAREST SUPPLY CENTER: Window Rock, Arizona

ACCESS ROAD: Rough, fair-weather; call ahead for conditions

MAP: *New Mexico Road & Recreation Atlas*, p. 34, F2

DIRECTIONS: From US 491 (formerly US 666) in Sheep Springs, go west on NM 134 for 17.5 miles to Crystal. Head south (left) on Reservation Road 321 for 7.5 miles to the campground.

Located in the Chuska Mountains on the Navajo Nation, Bowl Canyon makes a nice base camp for exploring the region. Window Rock, Ariz., the capital of the Navajo Nation, lies just across the border about 30 miles south of the town of Crystal. The spectacular Ancestral Puebloan ruins at Arizona's Canyon de Chelly National Monument are just 37 miles northwest of camp as the crow flies. Fishing is a major activity here, and mountain bikers can enjoy exploring the many unpaved roads.

The Bowl Canyon camp area is a loop overlooking Asaayi Lake. Massive boulders and cliffs of red rock line the water's edge. The stream that feeds the lake winds through wildflower-strewn fields.There are showers and two restrooms. Three campsites and the restrooms are wheelchair-accessible. Drinking water is available.

Reservations available. **Window Rock Sports Center, 928-871-6667.**

Dog Etiquette 101

Fellow dog owners, this is a cautionary tale for you.

My faithful companion, Chaos, a lab-mutt thing, accompanied me as I researched this book. He's a great camp dog: protective enough to keep strangers away in camp but easygoing enough to make friends wherever we go. Bottom line, barking or causing trouble in camp was never a concern. Then, toward the end of the research process, my husband and I acquired a smaller pooch named Zelda. As I left in winter for Chaco Canyon with Chaos to shoot a few more photos, I decided to let Zelda tag along. Arriving late at the park, I pitched camp and decided to save hiking for the dawn. All was going fine until the sun went down.

Unlike a lot of folks, I like camping in winter. Off-season, you can enjoy national parks in particular without crowds, even with peace and quiet.

So the sun has now set, the campfire is toasty, and Chaos is beside me as I settle in to read a book. But Zelda won't come near me. She's standing at the edge of the fire's glow, shivering. She won't come when I call, won't even sit in my lap. I realize she's afraid of the fire. Needless to say, this is the first strike against her as a camp dog. I had to give up my usual camp routine, douse the fire, and head into the tent; otherwise the little dog was going to freeze to death as the temperature dropped.

In my mummy bag, Chaos lies next to me and Zelda's on top of the footbox. Just as I begin to fall asleep, Zelda begins to shiver again. Fine, I put her in the bag with me—snug, but at least she warms up and goes to sleep. Several hours later, growling softly, Zelda wakes me up again. There are coyotes in our campsite. I'm terrified—not of the coyotes but that Zelda will cry out and wake the other campers. After a few tense moments, the critters outside move on, and peace again settles into the Frain tent. That was Zelda's second strike.

As planned, I rise before the sun to break camp before the road to the ruins reopens. Zelda strikes out when a fellow camper strolls past our site. Taking immediate offense, she proceeds to let the rest of Gallo Campground know about this major infraction. The canyon walls echo with her little terrier voice. I round her up as quickly as I can, but the damage is done. My fellow campers are awake, and I'm sure they'd have my head on a platter if only it weren't below freezing outside of their sleeping bags. I am back to Highway 550 in record time.

This episode taught me a valuable lesson: If you don't know how your dog will act in camp, don't choose a canyon as the test site. Pick a forest or streamside, where bad behavior can be absorbed or drowned out. Try to be as considerate as possible to other campers: If your pet can't hack it and behaves like Zelda, please leave the beastie at home.

7 COAL MINE CANYON

Gateway to Mount Taylor

LOCATION: 10 miles northeast of Grants
ELEVATION: 7,500 feet
NUMBER OF SITES: 17
RV NOTES: 30 feet maximum length
FEE: Yes
SEASON: May–September
NEAREST SUPPLY CENTER: Grants
ACCESS ROAD: Paved
MAP: *New Mexico Road & Recreation Atlas,*
p. 41, C8

SCENERY: ★★★
RVS: ★
TENTS: ★★★
SHADE: ★★★
PRIVACY: ★★★
FACILITIES: ★★★
CAMPGROUND ACTIVITIES: ★★
AREA ACTIVITIES: ★★★★★
WHEELCHAIR ACCESSIBILITY: ★★

DIRECTIONS: From Exit 85 on I-40 in Grants, go north on NM 124 for 1.35 miles. Turn onto NM 547, which will wind through town toward Mount Taylor. Drive 11 miles to the campground.

Coal Mine Canyon lies below 11,301-foot Mount Taylor, one of the Navajo's Four Sacred Mountains. Forest roads take you to trailheads up the mountain. The popular campground provides decently spaced sites that have picnic tables and fire rings. There are wheelchair-accessible restrooms and a short nature trail. Be aware that Coal Mine Canyon can be a popular weekend spot. No drinking water is available.

No reservations. **Mount Taylor Ranger District, 505-287-8833.**

8 BLUEWATER LAKE STATE PARK

Fishing, birding, and fossils

LOCATION: 6.3 miles southwest of Prewitt
ELEVATION: 7,400 feet
NUMBER OF SITES: 130
RV NOTES: 45 feet maximum length. Parking pads are packed gravel, and the main area is more easily navigated than Las Tusas.
FEE: Yes
SEASON: Year-round
NEAREST SUPPLY CENTER: Thoreau
ACCESS ROAD: Paved
MAP: *New Mexico Road & Recreation Atlas*, p. 40, C6
DIRECTIONS: From Exit 63 on I-40 near Prewitt, take NM 412 south for 6.3 miles to the park entrance.

SCENERY: ★★★★	
RVs: ★★★★	
TENTS: ★★★	
SHADE: ★★	
PRIVACY: ★★★	
FACILITIES: ★★★★★	
CAMPGROUND ACTIVITIES: ★★★	
AREA ACTIVITIES: ★★	
WHEELCHAIR ACCESSIBILITY: ★★★	

Bluewater is a fisherman's paradise. Stocked with catfish, rainbow and cutthroat trout, the lake is a popular spot for year-round fishing, including ice fishing during winter. Birdwatchers flock to Bluewater to seek out more than 68 identified species. Fossil hunters search for ancient snails and brachiopods in the shale and limestone that make up the valley walls, which catch the morning light. Mountain bikers camping on the western shore can bike into the Zuni Mountains via forest roads.

Parking, picnic areas, some campsites, the group shelter, restrooms, showers, and a playground are all wheelchair-accessible. The group shelter has tables, water, and grills and can accommodate 80 to 100.

Summer holidays can be very busy. Visitors can choose from two different camp environments: the main five campgrounds on the east side, accessed via NM 412, and the **Las Tusas** area on the western shore, accessed via NM 612. The 14 electric sites are in the main campground in **Canyonside**. **Piñon Cliff** is a reservation-only lakefront camp area; other eastern-shore areas are **Lakeside**, **Rim Rock**, and **North Point**. All developed sites have table and grills. Primitive campsites lie around the lake's edge west of North Point. Water is centrally located. There are dump stations on each side of the lake. Two boat ramps are available.

Reservations at 877-664-7787 or www.icampnm.com. **Park Manager,** 505-876-2391.

SCENIC DRIVE: VOLCANO ROAD AND SKY CITY

Begin this scenic journey in Gallup and head south on NM 602. The Zuni Indian Reservation surrounds the road. At the junction with NM 53, a right turn takes a little detour to the Zuni Pueblo and the homeland of the creators of the beautiful fetish carvings; a left turn continues on the tour heading past the Zuni Mountains, the sandstone bluff of El Morro National Monument, and the vast black lava flows of

El Malpais National Monument and Recreation Area. (If you have a high-clearance 4x4, you can detour onto FR C42, right after you cross the Continental Divide, which skirts the western edge of El Malpais and travels along a string of dormant volcano cones.) As you continue along NM 53 past the lava beds and arrive at Grants, take I-40 east to Exit 102. Follow the signs to Acoma Sky City (the ancient pueblo, not the casino). Sky City has been home to the Acoma for more than a thousand years and is said to be the oldest inhabited town in the United States. Backtrack to I-40, and about 10 miles farther east lies the Laguna Pueblo. You can see the St. Joseph Mission Church from the rest areas along the interstate.

Ancient dwellings in the Acoma Sky City have been handed down through families for centuries

9 OJO REDONDO

A beautiful glade

SCENERY: ★★★★
RVs: ★
TENTS: ★★★
SHADE: ★★★★
PRIVACY: ★★★
FACILITIES: ★★
CAMPGROUND ACTIVITIES: ★★
AREA ACTIVITIES: ★★
WHEELCHAIR ACCESSIBILITY: ★

LOCATION: 23 miles southeast of Thoreau
ELEVATION: 8,900 feet
NUMBER OF SITES: 19
RV NOTES: 30 feet maximum length
FEE: No
SEASON: Year-round, but may be inaccessible because of snow
NEAREST SUPPLY CENTER: Thoreau
ACCESS ROAD: Fair-weather; call ahead for conditions
MAP: *New Mexico Road & Recreation Atlas*, p. 40, C6

DIRECTIONS: From Exit 53 on I-40 near Thoreau, take NM 612 south for 17.5 miles to the junction of FR 178 and FR 180. Follow the right fork onto FR 178 and drive 8 miles to the campground.

Ojo Redondo inhabits a lovely, grassy glade surrounded by towering pines. The area is frequented by elk, deer, and lots of wildlife. The network of forest roads make for great mountain biking. Sites are basic, with tables and fire rings with grills. There are pit toilets. No drinking water is available.

No reservations. **Mount Taylor Ranger District, 505-287-8833.**

10 QUAKING ASPEN

Pine forest camping and mountain biking

LOCATION: 4.7 miles south of Fort Wingate
ELEVATION: 7,600 feet
NUMBER OF SITES: 20
RV NOTES: 30 feet maximum length
FEE: Yes
SEASON: Year-round but may be inaccessible because of snow
NEAREST SUPPLY CENTER: Gallup
ACCESS ROAD: Paved
MAP: *New Mexico Road & Recreation Atlas*, p. 40, B4
DIRECTIONS: From Exit 33 on I-40 near Navajo Wingate Village, drive south on NM 400 for about 10 miles to the campground entrance.

SCENERY:	★★★
RVs:	★★
TENTS:	★★★
SHADE:	★★★★★
PRIVACY:	★★★
FACILITIES:	★★
CAMPGROUND ACTIVITIES:	★★
AREA ACTIVITIES:	★★★★
WHEELCHAIR ACCESSIBILITY:	★

Although no aspens live here, you will still find plenty of shade in this pine- and oak-grove campground. A singletrack bike trail starts off the dirt road 0.5 mile north of the campground. The most popular time for the campground is the Fourth of July holiday. Sites have picnic tables and fire rings, and there are three toilets in the camp. Quaking Aspen is just 2 miles from the popular McGaffey fishing lake and about half an hour from Gallup. No drinking water is available.

No reservations. **Mount Taylor Ranger District, 505-287-8833.**

11 McGaffey

Fishing and cool forest camping

LOCATION: 7.4 miles south of Fort Wingate
ELEVATION: 8,000 feet
NUMBER OF SITES: 29
RV NOTES: No maximum length
FEE: Yes
SEASON: May–October
NEAREST SUPPLY CENTER: Gallup
ACCESS ROAD: Paved
MAP: *New Mexico Road & Recreation Atlas,* p. 40, B4

SCENERY: ★★★	
RVs: ★★	
TENTS: ★★★	
SHADE: ★★★★★	
PRIVACY: ★★★	
FACILITIES: ★★	
CAMPGROUND ACTIVITIES: ★★	
AREA ACTIVITIES: ★★★★	
WHEELCHAIR ACCESSIBILITY: ★	

DIRECTIONS: From Exit 33 on I-40 near Navajo Wingate Village, drive south on NM 400 for about 10.5 miles to the campground entrance.

This shady campground lies about 0.5 mile from McGaffey Lake, a popular fishing spot, provides a cool retreat in the Cibola National Forest. Sites have tables with grills, and the camp has restrooms with flush toilets. Gallup is about half an hour away. The Fourth of July holiday is the busiest time here. Drinking water is available.

Reservations are available. **Mount Taylor Ranger District, 505-287-8833.**

Lupine flourishes in the high country of New Mexico

12 RED ROCK STATE PARK

Red cliffs, museum, and Gallup base camp

LOCATION: 8 miles east of Gallup
ELEVATION: 6,700 feet
NUMBER OF SITES: 142
RV NOTES: No maximum length
FEE: Yes
SEASON: Year-round
NEAREST SUPPLY CENTER: Gallup
ACCESS ROAD: Paved
MAP: *New Mexico Road & Recreation Atlas,*
p. 40, B4
DIRECTIONS: From Gallup, drive east on I-40 to Exit 31. Follow the signs into the park.

SCENERY:	★★★★★
RVs:	★★★★
TENTS:	★★★
SHADE:	★★
PRIVACY:	★
FACILITIES:	★★★★
CAMPGROUND ACTIVITIES:	★★
AREA ACTIVITIES:	★★★★★
WHEELCHAIR ACCESSIBILITY:	★★★

Set at the base of bright red cliffs, Red Rock is the closest campground to Gallup. The park offers the Red Rock Museum, a nature trail, a small store, and a spectacular landscape. The rodeo arena on the grounds hosts not just rodeos but concerts, Native American ceremonials, and a wide variety of other events. All of the sites include electric and water hookup. There are two dump stations, some pull-thru parking areas, and paved parking pads. The camp has restrooms and showers.

Reservations at 877-664-7787. Drinking water is available. **Park Manager, 505-722-3829.**

13 EL MORRO NATIONAL MONUMENT

Inscription Rock and El Malpais

SCENERY: ★★★★★	
RVs: ★★	
TENTS: ★★★★★	
SHADE: ★★★	
PRIVACY: ★★	
FACILITIES: ★★★★	
CAMPGROUND ACTIVITIES: ★★★★	
AREA ACTIVITIES: ★★	
WHEELCHAIR ACCESSIBILITY: ★★★★★	

LOCATION: 42 miles southwest of Grants
ELEVATION: 7,100 feet
NUMBER OF SITES: 9
RV NOTES: 28 feet maximum length
FEE: Yes, April–November
SEASON: Year-round, but may be snow-covered in winter; no water off-season
NEAREST SUPPLY CENTER: Grants
ACCESS ROAD: Paved
MAP: *New Mexico Road & Recreation Atlas*, p. 40, D5
DIRECTIONS: From Grants, drive 42 miles southwest on NM 53.

Join the multitude who have camped over the centuries in the shadow of the massive sandstone bluff called El Morro. Many of the passersby and sometime residents have left their mark on the rock face, giving El Morro the nickname "Inscription Rock." Ancestral Puebloans, who left behind a 13th-century, 875-room pueblo on the top of the rock, also left petroglyphs. Starting with Don Juan de Oñate in 1605, other conquistadors, surveyors, railroad workers, members of the short-lived U.S. Camel Corps, emigrants, and travelers of all kinds scrawled more than 2,000 inscriptions. The National Park Service–administered El Morro National Monument includes a visitor center, and several trails leading past some of the most important signatures and inscriptions. One trail takes you up onto the mesa top to explore the ancient pueblo ruins and meander through bulbous rock formations worn smooth by millennia of rain.

Summer holiday weekends are the busiest times. Wheelchair-accessible facilities include one campsite, restrooms, the visitor center, and the interpretive trail, which has a slight grade. The campground includes tables, grills, a pit toilet, water spigots that are turned off in winter, and plenty of trees for shade. Pay phones are available at the visitor center.

No reservations. **El Morro Visitor Center, 505-783-4226.**

NORTHERN GILA

Wild West outlaws Billy the Kid and the Apache Kid appreciated the rugged wilderness of New Mexico's southern mountain ranges when they needed to disappear. Today, lovers of the outdoors and wild places can still meld into these mountains and not see a soul for days. Dominating this region are the rugged Mogollon Mountains and the country's first designated wilderness, the Gila—New Mexico's largest, at 558,014 acres—as well as the Apache Kid, Blue Range, Withington, and Aldo Leopold Wilderness Areas. The namesake of the last was a visionary forester and a founder of the wilderness movement in the United States, whose legacy is much in evidence in this part of the state. Leopold spearheaded the establishment of the

Those who have seen the 1997 movie Contact *will recognize the antennae of the Very Large Array*

Gila as the country's first wilderness in 1924 and in the process preserved what is now known as Gila Cliff Dwellings National Monument.

Area Campgrounds

Visitors to the Catwalk outside of Glenwood follow a walkway in a narrow canyon, hovering over a flowing river past bubblegum-colored boulders. High-mountain streams are popular with anglers. The ghost town of Mogollon offers a glimpse into the region's mining past. And in the middle of this mountainous high country lie the vast Plains of San Agustin, a virtually flat, dry lake bed. The giant radio dishes of the Very Large Array, one of the world's great astronomical radio observatories, spread out across this vast landscape, routinely intermixed with herds of pronghorn.

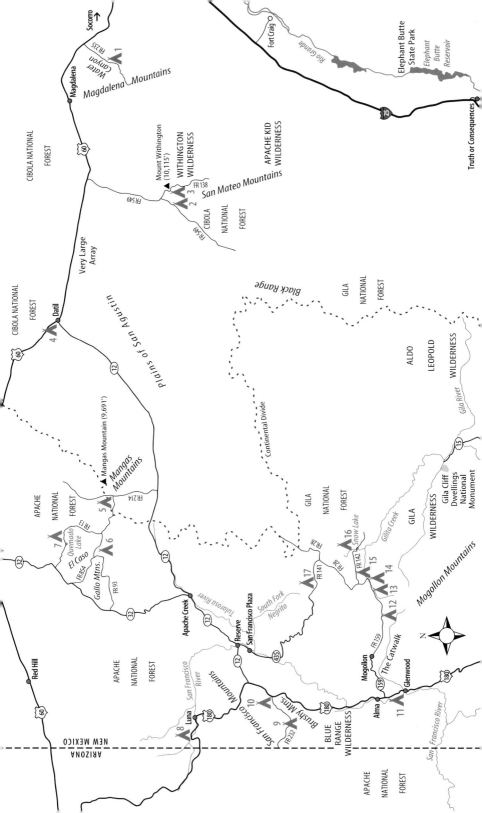

1 WATER CANYON

Forested canyon camping

🚶 🚲

LOCATION: 21 miles west of Socorro
ELEVATION: 7,000 feet
NUMBER OF SITES: 11
RV NOTES: Medium-sized RVs can fit, but there are no facilities
FEE: No
SEASON: Year-round
NEAREST SUPPLY CENTER: Socorro
ACCESS ROAD: Paved
MAP: *New Mexico Road & Recreation Atlas*, p. 47, B10
DIRECTIONS: From Exit 150 on I-25 in Socorro, stay on the main street and follow signs for US 60. From Exit 150, drive about 17 miles to FR 235. Turn left (southwest) onto FR 235. Drive 5.5 miles to the camp entrance.

> SCENERY: ★★★
> RVs: ★
> TENTS: ★★
> SHADE: ★★
> PRIVACY: ★★★
> FACILITIES: ★★
> CAMPGROUND ACTIVITIES: ★★
> AREA ACTIVITIES: ★★
> WHEELCHAIR ACCESSIBILITY: ★

Water Canyon is the closest campground to Socorro, the Bosque del Apache National Wildlife Refuge, and the historic town of Magdalena. Sites lie amid piñon, cedar, and juniper trees in the canyon bottom. A new trail to the top of Water Canyon begins in the camp. Sites include picnic tables and fire rings. There are vault toilets. The group shelter has four tables, and grills; call for reservations. No drinking water is available.
Magdalena Ranger District, 505-854-2281.

2 HUGHES MILL

Hike to Mount Withington Lookout

🚶 🚲

LOCATION: 30 miles southwest of Magdalena
ELEVATION: 8,100 feet
NUMBER OF SITES: 2, plus dispersed
RV NOTES: No more than one medium-sized RV could fit in the campground
FEE: No
SEASON: May–October
NEAREST SUPPLY CENTER: Magdalena
ACCESS ROAD: Rough dirt with sheer drop-offs in places; call ahead for conditions

> SCENERY: ★★★
> RVs: ★
> TENTS: ★★★
> SHADE: ★★★★
> PRIVACY: ★★★★★
> FACILITIES: ★
> CAMPGROUND ACTIVITIES: ★★★
> AREA ACTIVITIES: ★
> WHEELCHAIR ACCESSIBILITY: ★

MAP: *New Mexico Road & Recreation Atlas*, p. 47, C8
DIRECTIONS: From Magdalena, travel west for 12 miles on US 60, then turn south (left) onto FR 549. Drive about 17 miles to the fork where a left turn goes up to the Mount Withington Lookout. Take the right down the hill and drive about a mile to the campground.

Set among oak and pine trees, the camp sits high in the San Mateo Mountains. The trailhead for Trails #65 and #64 is in the campground, leading hikers 7 miles to the Mount Withington Lookout. The little campground has two picnic tables, fire rings, and a vault toilet. The camp area is almost flat. No drinking water is available.

No reservations. **Magdalena Ranger District, 505-854-2281.**

3 BEAR TRAP

Forested solitude

LOCATION: 29 miles southwest of Magdalena
ELEVATION: 8,600 feet
NUMBER OF SITES: 4, plus dispersed
RV NOTES: Medium-sized RVs can access the campground, but small campers are best
FEE: No
SEASON: May–September
NEAREST SUPPLY CENTER: Magdalena
ACCESS ROAD: Rough dirt with sheer drop-offs in places; call ahead for conditions

SCENERY: ★★★
RVs: ★
TENTS: ★★★
SHADE: ★★★★
PRIVACY: ★★★★★
FACILITIES: ★
CAMPGROUND ACTIVITIES: ★★★
AREA ACTIVITIES: ★★
WHEELCHAIR ACCESSIBILITY: ★

MAP: *New Mexico Road & Recreation Atlas*, p. 47, C8
DIRECTIONS: From Magdalena, travel west for 12 miles on US 60, then turn south (left) onto FR 549. Drive about 17 miles to the fork where a left turn goes up to the Mount Withington Lookout. Take the right down the hill and drive about 0.5 mile to the campground.

Bear Trap offers a pared-down wilderness experience. A small spring flows above the camp area. There are picnic tables, fire rings, and an outhouse. The ground is not very level. The trail to Mount Withington Lookout is about 0.5 mile away in Hughes Mill Campground.

No reservations. **Magdalena Ranger District, 505-854-2281.**

4 DATIL WELL NATIONAL RECREATION SITE
Nature trail, Datil Mountains, and the Very Large Array

LOCATION: 1.1 miles northwest of Datil
ELEVATION: 7,400 feet
NUMBER OF SITES: 22
RV NOTES: No maximum length; there are no hookups; the nearest dump station is in the town of Datil
FEE: Yes
SEASON: Year-round
NEAREST SUPPLY CENTER: Datil

SCENERY: ★★★
RVs: ★★
TENTS: ★★★★
SHADE: ★★★
PRIVACY: ★★★★
FACILITIES: ★★★★
CAMPGROUND ACTIVITIES: ★★
AREA ACTIVITIES: ★★★
WHEELCHAIR ACCESSIBILITY: ★★★

ACCESS ROAD: Paved and well-maintained gravel
MAP: *New Mexico Road & Recreation Atlas*, p. 47, A7
DIRECTIONS: From Datil, drive west on US 60 for 1 mile. Turn left onto the campground access road.

Datil Well was once one of fifteen wells along the old Magdalena cattle-drive trail between New Mexico and Arizona. Today the campground makes a great base camp for exploring the Datil Mountains and the Very Large Array (VLA) 15 miles away, made famous by the 1997 movie

Contact. Wildlife abounds in this area, including herds of pronghorn that frequent the Plains of San Agustin to the east. The campground is filled with piñon, cedar, and juniper trees. Families can also enjoy two short nature trails.

Sites, which are usually available, have picnic tables and grills. Twelve of the sites also have shelters. Restrooms and water hydrants are scattered throughout the area. Toilets and some campsites are fairly wheelchair-accessible, where gravel and space are sufficient that a wheelchair can navigate in fair weather.

For groups of up to 30 people, there is a shelter with three big picnic tables, a grill, a fire ring, and a pit toilet. Group visitors can tent-camp on the grassy area adjacent to the shelter, park an RV in the large parking lot, or occupy one of the developed sites and walk the short path to the group area.

No reservations. **BLM Socorro Field Office, 505-835-0412.**

5 VALLE TIO VENCES

Camp on the Continental Divide

LOCATION: 44 miles west of Datil on FR 214
ELEVATION: 8,200 feet
NUMBER OF SITES: 4 plus overflow
RV NOTES: No maximum length
FEE: No
SEASON: Year-round, but may be inaccessible because of snow
NEAREST SUPPLY CENTER: Datil
ACCESS ROAD: Fair weather; call ahead for conditions

SCENERY: ★★★
RVs: NR
TENTS: ★★
SHADE: ★★★★
PRIVACY: ★★★★
FACILITIES: ★★
CAMPGROUND ACTIVITIES: ★★
AREA ACTIVITIES: ★★
WHEELCHAIR ACCESSIBILITY: ★

MAP: *New Mexico Road & Recreation Atlas*, p. 46, B5
DIRECTIONS: From Datil, take NM 12 southwest 34 miles and turn right (north) onto FR 214. Drive 9.3 miles to the campground.

Set among the forested mesas of the Mangas Mountains, Valle Tio Vences is a popular camp for hikers along the Continental Divide Trail. About 4 miles northeast along the trail is the 9,691-foot summit of Mangas Mountain itself. Less than a mile south of the campground off FR 214 is FR 13, which heads west and north to Quemado Lake Recreation Area from the less frequently seen side.

The campground is thickly covered with pine needles, so it is possible to find a soft spot to pitch a tent. Expect to be visited by cattle during your stay. There are picnic tables, fire rings, and a pit toilet. No drinking water is available, although you could treat water available at Valle Tio Vences Spring, about a quarter-mile northeast of the site.

No reservations. **Quemado Ranger District, 505-773-4678.**

6 ARMIJO
Forested camping

LOCATION: 25 miles south of Quemado
ELEVATION: 7,800 feet
NUMBER OF SITES: Dispersed
RV NOTES: No maximum length
FEE: No
SEASON: April–November
NEAREST SUPPLY CENTER: Quemado
ACCESS ROAD: Very rough dirt road and virtually impassable when muddy; call ahead for conditions

SCENERY: ★★★
RVS: ★
TENTS: ★★★
SHADE: ★★★★★
PRIVACY: ★★★★
FACILITIES: ★
CAMPGROUND ACTIVITIES: ★★
AREA ACTIVITIES: ★
WHEELCHAIR ACCESSIBILITY: ★★★

MAP: *New Mexico Road & Recreation Atlas*, p. 46, B4
DIRECTIONS: From Quemado, drive south on NM 32 and turn left (east) on FR 854. Drive 4 miles to the campground.

The campground is spread out below tall pines. Wild turkeys, deer, and elk can be seen on occasion. Local forest roads offer great mountain biking. There are a few picnic tables and fire rings but no restroom. No drinking water is available.

No reservations. **Quemado Ranger District, 505-773-4678.**

7 QUEMADO LAKE
Rainbow trout and canoeing

LOCATION: 20 miles south of Quemado
ELEVATION: 7,800 feet
NUMBER OF SITES: 40, plus dispersed
RV NOTES: 42 feet maximum length; sites with electric and water hookups are in Juniper; the dump station is in Piñon
FEE: Yes
SEASON: May–October
NEAREST SUPPLY CENTER: Quemado
ACCESS ROAD: Paved

SCENERY: ★★★★
RVS: ★★★★
TENTS: ★★★★
SHADE: ★★★
PRIVACY: ★★★
FACILITIES: ★★★★
CAMPGROUND ACTIVITIES: ★★★
AREA ACTIVITIES: ★★
WHEELCHAIR ACCESSIBILITY: ★★★★

MAP: *New Mexico Road & Recreation Atlas*, p. 46, A4
DIRECTIONS: From Quemado, drive south on NM 32 for about 14 miles. Turn left (east) onto FR 13 and go 4 miles to the lake.

Tucked away in the Gallo Mountains, Quemado is a very popular recreation area. Visitors can fish, rent boats in the summer, hike around the lake, or trek 6 miles round-trip to the El Caso Lookout. Drinking water is available. On most holidays Juniper fills up quickly, so come as early as possible to secure a hookup site.

Lakeside **Juniper** has 18 sites with electricity and water hookups. There are also several tent-only sites. All parking pads are graded gravel, and sites have picnic tables and fire rings with grills. **Piñon** offers 22 sites with gravel pads but no hookups. All sites have picnic tables and fire rings with grills. The dump station is in this area. **El Caso** is primitive, with some tables and fire rings with grills. The trail to El Caso Lookout begins here.

There are two group sites. Each has a 28-by-20-foot shelter with picnic tables and large grills. Site A accommodates 30 people; Site B holds 75. Cove Day Use Area has a boat ramp and floating fishing dock, which is wheelchair-accessible, as are restrooms and, in fair weather, those campsites that have well-graded gravel pads.

No reservations. **Quemado Ranger District, 505-773-4678.**

8 HEAD OF THE DITCH

Aspens and agate hunting

LOCATION: 2 miles west of Luna
ELEVATION: 7,200 feet
NUMBER OF SITES: Dispersed
RV NOTES: RVs not recommended
FEE: No
SEASON: April–November
NEAREST SUPPLY CENTER: Reserve
ACCESS ROAD: Paved to the campground
MAP: *New Mexico Road & Recreation Atlas*,
p. 46, C2

SCENERY: ★★★
RVS: NR
TENTS: ★★
SHADE: ★★
PRIVACY: ★★★★
FACILITIES: ★
CAMPGROUND ACTIVITIES: ★★
AREA ACTIVITIES: ★
WHEELCHAIR ACCESSIBILITY: ★

DIRECTIONS: From Reserve, take NM 12 southwest for about 6 miles. At the junction, veer right and take US 180 northwest for about 14.5 miles to the campground, west of Luna.

Rock hounders take note. Campers come here to hunt for agates, relax to the sound of the river, and unwind under the golden aspens in the fall. In the San Francisco Mountains, the primitive campsites are spread out alongside the San Francisco River. Facilities include six tables and two outhouses.

No reservations. **Luna Work Center, 505-547-2612.**

9 PUEBLO PARK

CCC camp, archaeological sites, and a nature trail

LOCATION: 17 miles southwest of Reserve
ELEVATION: 6,200 feet
NUMBER OF SITES: 6, plus dispersed
RV NOTES: Smaller-sized RVs can fit
FEE: Yes
SEASON: April–November
NEAREST SUPPLY CENTER: Reserve
ACCESS ROAD: FR 232 is fair-weather; call ahead for conditions
MAP: *New Mexico Road & Recreation Atlas*, p. 46, D2
DIRECTIONS: From Reserve, take NM 12 southwest for about 6 miles. At the junction, veer left onto US 180 south. Go about 6 miles, turn right onto FR 232, and drive 5.5 miles to the campground.

SCENERY: ★★★
RVS: ★
TENTS: ★★★
SHADE: ★★★★★
PRIVACY: ★★★
FACILITIES: ★★
CAMPGROUND ACTIVITIES: ★★★
AREA ACTIVITIES: ★
WHEELCHAIR ACCESSIBILITY: ★

The camp is shaded by tall pines on the edge of the Blue Range Wilderness. The area was once a Civilian Conservation Corps project, as evidenced by the distinctive stone fire rings and nearby baseball diamond. The park features an interpretive trail exploring the culture of the Mogollon people, who once inhabited the area.

No drinking water is available. The park is very busy on holidays and in hunting season. Note that large groups need a special permit to camp here.

No reservations. **Glenwood Ranger District, 505-539-2481.**

10 Cottonwood

Camp in a shady ravine

Location: 12 miles southwest of Reserve
Elevation: 5,800 feet
Number of Sites: 5
RV Notes: RVs not recommended
Fee: No
Season: April–November
Nearest Supply Center: Reserve
Access Road: Paved
Map: *New Mexico Road & Recreation Atlas*,
p. 46, D2
Directions: From Reserve, take NM 12 southwest for about 6 miles. At the junction, veer left onto US 180 south. Go about 6 miles; the campground is on the right.

Scenery: ★★
RVs: NR
Tents: ★★
Shade: ★★★★★
Privacy: ★★★
Facilities: ★★
Campground Activities: ★
Area Activities: ★★★
Wheelchair Accessibility: ★

Lining the bottom of a shady ravine in the Brushy Mountains are campsites with tables and grills. Cottonwood is easily accessed if you need to get to a campground after dark, since the entrance is right off the highway. Choose a site farther into the campground to minimize road noise. There is a wheelchair-accessible toilet but no drinking water.

No reservations. **Glenwood Ranger District, 505-539-2481.**

Lizards are common throughout the state and can often be seen sunning themselves on rocks

11 BIGHORN

Base camp for Glenwood and Mogollon

LOCATION: 1 mile north of Glenwood on US 180
ELEVATION: 5,000 feet
NUMBER OF SITES: 5
RV NOTES: No maximum length
FEE: No
SEASON: Year-round
NEAREST SUPPLY CENTER: Glenwood
ACCESS ROAD: Paved
MAP: *New Mexico Road & Recreation Atlas,* p. 46, E2
DIRECTIONS: Go north from Glenwood a mile on US 180 and turn left into the campground.

SCENERY: ★★
RVs: ★
TENTS: ★★
SHADE: ★
PRIVACY: ★★
FACILITIES: ★★
CAMPGROUND ACTIVITIES: ★
AREA ACTIVITIES: ★★★★
WHEELCHAIR ACCESSIBILITY: ★

Bighorn lies just off US 180. It is a good base camp for exploring the historic towns of Glenwood and Mogollon, for hiking the breathtaking Catwalk deep into a slot canyon, or for journeying into the Gila Wilderness. Sites have picnic tables and fire rings. The vault toilet is wheelchair-accessible. No drinking water is available.

No reservations. **Glenwood Ranger District, 505-539-2481.**

12 BURSUM

Shady solitude

🚶🏽 🚴

LOCATION: 8 miles east of Mogollon
ELEVATION: 9,200 feet
NUMBER OF SITES: 2
RV NOTES: RVs not recommended
FEE: No
SEASON: May–October
NEAREST SUPPLY CENTER: Glenwood
ACCESS ROAD: The road past Mogollon is
dirt and closed all winter because of snow;
call ahead for conditions.

SCENERY: ★★★
RVs: NR
TENTS: ★★★
SHADE: ★★★★
PRIVACY: ★★★
FACILITIES: ★
CAMPGROUND ACTIVITIES: ★★
AREA ACTIVITIES: ★★★
WHEELCHAIR ACCESSIBILITY: ★

MAP: *New Mexico Road & Recreation Atlas*, p. 46, E3
DIRECTIONS: From US 180, 3.5 miles north of Glenwood, head east on
FR 159 to Mogollon, about 7 miles. Continue 8 miles past the village
to the campground.

Bursum sits high in the Mogollon Mountains on the edge of the Gila
Wilderness. Access to the Crest Trail is about a mile away. There is a picnic
table on either side of the road with fire rings. No drinking water is available.
No reservations. **Glenwood Ranger District, 505-539-2481.**

Old vehicles in the nearby living ghost town of Mogollon

MOGOLLON

Mogollon is a fascinating time capsule of the region's mining past. What is now a sleepy little hamlet hidden away in a deep, picturesque ravine was once a boomtown built primarily on the success of gold and silver strikes at the Little Fannie Mine. By 1902, the population was large enough to support fourteen saloons, seven restaurants, five stores, two hotels, and a few brothels. The mines of the area operated until World War I. Many of the original structures still stand, and several have been renovated. Scattered along the hillsides on the road down to Mogollon are ruins including tracks for moving ore, gate houses, and mining structures.

A word of caution: If you have any fear of heights or are not completely comfortable driving along a narrow road full of hairpin switchbacks, do not attempt to access Mogollon from the west off US 180. That being said, to get to town from Glenwood, drive north on US 180 for about 3.5 miles. Turn right onto NM 159 and continue 9 miles to Mogollon.

A renovated building displays relics of
Mogollon's mining past

13 BEN LILLY

Creekside camping

SCENERY: ★★★★
RVs: ★
TENTS: ★★★
SHADE: ★★★
PRIVACY: ★★★★
FACILITIES: ★★
CAMPGROUND ACTIVITIES: ★★
AREA ACTIVITIES: ★★★
WHEELCHAIR ACCESSIBILITY: ★

LOCATION: 16 miles east of Mogollon
ELEVATION: 7,950 feet
NUMBER OF SITES: 5
RV NOTES: No maximum length
FEE: No
SEASON: April–November
NEAREST SUPPLY CENTER: Reserve
ACCESS ROAD: May be closed because of snow; call ahead for conditions

MAP: *New Mexico Road & Recreation Atlas*, p. 46, E4
DIRECTIONS: From Reserve, travel south on NM 435. After about 5 miles, NM 435 changes to FR 141. After traveling about 25 miles total, the pavement ends. Continue on for another 11 miles to the junction with FR 28. Turn right onto FR 28 and drive 14 miles to Ben Lilly, past Willow Creek Campground.

A campground alongside Willow Creek, Ben Lilly offers fishing and sits only a mile from the Gila Wilderness. The sites, each containing a table and fire ring with grill, are large enough for a family or group to spread out comfortably. There are two vault toilets. Drinking water is available at Snow Lake.

No reservations. **Reserve Ranger District, 505-533-6232.**

14 WILLOW CREEK

Creekside camping in a beautiful meadow

LOCATION: 16.4 miles east of Mogollon
ELEVATION: 7,950 feet
NUMBER OF SITES: 6
RV NOTES: No maximum length
FEE: No
SEASON: April–November
NEAREST SUPPLY CENTER: Reserve
ACCESS ROAD: May be closed because of snow; call ahead for conditions

SCENERY: ★★★★	
RVs: ★	
TENTS: ★★★	
SHADE: ★★★	
PRIVACY: ★★★★	
FACILITIES: ★★	
CAMPGROUND ACTIVITIES: ★★	
AREA ACTIVITIES: ★★★	
WHEELCHAIR ACCESSIBILITY: ★	

MAP: *New Mexico Road & Recreation Atlas,* p. 46, E4
DIRECTIONS: From Reserve, travel south on NM 435. After about 5 miles, NM 435 changes to FR 141. After traveling about 25 miles total, the pavement ends. Continue on for another 11 miles to the junction with FR 28. Turn right onto FR 28 and drive 13 miles to the campground.

Dotted along the edge of the free-flowing Willow Creek, the campground offers fishing and several trailheads within a few miles that lead into the Gila Wilderness. All sites have a table and a fire ring with a grill. There are two vault toilets. Be prepared to ford the creek to access the campsites. If all of the sites at Willow Creek are full, try Ben Lilly Campground, a bit farther down the access road. Drinking water is available at Snow Lake.

No reservations. **Reserve Ranger District, 505-533-6232.**

15 GILITA

Fishing and trail into the Gila Wilderness

LOCATION: 17 miles east of Mogollon
ELEVATION: 7,950 feet
NUMBER OF SITES: 7
RV NOTES: No maximum length
FEE: No
SEASON: April–November
NEAREST SUPPLY CENTER: Reserve
ACCESS ROAD: May be closed because of snow; call ahead for conditions
MAP: *New Mexico Road & Recreation Atlas*, p. 46, E4
DIRECTIONS: From Reserve, travel south on NM 435. After about 5 miles, NM 435 changes to FR 141. After traveling about 25 miles total, the pavement ends. Continue on for another 11 miles to the junction with FR 28. Turn right onto FR 28 and drive 13 miles to Gilita.

Trail #151 begins at the end of Gilita Campground and leads into the Gila Wilderness and 24 miles one way to the Gila Cliff Dwellings. This trail is a favorite of hikers and horseback riders, although there are no equestrian facilities. Anglers can fish in Gilita Creek. Separated by stands of creekside brush and shaded by tall ponderosa pines, the secluded sites have tables and fire rings with grills. There are two vault toilets. Drinking water is available at Snow Lake.

SCENERY:	★★★
RVs:	★
TENTS:	★★★
SHADE:	★★★
PRIVACY:	★★★★
FACILITIES:	★★
CAMPGROUND ACTIVITIES:	★★★
AREA ACTIVITIES:	★★★
WHEELCHAIR ACCESSIBILITY:	★

No reservations. **Reserve Ranger District, 505-533-6232**.

16 DIPPING VAT AT SNOW LAKE

Mountaintop lake fishing

SCENERY: ★★★★
RVs: ★★
TENTS: ★★★
SHADE: ★★★
PRIVACY: ★★★
FACILITIES: ★★★
CAMPGROUND ACTIVITIES: ★★★
AREA ACTIVITIES: ★★★
WHEELCHAIR ACCESSIBILITY: ★★★

LOCATION: 32 miles southeast of Lower San Francisco Plaza
ELEVATION: 7,400 feet
NUMBER OF SITES: 40
RV NOTES: No maximum length; there are no RV facilities
FEE: Yes
SEASON: April–November
NEAREST SUPPLY CENTER: Reserve

ACCESS ROAD: Fair-weather; call ahead for conditions
MAP: *New Mexico Road & Recreation Atlas,* p. 46, E4
DIRECTIONS: From Reserve, travel south on NM 435. After about 5 miles, NM 435 changes to FR 141. After traveling about 25 miles total, the pavement ends. Continue on for another 11 miles to the junction with FR 28. Turn right onto FR 28 and drive 10 miles to the junction with FR 142. Take FR 142 east (left) and travel 6 miles to Snow Lake.

Set above 50-acre Snow Lake, Dipping Vat is popular with anglers fishing for rainbow trout, hikers and horseback riders heading into the Gila Wilderness, and people who come year after year just to enjoy the scenery. The lake is bordered by rolling, high-mountain meadows crisscrossed by clear streams. Wildlife and cattle are drawn to the abundant water.

Campsites, which are usually available, have fire rings, picnic tables, and gravel parking pads. There are no hookups, but water hydrants and vault toilets are scattered through the campground. The toilets and some campsites have maintained gravel pads and elevated fire rings for access by wheelchair.

The lake has a boat ramp for vessels with electric motors only. Note that there are no horse corrals.

No reservations. **Reserve Ranger District, 505-533-6232.**

17 SOUTH FORK NEGRITO

Streamside sites

LOCATION: 26 miles southeast of Lower San Francisco Plaza
ELEVATION: 7,450 feet
NUMBER OF SITES: 6
RV NOTES: No maximum length
FEE: No
SEASON: Year-round, but may be inaccessible because of snow
NEAREST SUPPLY CENTER: Reserve
ACCESS ROAD: May be closed because of snow; call ahead for conditions
MAP: *New Mexico Road & Recreation Atlas*, p. 46, D4
DIRECTIONS: From Reserve, travel south on NM 435. After about 5 miles, NM 435 changes to FR 141. After traveling about 25 miles total, the pavement ends. Continue for another 6 miles to the campground.

SCENERY: ★★★
RVS: ★
TENTS: ★★★
SHADE: ★★★★
PRIVACY: ★★★
FACILITIES: ★★
CAMPGROUND ACTIVITIES: ★★
AREA ACTIVITIES: ★★★
WHEELCHAIR ACCESSIBILITY: ★

The campground is dispersed along a bend in the South Fork Negrito, and FR 141 splits it in two. Either side offers sites that are off the road and along the running river. There are six picnic tables and fire rings marking the sites, and vault toilets are available. No drinking water is available.

No reservations. **Reserve Ranger District, 505-533-6232.**

The Catwalk, off Forest Road 159 near the historic town of Mogollon

SOUTHERN GILA AND SOUTHWEST

The Gila and Aldo Leopold Wilderness Areas encompass a large section of the high country in what's known as the Gila, providing unrivaled opportunities to hike for days in unspoiled nature. The Mogollon Mountains and the Black Range dominate this vast area, but smaller ranges like the Pinos Altos, Tularosas, Mimbres, and others also contribute to the region's rugged landscape, carved by the Gila and San Francisco River systems. Tucked into the beautiful West Fork Gila River canyon is Gila Cliff Dwellings National Monument, site of numerous Ancestral Puebloan structures and petroglyphs. To the south of the Gila, the high country descends into the plains of the Chihuahuan Desert, periodically interrupted by a small ridge. One odd break in this austere panorama is found at City of Rocks State Park, where ancient volcanic debris has eroded into what appear to be melting monoliths. Farther south, Rockhound State Park invites visitors to hunt for jasper, agate, and quartz crystals on the sides of the Little Florida Mountains. And then, almost as far south as you can travel in New Mexico before crossing into Old Mexico, you reach the site of Pancho Villa's famous raid in 1916 in the town of Columbus.

The Gila River carves dramatic canyons through the state's southwestern high country

Area Campgrounds

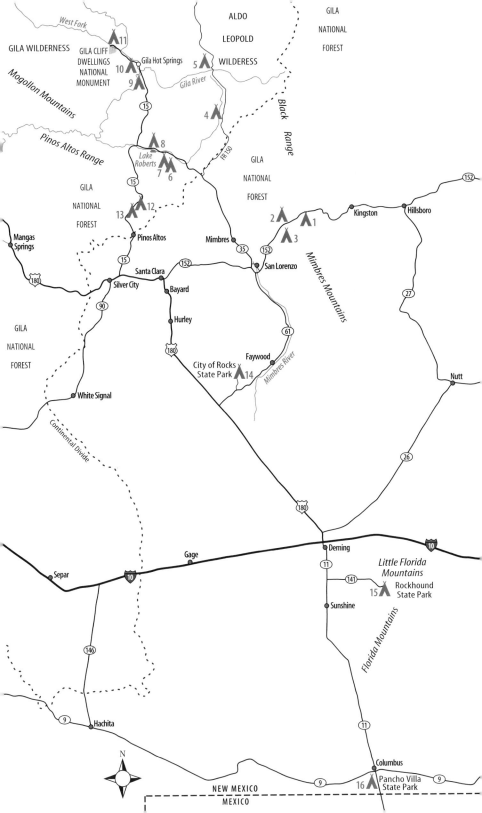

1 IRON CREEK

Pine forest camping in the Black Range

LOCATION: 8.1 miles west of Kingston
ELEVATION: 7,800 feet
NUMBER OF SITES: 15
RV NOTES: 28 feet maximum length
FEE: No
SEASON: Year-round; may be inaccessible in winter because of snow
NEAREST SUPPLY CENTER: Santa Clara
ACCESS ROAD: Paved; the drive is not for those with a fear of heights
MAP: *New Mexico Road & Recreation Atlas*, p. 47, G7
DIRECTIONS: From Kingston, take NM 152 west 8.1 miles to the campground.

SCENERY: ★★
RVs: ★★
TENTS: ★★★
SHADE: ★★★
PRIVACY: ★★
FACILITIES: ★★
CAMPGROUND ACTIVITIES: ★★
AREA ACTIVITIES: ★★★
WHEELCHAIR ACCESSIBILITY: ★★

Shaded by ponderosa pines and just off the highway, Iron Creek provides a base camp for accessing trailheads along NM 152. The campground provides tables, fire rings, and wheelchair-accessible toilets. No drinking water is available.

No reservations. **Silver City Ranger District, 505-388-8201.**

2 UPPER GALLINAS

Hike to the Black Range crest

LOCATION: 9 miles west of Kingston
ELEVATION: 6,700 feet
NUMBER OF SITES: Dispersed
RV NOTES: 28 feet maximum length
FEE: No
SEASON: Year-round; may be inaccessible because of snow
NEAREST SUPPLY CENTER: Santa Clara
ACCESS ROAD: Paved
MAP: *New Mexico Road & Recreation Atlas*, p. 47, G7
DIRECTIONS: From Kingston, drive west 9 miles on NM 152 to the campground.

SCENERY: ★★
RVS: ★
TENTS: ★★★
SHADE: ★★★★
PRIVACY: ★★★
FACILITIES: ★★
CAMPGROUND ACTIVITIES: ★★★
AREA ACTIVITIES: ★★★
WHEELCHAIR ACCESSIBILITY: ★★

Begin the hike on Trail #129 from the campground to the crest of the Black Range. The campsites are primitive, with a few tables, fire rings, and a wheelchair-accessible toilet. The campground lies parallel to NM 152. No drinking water is available.

No reservations. **Silver City Ranger District, 505-388-8201.**

3 LOWER GALLINAS

Camping in the Black Range

LOCATION: 9.5 miles west of Kingston
ELEVATION: 6,700 feet
NUMBER OF SITES: Dispersed
RV NOTES: 28 feet maximum length
FEE: No
SEASON: Year-round; may be inaccessible because of snow
NEAREST SUPPLY CENTER: Santa Clara
ACCESS ROAD: Paved
MAP: *New Mexico Road & Recreation Atlas*, p. 47, G7
DIRECTIONS: From Kingston, take NM 152 west 9.5 miles to the campground.

SCENERY:	★★★
RVs:	★
TENTS:	★★★
SHADE:	★★★★
PRIVACY:	★★★
FACILITIES:	★
CAMPGROUND ACTIVITIES:	★
AREA ACTIVITIES:	★★★
WHEELCHAIR ACCESSIBILITY:	★

Lower Gallinas is a primitive forested campground in the Black Range, offering tables, fire rings, and a toilet. The sites stretch out along a normally dry riverbed in a deep canyon; be aware of flash-flood danger during late-summer monsoons. No drinking water is available.

No reservations.
Silver City Ranger District, 505-388-8201.

A cholla in bloom near Lower Gallinas

SCENIC DRIVE: MINING IN SOUTHWESTERN NEW MEXICO

You can tour a major swath of New Mexico's mining past and present along this loop through the state's southwest. Begin at the Silver City Museum (312 West Broadway) to get acquainted with the region's mining history. Fill your gas tank in town, as there are virtually no facilities along this drive, then head east on US 180 for about 7.5 miles. Turn left onto NM 152 and drive about 5.5 miles to the overlook of the Chino copper mine, also called the Santa Rita mine. Whether you are fascinated or horrified by the sight, this operation is one of the country's largest open-pit mines. The pit is so deep that dump trucks with 12-foot-tall tires, each hauling almost a half-million pounds of excavated earth per load, look like toys.

Stay on NM 152 east through San Lorenzo and up into the Black Range, skirting the southern end of the Aldo Leopold Wilderness. The landscape mutates from desert grass dotted with yucca and piñon to deep, rocky crevasses lined with tall ponderosa pine, then back into high desert. The first town you reach east of the range, some 28 miles from the Chino mine, is Kingston. Built on mining silver, Kingston was once a rowdy Old West town, with a population of almost 7,000 in its heyday. In 1882, the town boasted a bank, 22 saloons, 14 groceries, three hotels, three newspapers, a brewery, gambling halls, a brothel, and an opera house. Some of the original structures still stand, although today only a handful of folks call Kingston home.

Another 8.5 miles east on NM 152 is Hillsboro, founded in 1877 and once the seat of Sierra County. The town's nearby Opportunity and Ready pay mines produced more than $12 million in gold and silver. Visitors today find a small artists' colony, complete with cafés and galleries housed in century-old adobes. From Hillsboro, turn south onto NM 27 and follow the highway into a treeless, rugged, yucca-strewn desert landscape, oddly named Lake Valley. About 17 miles south down the road is a large, well-preserved ghost town of the same name. The old Lake Valley school now houses a museum tracing the area's past through photographs, artifacts, illustrations, and newspaper articles. Fourteen miles south of Lake City is the junction with NM 26; bear right to take NM 26 the 29 miles to Deming.

Southeast of Deming you can actually try your hand at pulling riches from the earth. Head south on NM 11 from Deming about 5 miles, turn left (east) onto NM 141, and drive 9 miles to Rockhound State Park. Park visitors are actually invited to climb over the rocky Little Florida Mountains to collect semiprecious stones such as jasper, quartz, agate, and common opal. The 15-pound collection limit should allow you to gather enough sparkling tidbits to impress your friends. From back in Deming, US 180 will take you north the 54 miles to Silver City to complete the loop.

4 ROCKY CANYON

Remote forested canyon and a trailhead

SCENERY: ★★★
RVs: NR
TENTS: ★★
SHADE: ★★★★★
PRIVACY: ★★★★★
FACILITIES: ★
CAMPGROUND ACTIVITIES: ★★
AREA ACTIVITIES: ★
WHEELCHAIR ACCESSIBILITY: ★

LOCATION: 22.3 miles north of Mimbres
ELEVATION: 7,600 feet
NUMBER OF SITES: 2
RV NOTES: RVs not recommended
FEE: No
SEASON: Year-round; may be inaccessible because of snow
NEAREST SUPPLY CENTER: Santa Clara
ACCESS ROAD: Rough, fair-weather; high-clearance 4x4 recommended
MAP: *New Mexico Road & Recreation Atlas*, p. 46, F6
DIRECTIONS: From Mimbres, travel north about 10 miles on NM 35. Turn right and head north on FR 150 another 12.5 miles to the campground.

A lovely primitive campground set alongside a stream under a canopy of oaks and pines, Rocky Canyon offers a secluded getaway with opportunities to see deer, elk, and other wildlife. Access the #700 Trail leading into the Gila Wilderness. No drinking water is available.

No reservations. **Wilderness Ranger District, 505-536-2250.**

5 BLACK CANYON

Riverside glade and a trailhead

SCENERY: ★★★★
RVs: NR
TENTS: ★★
SHADE: ★★★
PRIVACY: ★★★
FACILITIES: ★
CAMPGROUND ACTIVITIES: ★★★
AREA ACTIVITIES: ★★
WHEELCHAIR ACCESSIBILITY: ★

LOCATION: 34 miles north of Mimbres
ELEVATION: 7,600 feet
NUMBER OF SITES: 3
RV NOTES: RVs not recommended
FEE: No
SEASON: Year-round; may be inaccessible because of snow
NEAREST SUPPLY CENTER: Santa Clara
ACCESS ROAD: Rough, fair-weather; high-clearance 4x4 recommended
MAP: *New Mexico Road & Recreation Atlas*, p. 46, F6
DIRECTIONS: From Mimbres, travel north about 10 miles on NM 35. Turn right and head north on FR 150 for 24 miles to the campground.

Black Canyon lies in a green glade alongside a river. The sites are very primitive, with just tables, fire rings, and a toilet. Access Trail #94 into the Gila Wilderness. No drinking water is available.

No reservations. **Wilderness Ranger District, 505-536-2250.**

6 SAPILLO (GROUP)

Dispersed pine grove camping

SCENERY: ★★★
RVs: ★
TENTS: ★★★
SHADE: ★★★★
PRIVACY: ★★★
FACILITIES: ★
CAMPGROUND ACTIVITIES: ★★★
AREA ACTIVITIES: ★★★
WHEELCHAIR ACCESSIBILITY: ★

LOCATION: 14 miles northwest of Mimbres
ELEVATION: 6,300 feet
NUMBER OF SITES: Dispersed
RV NOTES: No maximum length; the access road can be rough
FEE: No
SEASON: Year-round; may be inaccessible because of snow
NEAREST SUPPLY CENTER: Silver City
ACCESS ROAD: Fair-weather; call ahead for conditions

MAP: *New Mexico Road & Recreation Atlas*, p. 46, G6
DIRECTIONS: From Mimbres, travel 14 miles northwest along NM 35 to the access road, on the left.

A large dispersed area set among ponderosa pine and juniper, Sapillo can accommodate up to 50 people. Access nearby Lake Roberts for fishing and boating, or hike into the Gila Wilderness. The Continental Divide Trail passes near the fence that borders the campground. There are picnic tables, fire rings, and two new vault toilets. No drinking water is available.

Call for reservations. **Wilderness Ranger District, 505-536-2250.**

7 UPPER END

Water's-edge camping at Lake Roberts

LOCATION: 19.7 miles northwest of Mimbres
ELEVATION: 6,050 feet
NUMBER OF SITES: 12
RV NOTES: No maximum length
FEE: Yes
SEASON: May–October
NEAREST SUPPLY CENTER: Silver City
ACCESS ROAD: Paved

SCENERY: ★★★
RVs: ★
TENTS: ★★★
SHADE: ★★★★
PRIVACY: ★★★
FACILITIES: ★
CAMPGROUND ACTIVITIES: ★★★
AREA ACTIVITIES: ★★★★★
WHEELCHAIR ACCESSIBILITY: ★

MAP: *New Mexico Road & Recreation Atlas*, p. 46, G6
DIRECTIONS: From Mimbres, drive north on NM 35 for 19.7 miles to the campground entrance, on the left.

Situated along the shore of Lake Roberts, Upper End provides fishing access and well-spaced campsites under tall pines. There are tables, fire rings, and two new restrooms with running water. Drinking water is available.

No reservations. **Wilderness Ranger District, 505-536-2250.**

8 MESA

Sites overlooking Lake Roberts

LOCATION: 20.4 miles northwest of Mimbres
ELEVATION: 6,200 feet
NUMBER OF SITES: 24
RV NOTES: 28 feet maximum length
FEE: Yes
SEASON: May–October
NEAREST SUPPLY CENTER: Silver City
ACCESS ROAD: Paved
MAP: *New Mexico Road & Recreation Atlas*, p. 46, G5

SCENERY:	★★★★
RVs:	★★★
TENTS:	★★★
SHADE:	★
PRIVACY:	★★★
FACILITIES:	★★
CAMPGROUND ACTIVITIES:	★★★
AREA ACTIVITIES:	★★★
WHEELCHAIR ACCESSIBILITY:	★★

DIRECTIONS: From Mimbres, travel north on NM 35 for 20.4 miles to the campground entrance, on the left.

Mesa is a developed campground on a bluff overlooking the aquamarine waters of Lake Roberts, a popular fishing location. Holiday weekends are busy. A boat ramp, toilets, and drinking water are available, and sites have picnic tables and grills. Gila Cliff Dwellings National Monument is a short drive to the north along NM 15.

No reservations. **Wilderness Ranger District, 505-536-2250.**

9 GRAPEVINE

Riverside camping and fishing

SCENERY: ★★★
RVS: NR
TENTS: ★★
SHADE: ★★★★
PRIVACY: ★★★★★
FACILITIES: ★
CAMPGROUND ACTIVITIES: ★★
AREA ACTIVITIES: ★★★★
WHEELCHAIR ACCESSIBILITY: ★

LOCATION: 43 miles north of Silver City
ELEVATION: 5,600 feet
NUMBER OF SITES: Dispersed
RV NOTES: RVs not recommended
FEE: No
SEASON: Year-round; may be inaccessible because of snow
NEAREST SUPPLY CENTER: Silver City
ACCESS ROAD: Paved to the campground, which is a network of fair-weather roads

MAP: *New Mexico Road & Recreation Atlas*, p. 46, F5
DIRECTIONS: From Silver City, drive east 2 miles on US 180 to NM 15. Turn left (north) and go 26 miles, then turn left again to continue north on NM 15, about 17 miles to the campground.

Laid out along the stocked Gila River, Grapevine is popular as a fishing spot and a nice overflow area for the Gila Cliff Dwellings National Monument campgrounds 5 miles to the north. The sites are primitive and well-shaded. There are a few tables, fires rings, and toilets. No drinking water is available.
No reservations. **Wilderness Ranger District, 505-536-2250.**

10 FORKS

Secluded fishing in the Gila River

LOCATION: 43.5 miles north of Silver City
ELEVATION: 5,500 feet
NUMBER OF SITES: Dispersed
RV NOTES: Any size RV can fit in the upper camp area, but the road to the lower areas may be too steep and rough to access
FEE: No
SEASON: Year-round; may be inaccessible because of snow
NEAREST SUPPLY CENTER: Silver City
ACCESS ROAD: Paved to the campground. In the camp the roads are fair-weather and can be quite rough. Roads to the riverside are quite steep.
MAP: *New Mexico Road & Recreation Atlas*, p. 46, F5
DIRECTIONS: From Silver City, drive east 2 miles on US 180 to NM 15. Turn left (north) and go 26 miles, then turn left again to continue north on NM 15, about 17.5 miles to the campground.

SCENERY: ★★★★
RVs: ★
TENTS: ★★
SHADE: ★★
PRIVACY: ★★★★★
FACILITIES: ★
CAMPGROUND ACTIVITIES: ★★
AREA ACTIVITIES: ★★★★
WHEELCHAIR ACCESSIBILITY: ★

Forks is a network of rough dirt roads that weave in and out of primitive campsites tucked in the trees and scrub lining a beautiful bend in the Gila River. Though not far from the road, Forks provides a beautiful, quiet getaway for people who want to car-camp but are willing to rough it. The Gila Cliff Dwellings National Monument is only a short drive up NM 15.

Toilets and fire rings are scattered through the area. No drinking water is available.

No reservations. **Wilderness Ranger District, 505-536-2250.**

11 GILA CLIFF DWELLINGS NATIONAL MONUMENT

Hike amid 700-year-old cliff dwellings

LOCATION: About 50 miles north of Silver City

ELEVATION: 5,700 feet

NUMBER OF SITES: 15

RV NOTES: 20 feet maximum length; vehicles over 20 feet should use NM 35 because NM 15 has very sharp turns and a steep grade

FEE: No

SEASON: Year-round; may be inaccessible because of snow

NEAREST SUPPLY CENTER: Silver City

ACCESS ROAD: Paved

MAP: *New Mexico Road & Recreation Atlas*, p. 46, F5

DIRECTIONS: From Silver City, drive east 2 miles on US 180 to NM 15. Turn left (north) and go 26 miles, then turn left to continue north on NM 15, and go about 24 miles to the park.

SCENERY: ★★★★	
RVS: ★★	
TENTS: ★★★	
SHADE: ★★★	
PRIVACY: ★★★	
FACILITIES: ★★★★	
CAMPGROUND ACTIVITIES: ★★★★	
AREA ACTIVITIES: ★★★	
WHEELCHAIR ACCESSIBILITY: ★★★★	

People of the Mogollon culture inhabited the canyons around the Gila River more than 700 years ago, leaving behind amazing structures tucked into the cliff faces of the area. Today, visitors can hike a trail to a large complex built high into a cliff side, and even enter some of the buildings once inhabited by these Ancestral Puebloan people. A visitor center offers interpretive programs and has a small gift store and phones. Trails of varying length and difficulty take hikers into the Gila Wilderness, the first federally designated wilderness area in the nation. A short trail leads to a nearby hot spring, one of many in the area. The park is a popular starting point for horseback trips into the wilderness.

The two campgrounds, **Upper Scorpion** and **Lower Scorpion**, lie near the end of the park access road, within walking distance of the ruins and only a few hundred yards from the West Fork Gila River. Even though they are right on the park road, the campgrounds become noticeably remote once the ruins close to visitors in the late afternoon. Campers are left with the running river and the wild sounds of a night spent on the edge of the Gila Wilderness. Photographers, note that the cliff dwellings generally catch the afternoon light.

Both campgrounds have picnic tables, grills, running water, and flush toilets. The Trail to the Past, leading to a two-room cliff dwelling and pictographs, starts from the Lower Scorpion parking area. Camping is also permitted in the **TJ Corral** equestrian areas. The visitor center, toilets, and the Trail to the Past are all wheelchair-accessible. Summer holidays can be very busy; Forks and Grapevine Campgrounds to the south can serve as overflow.

No reservations. **National Park Service visitor center, 505-536-9461.**

Ancient history awaits just a short stroll from your campsite

12 McMILLAN

Creekside forested sites

Location: 8.5 miles north of Silver City
Elevation: 6,700 feet
Number of Sites: 3
RV Notes: RVs not recommended
Fee: No
Season: Year-round; may be inaccessible because of snow
Nearest Supply Center: Silver City
Access Road: Paved to the access road, which is fair-weather; call ahead for conditions
Map: *New Mexico Road & Recreation Atlas*, p. 46, G5
Directions: From Silver City, drive east 2 miles on US 180 to NM 15. Turn left (north) and go 8.5 miles to the campground.

SCENERY: ★★
RVs: NR
TENTS: ★★
SHADE: ★★★★★
PRIVACY: ★★★
FACILITIES: ★
CAMPGROUND ACTIVITIES: ★
AREA ACTIVITIES: ★★★★★
WHEELCHAIR ACCESSIBILITY: ★

The campsites are right off the road and stretch along the creek in fairly dense woods. Trails heading east and west into the Pinos Altos Range start within a couple of miles north along NM 15. The camp offers tables, fire rings, and toilets. No drinking water is available.

No reservations. **Silver City Ranger District, 505-388-8201.**

13 CHERRY CREEK

Creekside forested sites

Location: 8.5 miles north of Silver City
Elevation: 6,700 feet
Number of Sites: 12
RV Notes: RVs not recommended
Fee: No
Season: Year-round but may be inaccessible because of snow
Nearest Supply Center: Silver City
Access Road: Paved to the access road, which is fair-weather; call ahead for conditions
Map: *New Mexico Road & Recreation Atlas*, p. 46, G5
Directions: From Silver City, drive east 2 miles on US 180 to NM 15. Turn left (north) and go 8.5 miles to the campground.

SCENERY: ★★
RVs: NR
TENTS: ★★
SHADE: ★★★★★
PRIVACY: ★★★
FACILITIES: ★
CAMPGROUND ACTIVITIES: ★
AREA ACTIVITIES: ★★★★★
WHEELCHAIR ACCESSIBILITY: ★

The campsites are right off the road and stretch along the creek in fairly dense woods. The canyon is scenic, and the Continental Divide National Scenic Trail crosses NM 15 just a couple miles south of this camp and north of Pinos Altos Mountain. Sites have tables, fire rings, and toilets. No drinking water is available.

No reservations. **Silver City Ranger District, 505-388-8201.**

14 CITY OF ROCKS STATE PARK
Very private sites in a surreal landscape

LOCATION: 30 miles northwest of Deming
ELEVATION: 5,200 feet
NUMBER OF SITES: 52; no overflow
RV NOTES: No maximum length. There is no dump station.
FEE: Yes
SEASON: Year-round
NEAREST SUPPLY CENTER: Bayard
ACCESS ROAD: Paved

SCENERY: ★★★★★
RVs: ★★★★
TENTS: ★★★★★
SHADE: ★
PRIVACY: ★★★★★
FACILITIES: ★★★★★
CAMPGROUND ACTIVITIES: ★★
AREA ACTIVITIES: ★
WHEELCHAIR ACCESSIBILITY: ★★★★

MAP: *New Mexico Road & Recreation Atlas*, p. 52, B6
DIRECTIONS: From Deming, take US 180 northwest for 24 miles. Turn right and head northeast on NM 61 for 4 miles to the park access road.

"Stonehenge slightly melted" would be one way to describe the landscape at City of Rocks. Ancient volcanic eruptions and subsequent erosion have created several acres of topsy-turvy monoliths. Visitors can hike between them, crawl on them, and, of course, photograph them. Because the campsites are scattered among these boulders, it is possible to never know there is another soul in the campground. The adventurous can also explore a cactus garden and several trails.

Easter is the busiest time. Three sites, in addition to the visitor center, showers, and restrooms, are wheelchair-accessible. A 35-foot-long group shelter accommodates up to 100 people and 30 vehicles.

The campground is basically laid out in one large loop with a smaller RV loop near the visitor center (which has phones). The showers are in the visitor center building complex. There are 10 electric sites, and water pumps are scattered throughout the campground. All sites have picnic tables and fire rings with grills.

The campground gate is closed 9 p.m.–7 a.m. Reservations can be made at 877-664-7787 or www.icampnm.com. **Park Manager, 505-536-2800**.

Hiking among the boulders offers photographers countless phenomenal images

15 ROCKHOUND STATE PARK

Hunt for semiprecious stones

LOCATION: 13 miles southeast of Deming
ELEVATION: 4,450 feet
NUMBER OF SITES: 35
RV NOTES: No maximum length; there are 29 electric sites
FEE: Yes
SEASON: Year-round
NEAREST SUPPLY CENTER: Deming
ACCESS ROAD: Paved
MAP: *New Mexico Road & Recreation Atlas*, p. 53, D8
DIRECTIONS: From Deming, take NM 11 south for 5 miles. Turn left and head east on NM 141 and NM 497 for about 9 miles to the park entrance.

SCENERY: ★★★
RVS: ★★★★
TENTS: ★★★★★
SHADE: ★★★★★
PRIVACY: ★★
FACILITIES: ★★★★★
CAMPGROUND ACTIVITIES: ★★
AREA ACTIVITIES: ★★★★
WHEELCHAIR ACCESSIBILITY: ★★★★

Set at the foot of the Little Florida Mountains, Rockhound provides just what the name implies, great rock-hounding opportunities. Trails lead up onto a small mountain where rock hunters can find varieties of silica, minerals, quartz crystals, chalcedony, agate, and common opal. Feel free to take home up to 15 pounds of rocks for a personal collection. The campground offers a visitor center and is not too far from the town of Deming and the village of Columbus, where Pancho Villa made his famous raid in 1916.

From November through March, securing a site can be tough. The campground offers deluxe accommodations, providing showers, shelters, phones, picnic tables, and grills. Drinking water is available. The restrooms, visitor center, and group shelter are wheelchair-accessible. A group shelter accommodates up to 60 people and is fitted with four electric hookups, two water hydrants, nine tables, and a big grill.

Gate closed from sunset to 7:30 a.m. Reservations at 877-664-7787 or www.icampnm.com. **Park Manager, 505-546-6182.**

16 PANCHO VILLA STATE PARK

Cacti and the famous raid site

LOCATION: 31 miles south of Deming
ELEVATION: 4,050 feet
NUMBER OF SITES: 62
RV NOTES: No maximum length; all
62 sites are pull-thrus with electric
FEE: Yes
SEASON: Year-round
NEAREST SUPPLY CENTER: Deming
ACCESS ROAD: Paved

SCENERY: ★★★★
RVS: ★★★★
TENTS: ★★★
SHADE: ★★
PRIVACY: ★★
FACILITIES: ★★★★★
CAMPGROUND ACTIVITIES: ★★
AREA ACTIVITIES: ★
WHEELCHAIR ACCESSIBILITY: ★★★

MAP: *New Mexico Road & Recreation Atlas,* p. 53, E8
DIRECTIONS: From Deming, drive south on NM 11 for 35 miles to the park.

Camp in the same location, in the northern Chihuahuan Desert, where Mexican revolutionary Pancho Villa made his famous raid in 1916 just north of the Mexican border. At the northern end of the campground, visitors can view a number of buildings from the time of the raid, as well as a variety of period vehicles. History and auto buffs can check out a 1916 Dodge touring car like the one Gen. John J. "Black Jack" Pershing used as he pursued Pancho Villa, a 1915 first-generation 4-wheel-drive truck, a 1915 Dodge full of bullet holes from the actual raid, and a1915 Jeffrey-Quad armored car.

The campground also boasts an impressive variety of cacti. Call ahead to find out when different species are in bloom. April and May are generally good times to catch blossoms.

The visitor center (which has phones), group shelter, restrooms, showers, playground, and Site #19 are all wheelchair-accessible. Children can enjoy the playground, and families will enjoy interpretive trails and programs. Drinking water is available, and there is also a primitive, grassy tent area.

Reservations at 877-664-7787 or www.icampnm.com. **Park Manager, 505-531-2711.**

LOWER RIO GRANDE

As it has been for centuries, the Rio Grande is the lifeline for much of New Mexico. Most of the historic pueblos grew up along the river's banks. The Spanish colonists' Camino Real followed the Rio Grande from Mexico to Santa Fe. Today the lower Rio Grande irrigates New Mexico's farms and pro-

vides water-based recreation for a desert state. Dams created a series of lakes including Elephant Butte, the state's largest. The Bosque del Apache National Wildlife Refuge is a winter habitat for sandhill cranes, ducks, geese, and wading birds. Historical sites dot the Rio Grande Valley, including Fort Craig, the Valverde Battlefield Civil War site, and Fort Selden, which was home to the legendary Buffalo Soldiers. Visible in the distance beyond the river are mountains including the San Mateo Mountains to the west of Elephant Butte and the jagged Organ Mountains east of Las Cruces.

Elephant Butte State Park

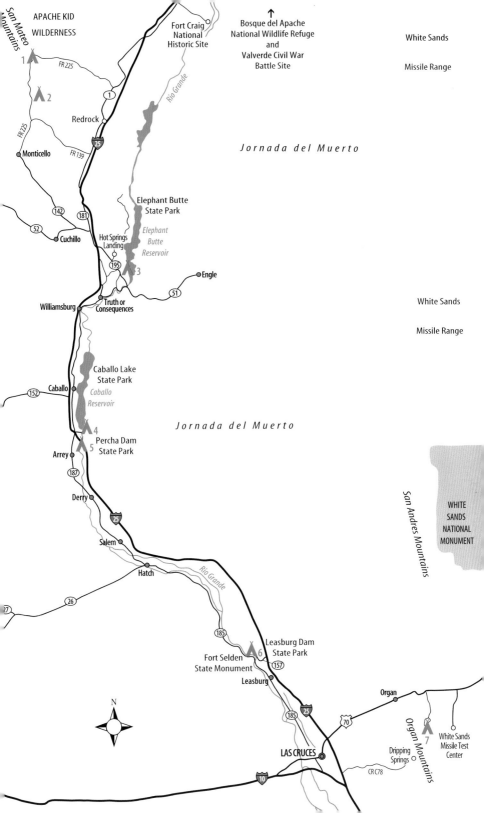

1 SPRINGTIME

Shady camping and trailhead

LOCATION: 17 miles north of Monticello
ELEVATION: 7,400 feet
NUMBER OF SITES: 4
RV NOTES: RVs not recommended
FEE: No
SEASON: Year-round, but may be inaccessible because of snow
NEAREST SUPPLY CENTER: Truth or Consequences
ACCESS ROAD: Fair-weather; call ahead for conditions
MAP: *New Mexico Road & Recreation Atlas,* p. 47, D9
DIRECTIONS: From Truth or Consequences, drive north on I-25 for about 22 miles to Exit 100 at Redrock. Off the exit, take NM 1 north and go about 5 miles. Turn left onto FR 225. Follow FR 225 west for about 14 miles to the campground.

Campsites have Adirondack shelters and grills, and there is one outhouse. Access the Apache Kid Wilderness, the Crest Trail, and San Mateo Peak Lookout by hiking or horseback riding along Trail #43.

No reservations. **Magdalena Ranger District, 505-854-2281.**

SCENERY: ★★★
RVs: NR
TENTS: ★★★★
SHADE: ★★★★★
PRIVACY: ★★★★
FACILITIES: ★★
CAMPGROUND ACTIVITIES: ★★
AREA ACTIVITIES: ★
WHEELCHAIR ACCESSIBILITY: ★

2 LUNA PARK
Secluded lunar landscape

LOCATION: 10.5 miles north of Monticello
ELEVATION: 6,950 feet
NUMBER OF SITES: 2
RV NOTES: RVs not recommended
FEE: No
SEASON: Year-round, but may be inaccessible because of snow
NEAREST SUPPLY CENTER: Truth or Consequences
ACCESS ROAD: Fair-weather; call ahead for conditions
MAP: *New Mexico Road & Recreation Atlas*, p. 47, D9
DIRECTIONS: From Truth or Consequences, drive north on I-25 to Exit 83 at Hot Springs Landing. Drive north on NM 181 to the junction with NM 52 and go west toward Cuchillo for about 2 miles. Veer right onto NM 142 north toward Monticello and travel for about 14 miles. At Monticello, turn right (northeast) onto FR 225 and travel about 10.5 miles to the campground.

SCENERY: ★★★★
RVs: NR
TENTS: ★★★
SHADE: ★★★
PRIVACY: ★★★★★
FACILITIES: ★★
CAMPGROUND ACTIVITIES: ★★
AREA ACTIVITIES: ★
WHEELCHAIR ACCESSIBILITY: ★

Camp at the base of bulbous, volcanic rocks and hike into small canyons between the monoliths. The little camp has fire rings, picnic tables, and an outhouse.

No reservations. **Magdalena Ranger District, 505-854-2281**.

3 ELEPHANT BUTTE STATE PARK

Watery desert playground

LOCATION: 5 miles northeast of Truth or Consequences

ELEVATION: 4,500 feet

NUMBER OF SITES: 132; overflow available

RV NOTES: No maximum length; all sites in the new South Monticello area are pull-thrus with hookups; the main campground has only a few pull-thru sites

FEE: Yes

SEASON: Year-round

NEAREST SUPPLY CENTER: Truth or Consequences

ACCESS ROAD: Paved

MAP: *New Mexico Road & Recreation Atlas*, p. 47, F10

DIRECTIONS: From Exit 83 on I-25, travel 3 miles southeast on NM 195 to the park entrance.

SCENERY: ★★★★★
RVS: ★★★★★
TENTS: ★★★★
SHADE: ★★★
PRIVACY: ★★
FACILITIES: ★★★★★
CAMPGROUND ACTIVITIES: ★★★★★
AREA ACTIVITIES: ★★★★★
WHEELCHAIR ACCESSIBILITY: ★★★★★

More than 40 miles long, Elephant Butte Lake beckons water-sports enthusiasts year-round. The 200 miles of shoreline provide a variety of different camping environments and quiet coves for fishing. The lake's name comes from an ancient volcanic core that protrudes from the lake's surface close to the dam. Nearby Truth or Consequences is famous for its hot springs and resort atmosphere. At the northern end of the park lie the ruins of Fort Craig, a major defensive structure along the Camino Real, and the Valverde Civil War site. The world-famous Bosque del Apache National Wildlife Refuge, the wintering grounds for sandhill cranes and migrating waterfowl, straddles the Rio Grande just north of the lake. The various marinas offer houseboats, fishing boats, personal watercraft, and other water toys for rent. Visitors can hike along the Rio Grande below the dam on either a paved or primitive trail. When it comes to water fun, Elephant Butte has a little of everything.

The visitor center, group shelter, restrooms, showers, courtesy dock (water level permitting), interpretive trail along the river below the dam, playground, and visitor center (which has phones) are all wheelchair-accessible. Two areas at the end of Ridge Road, and one at Hot Springs Landing, are available for groups. They have vault toilets, picnic tables, and grills, but no electric hookups. Campers can use showers in the main campground areas.

From Easter to Labor Day, try to arrive before the weekend or make a reservation if you want a hookup site. All developed sites have a shelter, picnic table, and possibly water and electric. The entrance to the main campground and the visitor center are near the Marina Del Sur. The main camp area, which includes Desert Cove, Quail Run, and Lion's Beach electric areas, has 92 electric hookup sites, water, and a dump station with hard-packed surface roads. The new **South Monticello Recreation Area** boasts spacious pull-thru RV sites with electric and water hookups and a dump station. Below the dam along the Rio Grande, **Paseo del Rio** offers shelters and picnic tables but no hookups. The area has a paved, wheelchair-accessible trail and a primitive, riverside trail. There is a shower/restroom facility and vault toilets. The access road is hard-packed. Up and down the shoreline are miles and miles of primitive camping spots on the white, sandy beach. These areas are pack in/pack out, and four-wheel drives are recommended, as passenger cars can get stuck in the sand.

Reservations at 877-664-7787 or www.icampnm.com. **Park Manager**, **505-744-5421**.

4 CABALLO LAKE STATE PARK

Fishing, eagles, and cacti

LOCATION: 16 miles south of Truth or Consequences
ELEVATION: 4,100 feet
NUMBER OF SITES: 64; overflow available
RV NOTES: No maximum length; sites with water, electric, and sewer hookups are in the Palomino and Riverside Loops; parking pads are graded gravel
FEE: Yes
SEASON: Year-round
NEAREST SUPPLY CENTER: Williamsburg
ACCESS ROAD: Paved
MAP: *New Mexico Road & Recreation Atlas*, p. 47, G9
DIRECTIONS: From Truth or Consequences, travel south on I-25 for about 16 miles to Exit 59. The entrance to the campground is just to the east of the exit.

SCENERY: ★★★★	
RVS: ★★★★★	
TENTS: ★★★	
SHADE: ★★★	
PRIVACY: ★★★	
FACILITIES: ★★★★★	
CAMPGROUND ACTIVITIES: ★★★	
AREA ACTIVITIES: ★★★	
WHEELCHAIR ACCESSIBILITY: ★★★★	

The fishing is peaceful along the Rio Grande in the Riverside Area below the dam

Caballo offers campers two very different environments. The campgrounds north of the visitor center look out over the lake and the dry, mountainous terrain on the opposite shore. The sites in the Riverside area below the dam sit among trees and reeds along the banks of the free-flowing Rio Grande. The foothills on the lake's eastern shore provide a home for nesting bald and golden eagles in late October. Visitors can explore two cactus gardens where many of the cacti bloom in late March and early April (call ahead for bloom dates). Photographers can catch afternoon light falling on the western face of the Caballo foothills. And of course fishing and boating are extremely popular in this large lake.

Holiday weekends are usually quite busy. Non-hookup and primitive sites are normally available. The Rally group site, located in the Riverside area, accommodates 170 people with a 60-by-60-foot shelter, 20 picnic tables, and 40 feet of grills. Fifty-four electric hookup sites lie adjacent to it. The visitor center, some fishing access, some campsites, the playground, the group shelter, restrooms, and showers are all wheelchair-accessible.

All of the developed sites in the **Palomino**, **Appaloosa**, and **Stallion** loops in the main campground, and in the loop in **Riverside** area, have electric and water hookup. Six sites in each of the Palomino Loop and Riverside areas have water, electric, and sewer hookups. Showers are located in the Appaloosa, Stallion, and Riverside Loops. **Upper Flats** and the **Percha Flats** are primitive camping areas, providing fire rings and vault toilets. There are also primitive sites along the river in the Riverside area. The boat ramp is below the Palomino area.

Reservations at 877-664-7787 or www.icampnm.com. **Park Manager, 505-743-3942.**

5 PERCHA DAM STATE PARK

Shady riverside campground

SCENERY: ★★★★
RVs: ★★★★
TENTS: ★★★★
SHADE: ★★★★
PRIVACY: ★★★
FACILITIES: ★★★★★
CAMPGROUND ACTIVITIES: ★★
AREA ACTIVITIES: ★★★
WHEELCHAIR ACCESSIBILITY: ★★★

LOCATION: 21 miles south of Truth or Consequences
ELEVATION: 4,200 feet
NUMBER OF SITES: 26
RV NOTES: No maximum length
FEE: Yes
SEASON: Year-round
NEAREST SUPPLY CENTER: Williamsburg
ACCESS ROAD: Paved
MAP: *New Mexico Road & Recreation Atlas*, p. 47, H9

DIRECTIONS: From Truth of Consequences, drive 21 miles south on I-25 to Exit 59. The entrance to Percha is about a mile south on NM 187.

Fishing, watching wildlife, and relaxing draw visitors and campers to Percha. Sites lie below mature cottonwood, salt cedar, and Russian olive trees, overlooking the small dam and river below. Holidays are usually busy.

Some campsites, restrooms, showers, the playground, and fishing access are wheelchair-accessible. Percha has 29 electric and water hookup sites. Showers are near the park entrance. The playground is at the southern end of the park next to the river.

Reservations at 877-664-7787 or www.icampnm.com. **Park Manager, 505-743-3942.**

6 LEASBURG DAM STATE PARK

Fishing, Fort Selden, and the Buffalo Soldiers

LOCATION: 15 miles north of Las Cruces
ELEVATION: 3,960 feet
NUMBER OF SITES: 24; no overflow area
RV NOTES: No maximum length
FEE: Yes
SEASON: Year-round
NEAREST SUPPLY CENTER: Las Cruces
ACCESS ROAD: Paved

SCENERY: ★★
RVs: ★★★★
TENTS: ★★★★
SHADE: ★★★
PRIVACY: ★★
FACILITIES: ★★★★★
CAMPGROUND ACTIVITIES: ★★
AREA ACTIVITIES: ★★★★★
WHEELCHAIR ACCESSIBILITY: ★★★★

MAP: *New Mexico Road & Recreation Atlas,* p. 53, B11
DIRECTIONS: From Las Cruces, drive 15 miles north on I-25. Take Exit 19 and follow NM 157 to the park.

Leasburg makes an excellent base camp for exploring Las Cruces, the Organ Mountains, and south-central New Mexico. The park lies alongside the Rio Grande, offering premium amenities. Every facility is ADA compliant. Visitors can fish, wander the cactus gardens, or explore nearby Fort Selden, a 19th-century territorial outpost and home to the famous Buffalo Soldiers. Sites with hookups are very popular; reservations are recommended.

Restrooms, shower, playground, group shelter, and interpretive trails are all wheelchair-accessible. A 30-by-30-foot group shelter accommodates up to 100 people, with a giant grill, water, and five adjoining campsites. Reservations are required.

Leasburg offers 17 sites with electric and water hookup. Ten of those hookup sites have 15-by-30-foot, level concrete parking pads. The dump station is next to the visitor center, where a courtesy phone with Internet access is available. All sites have picnic tables and grills, and most have shelters. Drinking water is available. A large cactus garden next to the visitor center has a trail running through it.

The gate is closed from sunset to 7 a.m. Reservations at 877-664-7787 or www.icampnm.com. **Park Manager, 505-524-4068.**

7 AGUIRRE SPRINGS

Rugged mountains, lush canyons, and White Sands Missile Range

LOCATION: 7.7 miles southeast of Organ
ELEVATION: 5,650 feet
NUMBER OF SITES: 54
RV NOTES: 32 feet maximum length
FEE: Yes
SEASON: Year-round
NEAREST SUPPLY CENTER: Las Cruces
ACCESS ROAD: Paved
MAP: *New Mexico Road & Recreation Atlas*,
p. 54, C4

SCENERY: ★★★★★
RVs: ★★
TENTS: ★★★★★
SHADE: ★★★
PRIVACY: ★★★★
FACILITIES: ★★★
CAMPGROUND ACTIVITIES: ★★★
AREA ACTIVITIES: ★★★★★
WHEELCHAIR ACCESSIBILITY: ★★★

DIRECTIONS: From I-25 in Las Cruces, take US 70 east for 14.5 miles over the San Agustin Pass. Turn right (south) at the sign for Aguirre Springs. Drive about 5 miles to the campground entrance.

Nestled at the base of the rugged Organ Mountains, this campground faces the Jornada del Muerto, White Sands Missile Range, and the Sacramento Mountains in the distance. Trails winding up the mountainside take visitors from a Chihuahuan Desert environment into often lush canyons. Two good trails begin at the camp, one a 6-mile, one-way climb to the top, the other a 4.5-mile loop. The Cox visitor center is on the other side of the mountains at Dripping Springs. Sites have picnic tables, fire rings, and tent pads. Most of the campground has some shade from trees.

Reservations for groups only. **BLM Las Cruces, 505-525-4300.**

Opposite: Poppies bloom at the foot of the Organ Mountains

SOUTH CENTRAL

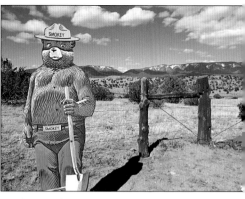

At the Smokey Bear rescue site near Capitan Mountain

The mountains of south central New Mexico lord over an unusual landscape. To the west lies the immense, dry, windswept Tularosa Basin, home of White Sands National Monument. Also to the west, the Malpais Lava Beds look like a river of black rock. Less harsh, the east slope of the mountains is home to excellent fishing rivers and plenty of trails through densely forested hills and canyons. The area is a resort for lowlanders for hundreds of miles around it, who come to ski in winter and to escape the heat in summer. Sierra Blanca Peak, at 11,973 feet, looms beside the White Mountain Wilderness on the Mescalero Apache Indian Reservation and is visible from great distances in this region.

This area hosted lots of history. Both the Lincoln County War and key events in the life of Billy the Kid took place around the town of Lincoln. White Oaks retains the flavor of its mining glory days. The first explosion of an atomic bomb occurred at the Trinity Site, just west of the Oscura Mountains. The real Smokey the Bear was rescued after a forest fire in the Capitan Mountains. In the late 1800s, Apaches used the canyons above Alamogordo as strongholds while fighting the U.S. Army. Today, their descendants remain in the heart of the Sacramento Mountains.

Area Campgrounds

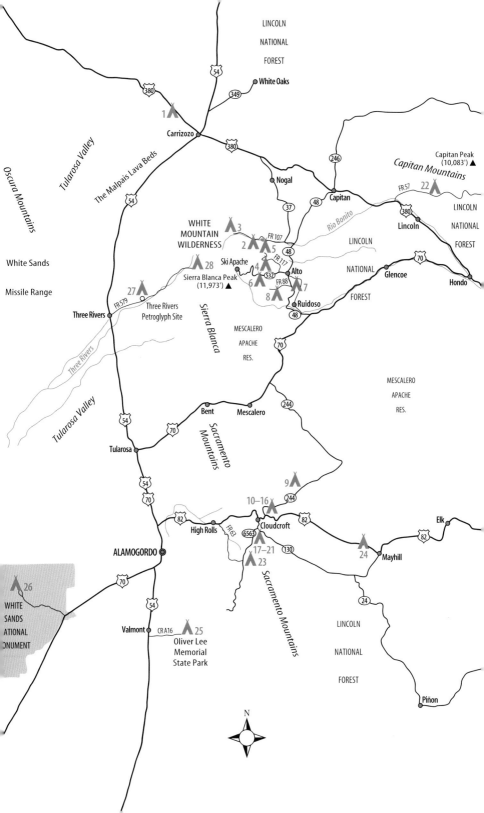

1 VALLEY OF FIRES RECREATION AREA

Lava flows and rugged mountains near the Trinity Site

LOCATION: 4 miles northwest of Carrizozo
ELEVATION: 5,400 feet
NUMBER OF SITES: 23; no overflow
RV NOTES: No maximum length; hookup sites have long, paved parking pads
FEE: Yes
SEASON: Year-round
NEAREST SUPPLY CENTER: Carrizozo
ACCESS ROAD: Paved

SCENERY: ★★★★★	
RVs: ★★★★	
TENTS: ★★★★★	
SHADE: ★★★★	
PRIVACY: ★★★	
FACILITIES: ★★★★	
CAMPGROUND ACTIVITIES: ★★★	
AREA ACTIVITIES: ★★★★★	
WHEELCHAIR ACCESSIBILITY: ★★★★	

MAP: *New Mexico Road & Recreation Atlas*, p. 49, D7
DIRECTIONS: From Carrizozo, take US 380 northwest 4 miles to the campground.

"Surreal" and "dramatic" describe the landscape around the Valley of Fires. The campground is an island in a 2,000-year-old lava flow. From a promontory in the camp, visitors can clearly see the peaks of the Sierra Blanca to the southeast and the Tularosa Basin and San Andres Mountains to the southwest. About 35 miles to the west, just beyond the Oscura Mountains, lies the Trinity Site, where the first atomic bomb was exploded in July 1945. The valley makes a great base camp for exploring this wide-open region. Take day trips to the historic town of White Oaks, Smokey Bear Historical Park in Capitan, or Bosque del Apache National Wildlife Refuge, just to name a few.

Valley of Fires is an amazing location for photos of expansive vistas as well as close-ups of lava rocks and the life forms they host. The sun sets over the lava flow and the Tularosa Basin beyond, and rises over the Sierra Blanca. To get good contrast between the jet-black lava rocks and the plant life or creatures on their surfaces, use a polarizing filter to reduce light reflection off the rock.

The first section of the campground has 15 hookup sites with electric and water, as well as shelters, tables, and grills. The visitor center and restrooms with running water are in this area. Past the hookup sites is a loop of seven tent sites virtually in the lava flow, with tables, shelters, and grills. The area has a vault toilet. If it is windy, choose a tent site in the tent-only loop, where lava rocks provide good shelter. Restrooms, the nature trail, and campsites near the visitor center are wheelchair-accessible. Two group shelters can accommodate 40 people each. Summer weekends can be very busy.

No reservations. **Visitor center, 505-648-2241**.

The dark rocks of the Malpais Lava Beds are great for photography

2 South Fork

Trout and White Mountain Trailheads

Location: 15.5 miles northwest of Ruidoso
Elevation: 7,500 feet
Number of Sites: 60
RV Notes: 35 feet maximum length; an RV with a car is considered one vehicle
Fee: Yes
Season: April–October
Nearest Supply Center: Ruidoso
Access Road: Maintained dirt

Scenery: ★★★★	
RVs: ★★	
Tents: ★★★	
Shade: ★★★★	
Privacy: ★★★	
Facilities: ★★★★	
Campground Activities: ★★★	
Area Activities: ★★★★★	
Wheelchair Accessibility: ★★★★	

Map: *New Mexico Road & Recreation Atlas*, p. 49, E7
Directions: From Ruidoso, take NM 48 north 9 miles. Just past the Bonita Park Nazarene camp, turn left onto NM 37, go 1.5 miles, then bear left onto FR 107 to continue west for 5 miles. Pass Bonito Lake and go about another mile to the campground, on the left.

Set in a pine-shaded valley in the Sierra Blanca, South Fork is a popular fishing and hiking destination. Anglers can throw a line into the South Fork Rio Bonito, Bonito Creek, or nearby Bonito Lake. Hikers can head into the White Mountain Wilderness via the South Fork Trail or the Argentina/Bonito Trail a few miles away.

Sites have tables and fire grills. The campground offers restrooms, trailhead parking, and drinking water. Only two vehicles are allowed per site. The tent-only area is near the South Fork trailhead. Two campsites, restrooms, and fishing access at nearby Bonito Lake are wheelchair-accessible. Heaviest use occurs on weekends during July and August.

No reservations. **Smokey Bear Ranger District, 505-257-4095.**

Bonito Lake

3 Argentina/Bonito Trailhead

White Mountain access and equestrian adventures

Location: 18 miles northwest of Ruidoso
Elevation: 7,500 feet
Number of Sites: Dispersed
RV Notes: There is enough pull-off space for RVs and trailers
Fee: No
Season: May–October
Nearest Supply Center: Ruidoso
Access Road: Fair-weather; call ahead for conditions

Scenery: ★★★
RVs: ★
Tents: ★★
Shade: ★★★★
Privacy: ★★
Facilities: ★★
Campground Activities: ★★★
Area Activities: ★★★★
Wheelchair Accessibility: ★

Map: *New Mexico Road & Recreation Atlas*, p. 49, E7
Directions: From Ruidoso, take NM 48 north 9 miles. Just past the Bonita Park Nazarene camp, turn left onto NM 37, go 1.5 miles, then bear left onto FR 107 and drive to the end of the road. (Note that along FR 107 you will encounter a cluster of buildings as the road zigzags. Continue to weave your way west even though it may feel like you are entering someone's property.)

Argentina/Bonito is a popular access point for trails into the White Mountain Wilderness. The four horse corrals make the campground popular for equestrian adventures. Tents can be pitched in the meadow among pines and aspens. No drinking water is available.

No reservations. **Smokey Bear Ranger District, 505-257-4095.**

4 SKYLINE

Mountain vistas

LOCATION: 7 miles northwest of Alto
ELEVATION: 9,000 feet
NUMBER OF SITES: 17
RV NOTES: RVs not recommended
FEE: No
SEASON: May–November, but may open late or close early depending upon snow
NEAREST SUPPLY CENTER: Ruidoso
ACCESS ROAD: Rough gravel; call ahead for conditions
MAP: *New Mexico Road & Recreation Atlas*, p. 49, E8
DIRECTIONS: From Ruidoso, take NM 48 north 4 miles, turn left (west) onto NM 532, drive 1 mile, then turn right (north) onto FR 117 and continue 4 miles to the campground. The last couple miles may be rough.

SCENERY: ★★★★	
RVs: NR	
TENTS: ★★	
SHADE: ★★★	
PRIVACY: ★★	
FACILITIES: ★★	
CAMPGROUND ACTIVITIES: ★★	
AREA ACTIVITIES: ★★	
WHEELCHAIR ACCESSIBILITY: ★	

Perched at 9,000 feet, Skyline overlooks the peaks of the Sierra Blanca, preserved in the White Mountain Wilderness. Although the views are lovely, exposure is an issue during monsoon season. In July and August, it's important for campers to be aware of lightning danger. Sites have fireplaces and tables. There are vault toilets, but no drinking water is available.

No reservations. **Smokey Bear Ranger District, 505-257-4095.**

5 MONJEAU

Mountain views and a CCC lookout tower

LOCATION: 7 miles northwest of Alto
ELEVATION: 9,500 feet
NUMBER OF SITES: 4
RV NOTES: RVs not recommended
FEE: No
SEASON: Open May–November, but may open late or close early because of snow
NEAREST SUPPLY CENTER: Ruidoso
Access Road: Rough; call ahead for conditions
MAP: *New Mexico Road & Recreation Atlas*, p. 49, E7

DIRECTIONS: From Ruidoso, take NM 48 north 4 miles, turn left (west) onto NM 532, drive 1 mile, then turn right (north) onto FR 117 and continue 5 miles to the campground. The last few miles may be rough.

Monjeau provides access to an old 9,641-foot lookout tower of the same name built by the Civilian Conservation Corps (CCC). From the tower, you can enjoy 360-degree views of the White Mountain Wilderness, Sierra Blanca Peak, and Ruidoso. Hike along the Crest and Mills Trails in the White Mountain Wilderness. During July and August, the storms of the monsoon season bring rain as well as extreme risk from lightning, so be cautious when choosing a campsite. Sites, set among boulders and aspens, have fireplaces and tables. All sites are technically walk-ins. There are vault toilets but no drinking water.

No reservations. **Smokey Bear Ranger District, 505-257-4095.**

SCENERY:	★★★★★
RVs:	NR
TENTS:	★★
SHADE:	★★★
PRIVACY:	★★★
FACILITIES:	★★
CAMPGROUND ACTIVITIES:	★★★
AREA ACTIVITIES:	★★
WHEELCHAIR ACCESSIBILITY:	★

6 Oak Grove

Pretty mountain getaway

Location: 5 miles west of Alto
Elevation: 8,300 feet
Number of Sites: 30
RV Notes: RVs over 18 feet are not recommended because of the grade of the access road
Fee: Yes
Season: May–September
Nearest Supply Center: Ruidoso
Access Road: Paved
Map: *New Mexico Road & Recreation Atlas*, p. 49, E8
Directions: From Ruidoso, take NM 48 north 4 miles, turn left (west) onto NM 532, and drive 5 miles to the campground.

Scenery: ★★★★
RVs: ★
Tents: ★★★
Shade: ★★★
Privacy: ★★★
Facilities: ★★★
Campground Activities: ★★★
Area Activities: ★★★
Wheelchair Accessibility: ★

Oak Grove lies off the road that leads to Ski Apache and makes a nice base camp for exploring nearby Ruidoso. View Sierra Blanca Peak (11,973 feet) from nearby Windy Vista Overlook. A variety of trailheads are in the area. The campground is newly remodeled and sites have grills and tables. Many sites border an open field surrounded by pines and aspens. There are vault toilets, but no drinking water is available.

No reservations. **Smokey Bear Ranger District, 505-257-4095.**

7 Sam Tobias Memorial (Group)

Large-group camping

Location: 0.6 mile northwest of Ruidoso
Elevation: 6,950 feet
Number of Sites: Accommodates up to 250
RV Notes: No maximum length
Fee: Yes
Season: May–September
Nearest Supply Center: Ruidoso
Access Road: Paved

Scenery: ★★
RVs: ★★★
Tents: ★★★
Shade: ★★
Privacy: ★★
Facilities: ★★★★
Campground Activities: ★★
Area Activities: ★★★★★
Wheelchair Accessibility: ★★★

Map: *New Mexico Road & Recreation Atlas*, p. 49, E8
Directions: From the Smokey Bear Ranger District office on NM 48 in Ruidoso, take FR 88 about a mile north to the campground.

This cluster of three pavilions can accommodate up to 250 people. Each shelter has water, electric, and lots of space for RV parking. This group area is close to the town of Ruidoso, where golf, winter sports, and a nearby performing arts theater are among the attractions.

Reservations required. **Smokey Bear Ranger District, 505-257-4095.**

8 Cedar Creek

Shady tent sites

Location: 4.6 miles northwest of Ruidoso
Elevation: 7,000 feet
Number of Sites: Dispersed
RV Notes: RVs not recommended
Fee: No
Season: Year-round, but may be inaccessible because of snow
Nearest Supply Center: Ruidoso
Access Road: Fair-weather; call ahead for conditions

Scenery: ★★★
RVs: NR
Tents: ★★★
Shade: ★★★★★
Privacy: ★★★★★
Facilities: ★★
Campground Activities: ★
Area Activities: ★★★★★
Wheelchair Accessibility: ★

Map: *New Mexico Road & Recreation Atlas*, p. 49, E8
Directions: From the Smokey Bear Ranger District office on NM 48 in Ruidoso, take FR 88 about 4 miles west to the dispersed area.

Situated in a heavily forested ravine, Cedar Creek offers solitude in a primitive setting. The campground makes a nice base camp for exploring Ruidoso, which is only minutes away and offers many activities. No drinking water is available.

Reservations required. **Smokey Bear Ranger District, 505-257-4095.**

9 SILVER LAKE

Family-oriented lakeside camping

LOCATION: 10 miles northeast of Cloudcroft
ELEVATION: 7,700 feet
NUMBER OF SITES: 55 RV sites plus primitive tent sites over 200 acres
RV NOTES: No maximum length
FEE: Yes
SEASON: April–mid-October
NEAREST SUPPLY CENTER: Cloudcroft
ACCESS ROAD: Paved to the campground
MAP: *New Mexico Road & Recreation Atlas*, p. 49, G8
DIRECTIONS: From Cloudcroft, take NM 244 northeast 10 miles. The entrance to the campground is on the left.

SCENERY: ★★★
RVs: ★★★★★
TENTS: ★★★
SHADE: ★★★★
PRIVACY: ★★★
FACILITIES: ★★★
CAMPGROUND ACTIVITIES: ★★★
AREA ACTIVITIES: ★★★★★
WHEELCHAIR ACCESSIBILITY: ★★

Silver Lake is a hugely popular campground on the Mescalero Apache Reservation, not far from the mountain resort town of Cloudcroft. Many families come back year after year. The campground wraps around a lake and offers plenty of pine trees for shade, along with large grassy areas. Various paths meander through the park. In the lake, campers can fish for rainbow trout. Note that the required fishing permit can be purchased in the on-site convenience store; no New Mexico license is needed.

The sites are all first-come, first-served, and the only way to secure an RV site on a weekend in June, July, or August is to arrive as early as you can —on Thursday, if possible. Closely packed, all 55 RV sites have water and electric hookups, and 25 of these also provide sewer hookup. There are restrooms with showers and a dump station. Wheelchair ramps lead to both restrooms. Primitive camping is also possible.

No reservations. **Mescalero Apache Reservation Office, 505-464-4494.**

10 SILVER

Forested RV camping

LOCATION: 2 miles northeast of Cloudcroft
ELEVATION: 9,000 feet
NUMBER OF SITES: 32
RV NOTES: 32 feet maximum length; no hookups
FEE: Yes
SEASON: Mid-April to October
NEAREST SUPPLY CENTER: Cloudcroft
ACCESS ROAD: Paved
MAP: *New Mexico Road & Recreation Atlas*, p. 49, G8
DIRECTIONS: From Cloudcroft, take NM 244 northeast 2 miles to a right onto the campground's access road.

SCENERY: ★★★	
RVs: ★★★	
TENTS: ★★	
SHADE: ★★★★★	
PRIVACY: ★★	
FACILITIES: ★★★	
CAMPGROUND ACTIVITIES: ★★	
AREA ACTIVITIES: ★★★★★	
WHEELCHAIR ACCESSIBILITY: ★★★★	

Set in the pine forests of the Sacramento Mountains and close to Cloudcroft, Silver is an RV-friendly campground offering a completely paved road and parking pads. There is a full-time host and a nature trail, and water is available at the fee station. The restrooms and campsites are wheelchair-accessible. Available showers and a dump station are in the Silver Overflow area.

No reservations. **Sacramento Ranger District, 505-682-2551.**

11 SADDLE

Forested RV camping

LOCATION: 2 miles northeast of Cloudcroft
ELEVATION: 9,000 feet
NUMBER OF SITES: 17
RV NOTES: 32 feet maximum length;
no hookups
FEE: Yes
SEASON: Mid-April to October
NEAREST SUPPLY CENTER: Cloudcroft
ACCESS ROAD: Paved

SCENERY: ★★★
RVs: ★★★
TENTS: ★★
SHADE: ★★★★★
PRIVACY: ★★
FACILITIES: ★★★
CAMPGROUND ACTIVITIES: ★★
AREA ACTIVITIES: ★★★★★
WHEELCHAIR ACCESSIBILITY: ★★★★

MAP: *New Mexico Road & Recreation Atlas*, p. 49, G8
DIRECTIONS: From Cloudcroft, take NM 244 north 2 miles
to a right onto the access road.

Saddle is virtually identical to Silver Campground. Set in the pine forests of the Sacramento Mountains and close to Cloudcroft, Saddle is an RV-friendly campground offering a completely paved road and parking pads. There is a nearby nature trail, and water is available at the fee station. The restrooms and campsites are wheelchair-accessible. Available showers and a dump station are in the Silver Overflow area.

No reservations. **Sacramento Ranger District, 505-682-2551.**

Echoes of the Old West are a common sight along New Mexico's byways

12 APACHE

Forested RV camping

LOCATION: 2 miles northeast of Cloudcroft
ELEVATION: 8,900 feet
NUMBER OF SITES: 26
RV NOTES: 32 feet maximum length;
no hookups
FEE: Yes
SEASON: Mid-April to October
NEAREST SUPPLY CENTER: Cloudcroft
ACCESS ROAD: Paved
MAP: *New Mexico Road & Recreation Atlas*, p. 49, G8
DIRECTIONS: From Cloudcroft, take NM 244 north 2 miles
to a right onto the access road.

SCENERY: ★★★
RVS: ★★★
TENTS: ★★
SHADE: ★★★★★
PRIVACY: ★★
FACILITIES: ★★★
CAMPGROUND ACTIVITIES: ★★
AREA ACTIVITIES: ★★★★★
WHEELCHAIR ACCESSIBILITY: ★★★★

Apache is virtually identical to Silver and Saddle Campgrounds. Set in the pine forests of the Sacramento Mountains and close to Cloudcroft, Apache is an RV-friendly campground offering a completely paved road and parking pads. There is a nearby nature trail, and water is available at the fee station. The restrooms and campsites are wheelchair-accessible. Available showers and a dump station are in the Silver Overflow area.

No reservations. **Sacramento Ranger District, 505-682-2551.**

Sunset over the Sacramento Mountains

13 SILVER OVERFLOW
Forested RV camping

🚵 🏃

LOCATION: 2 miles northeast of Cloudcroft
ELEVATION: 8,900 feet
NUMBER OF SITES: 52
RV NOTES: No maximum length; no hookups
FEE: Yes
SEASON: May–September
NEAREST SUPPLY CENTER: Cloudcroft
ACCESS ROAD: Paved
MAP: *New Mexico Road & Recreation Atlas*, p. 49, G8
DIRECTIONS: From Cloudcroft, take NM 244 north 2 miles to a right turn into the campground.

SCENERY: ★★★
RVs: ★★★
TENTS: ★★
SHADE: ★★★★★
PRIVACY: ★★
FACILITIES: ★★★
CAMPGROUND ACTIVITIES: ★★
AREA ACTIVITIES: ★★★★★
WHEELCHAIR ACCESSIBILITY: ★★★★

In this popular resort district close to Cloudcroft, RV campers, latecomers, and those requiring paved facilities ensure that this separate camp area, set in the pine forests of the Sacramento Mountains, is usually occupied. Basically a large parking lot with sites placed along the pavement's edge, Silver Overflow also houses a dump station and showers shared by the Silver, Saddle, and Apache Campgrounds.

Sites have tables and fire rings. Water is available at the fee station.

No reservations. **Sacramento Ranger District, 505-682-2551**.

Visitors are welcome at Apache Point Observatory (right) and the National Solar Observatory at Sacramento Peak, both at the southern end of NM 6563 (Sunspot Highway)

14 PINES

Forested campsites encircling open space

LOCATION: 1 mile northeast of Cloudcroft
ELEVATION: 8,800 feet
NUMBER OF SITES: 48
RV NOTES: 16 feet maximum length
FEE: Yes
SEASON: May–October
NEAREST SUPPLY CENTER: Cloudcroft
ACCESS ROAD: Gravel
MAP: *New Mexico Road & Recreation Atlas,* p. 49, G8
DIRECTIONS: From Cloudcroft, take NM 244 north about 1 mile to a left into the campground.

SCENERY: ★★★	
RVs: ★★★	
TENTS: ★★★	
SHADE: ★★★	
PRIVACY: ★★★	
FACILITIES: ★★★	
CAMPGROUND ACTIVITIES: ★★	
AREA ACTIVITIES: ★★★★★	
WHEELCHAIR ACCESSIBILITY: ★★	

Close to the mountain town of Cloudcroft, Pines is a loop road around an open field with campsites situated on the outside of the loop. There is more space between sites than at Silver, Saddle, or Apache, which are all in the same area. Sites have picnic tables and grills, and water is available. Pines is nice for tent camping. After a recent renovation, the campground is wheelchair-accessible. No drinking water is available.

No reservations **Sacramento Ranger District, 505-682-2551.**

Wild iris thrive in wet high-elevation locations

15 UPPER FIR (GROUP)
Pine forest camping

LOCATION: 1 mile northeast of Cloudcroft
ELEVATION: 8,800 feet
NUMBER OF SITES: Accommodates up to 200
RV NOTES: 16 feet maximum length
FEE: Yes
SEASON: May–October
NEAREST SUPPLY CENTER: Cloudcroft
ACCESS ROAD: Paved

SCENERY: ★★★
RVs: ★★★
TENTS: ★★
SHADE: ★★★★
PRIVACY: ★★
FACILITIES: ★★★
CAMPGROUND ACTIVITIES: ★★
AREA ACTIVITIES: ★★★★★
WHEELCHAIR ACCESSIBILITY: ★★★

MAP: *New Mexico Road & Recreation Atlas*, p. 49, G8
DIRECTIONS: From Cloudcroft, take NM 244 north about 1 mile to a right into the campground.

Upper Fir was renovated in 2002. The updated pavilion has picnic tables, grills, a concrete floor, water, and a bearproof food locker. The parking pads are all paved.

Reservations required at 877-444-6777 or ReserveUSA.com. **Sacramento Ranger District, 505-682-2551.**

16 LOWER FIR (GROUP)
Forested group environment

LOCATION: 1 mile northeast of Cloudcroft
ELEVATION: 8,800 feet
NUMBER OF SITES: Accommodates up to 200
RV NOTES: 16 feet maximum length
FEE: Yes
SEASON: May–October
NEAREST SUPPLY CENTER: Cloudcroft
ACCESS ROAD: Fair-weather; call ahead for conditions

SCENERY: ★★★
RVs: ★★★
TENTS: ★★
SHADE: ★★★★
PRIVACY: ★★
FACILITIES: ★★★
CAMPGROUND ACTIVITIES: ★★
AREA ACTIVITIES: ★★★★★
WHEELCHAIR ACCESSIBILITY: ★★★

MAP: *New Mexico Road & Recreation Atlas*, p. 49, G8
DIRECTIONS: From Cloudcroft, take NM 244 north about 1 mile to a right into the campground.

Like its neighboring group site, Upper Fir, Lower Fir was renovated in 2002. The improved pavilion has picnic tables, grills, a concrete floor, water, and a bearproof food locker. Parking pads are paved.

Reservations required at 877-444-6777 or ReserveUSA.com. **Sacramento Ranger District, 505-682-2551.**

17 DEERHEAD

Hiking and Cloudcroft

SCENERY: ★★★
RVs: NR
TENTS: ★★★
SHADE: ★★★★
PRIVACY: ★★★
FACILITIES: ★★
CAMPGROUND ACTIVITIES: ★★★
AREA ACTIVITIES: ★★★★★
WHEELCHAIR ACCESSIBILITY: ★

LOCATION: Southern edge of Cloudcroft
ELEVATION: 8,700 feet
NUMBER OF SITES: 29
RV NOTES: RVs not recommended because of steep access, sharp turns, and limited parking
FEE: Yes
SEASON: May–October
NEAREST SUPPLY CENTER: Cloudcroft
ACCESS ROAD: Gravel
MAP: *New Mexico Road & Recreation Atlas*, p. 49, G8

DIRECTIONS: Take NM 130 south through Cloudcroft to the campground.

Right off the highway in a densely forested canyon bottom, Deerhead is a tent campground. Sites, many of which are nicely separated by trees or space, have picnic tables, fire rings, and some pedestal grills. There are toilets and drinking water. Access the trailheads for the 27-mile Rim Trail and Sunspot Solar Observatory Trail. No drinking water is available.

No reservations. **Sacramento Ranger District, 505-682-2551.**

18 SLEEPY GRASS

Pretty forested canyon

🎿🚴 👫

SCENERY: ★★★
RVs: ★
TENTS: ★★★
SHADE: ★★★
PRIVACY: ★★★
FACILITIES: ★★
CAMPGROUND ACTIVITIES: ★★
AREA ACTIVITIES: ★★★★★
WHEELCHAIR ACCESSIBILITY: ★

LOCATION: 1.4 miles south of Cloudcroft

ELEVATION: 8,800 feet

NUMBER OF SITES: 45

RV NOTES: Smaller RVs can find space to park near the walk-in sites

FEE: Yes

SEASON: May–October

NEAREST SUPPLY CENTER: Cloudcroft

ACCESS ROAD: Fair-weather; call ahead for conditions

MAP: *New Mexico Road & Recreation Atlas,* p. 49, G8

DIRECTIONS: From US 82 in Cloudcroft, take NM 130 south 1.4 miles to FR 24B and veer left into the camp area, all along Apache Canyon.

Sleepy Grass stretches for a mile along a forested canyon bottom. These walk-in sites, laid out along the dirt road that runs the length of the camp, have picnic tables, grills, and plenty of grass. There are toilets and a mile-long picnic area at the end of the campground. Sleepy Grass also hosts an interpretive trail specifically designed for the visually impaired. No water is available.

No reservations. **Sacramento Ranger District, 505-682-2551.**

19 SLIDE (GROUP)

Rim Trail and secluded camping

LOCATION: 2 miles south of Cloudcroft
ELEVATION: 8,700 feet
NUMBER OF SITES: Accommodates up to 90
RV NOTES: No maximum length but parking is limited, holding up to 50 vehicles
FEE: Yes
SEASON: May–October
NEAREST SUPPLY CENTER: Cloudcroft
ACCESS ROAD: Gravel

SCENERY: ★★★	
RVs: ★★★	
TENTS: ★★	
SHADE: ★★★★	
PRIVACY: ★★★★	
FACILITIES: ★★★	
CAMPGROUND ACTIVITIES: ★★	
AREA ACTIVITIES: ★★★★★	
WHEELCHAIR ACCESSIBILITY: ★★★	

MAP: *New Mexico Road & Recreation Atlas*, p. 49, G8
DIRECTIONS: From US 82 in Cloudcroft, take NM 130 south 2 miles to NM 6563, then turn right and right again around the bend to the campground.

Set among pines and aspens, Slide is a secluded, dispersed group-camping area. There is a pavilion with water, tables, fire rings, and toilets. The road in and the parking area are dirt. A trailhead for the 27-mile Rim Trail begins in the camp.

Reservations required at 877-444-6777 or ReserveUSA.com. **Sacramento Ranger District, 505-682-2551**.

Indian paintbrush add a splash of color to the forest landscape

20 ASPEN (GROUP)

Dispersed group area

LOCATION: 1.4 miles south of Cloudcroft
ELEVATION: 8,700 feet
NUMBER OF SITES: Accommodates up to 70
RV NOTES: No maximum length, but the area is better suited for tent camping
FEE: Yes
SEASON: May–October
NEAREST SUPPLY CENTER: Cloudcroft

SCENERY: ★★★
RVs: ★
TENTS: ★★★
SHADE: ★★★★
PRIVACY: ★★★★
FACILITIES: ★★
CAMPGROUND ACTIVITIES: ★★
AREA ACTIVITIES: ★★★★★
WHEELCHAIR ACCESSIBILITY: ★

ACCESS ROAD: Fair-weather; call ahead for conditions
MAP: *New Mexico Road & Recreation Atlas*, p. 49, G8
DIRECTIONS: From US 82 in Cloudcroft, take NM 130 south 1.4 miles to FR 24B and veer left. The campground is on the right.

Aspen Group offers primitive, dispersed camping within a 5-acre area with shade from pines and aspens. Sites have picnic tables and fire rings. Water is available in nearby Sleepy Grass.
Reservations required at 877-444-6777 or ReserveUSA.com. **Sacramento Ranger District, 505-682-2551.**

21 BLACK BEAR (GROUP)

Dispersed group area

LOCATION: 1.4 miles south of Cloudcroft
ELEVATION: 8,700 feet
NUMBER OF SITES: Accommodates up to 70
RV NOTES: No maximum length, but the area is better suited for tent camping
FEE: Yes
SEASON: May–October
NEAREST SUPPLY CENTER: Cloudcroft

SCENERY: ★★★
RVs: ★
TENTS: ★★★
SHADE: ★★★★
PRIVACY: ★★★★
FACILITIES: ★★
CAMPGROUND ACTIVITIES: ★★
AREA ACTIVITIES: ★★★★★
WHEELCHAIR ACCESSIBILITY: ★

ACCESS ROAD: Fair-weather; call ahead for conditions
MAP: *New Mexico Road & Recreation Atlas*, p. 49, G8
DIRECTIONS: From US 82 in Cloudcroft, take NM 130 south 1.4 miles to FR 24B and veer left. The campground is on the right.

Black Bear offers primitive, dispersed camping over a large, grassy area with shade from pines and aspens. Sites have picnic tables and fire rings. Water is available in nearby Sleepy Grass.

Reservations required at 877-444-6777 or ReserveUSA.com. **Sacramento Ranger District, 505-682-2551**.

BILLY THE KID IN NEW MEXICO

It may be hard to see why a state would adopt a notorious fugitive as one of its favorite sons. But then it's hard to find more famous an Old West figure than Billy the Kid (1860?–1881), a.k.a. Henry McCarty or William H. Bonney, the orphaned drifter and ranch hand turned outlaw. Whether you believe him to be a bad seed or just a victim of circumstance looking for justice, Billy's short, violent life and legend still fascinate history buffs.

Beside the visitor center in Silver City stands a replica of the kind of rustic log cabin Billy would have lived in during the early 1870s. After his mother died there in 1874, he roamed Arizona and New Mexico. The well-preserved historic district of Lincoln looks much as it did when Billy One of the marble markers outside the Old Lincoln County Courthouse Museum

walked those streets a few years later, working as a loyal ranch hand for John Tunstall, one of Lincoln County's newer entrepreneurs. In 1878, after Tunstall had been gunned down by supporters of business rivals L.G. Murphy and James Dolan, the Lincoln County War began. Billy vowed revenge, and, joining a vigilante gang, killed Sheriff William Brady and others thought to be behind Tunstall's murder.

The Old Lincoln County Courthouse, scene of one of Billy's most daring escapes and deadly shootouts, is now a museum. Little marble blocks on the courthouse grounds mark the locations where Billy's victims, both deputy sheriffs, fell when in April 1881 he escaped his hanging for killing Brady.

Certainly the most contested spot on the Billy the Kid tour is his "grave" in Fort Sumner, on New Mexico's eastern plains. The story goes that Pat Garrett, new sheriff of Lincoln County, found and shot Billy dead in July 1881. But long-standing debate surrounds whether Garrett actually killed Billy, and whose body is in the grave. In 2003, local officials, working with state agencies, launched a project to try to exhume various remains and conduct DNA analysis. Maybe one element of the story will soon lose some of its mystery, but the legend will probably lose none of its allure.

22 BACA

Capitan Peak, Smokey Bear, and Billy the Kid

Ruins of a ranch house fireplace adjoin Baca Campground.

LOCATION: 17 miles northeast of Capitan
ELEVATION: 6,400 feet
NUMBER OF SITES: Dispersed
RV NOTES: RVs are not recommended, but pop-up trailers can fit
FEE: No
SEASON: Year-round, but may be inaccessible because of snow
NEAREST SUPPLY CENTER: Lincoln
ACCESS ROAD: Fair-weather; call ahead for conditions
MAP: *New Mexico Road & Recreation Atlas*, p. 49, D9
DIRECTIONS: From the village of Capitan drive 10 miles east on US 380, then turn left (northeast) on FR 57. Travel about 7 miles to the campground.

SCENERY:	★★★★★
RVs:	★
TENTS:	★★
SHADE:	★★★
PRIVACY:	★★★★★
FACILITIES:	★
CAMPGROUND ACTIVITIES:	★★
AREA ACTIVITIES:	★★★★
WHEELCHAIR ACCESSIBILITY:	★

Baca was once a Civilian Conservation Corps (CCC) camp and boasts views of Capitan Peak to the northeast. To the south a few miles is the town of Lincoln, site of major events in the Lincoln County War and the life of Billy the Kid. With a short drive to the west, families can explore Smokey Bear Historical Park in Capitan.

The camp is very primitive, with just scattered fire rings and an outhouse, but there are plenty of secluded spots among the piñon and alligator juniper. There is a large central field for kicking around a ball or really spreading out as a large group. The road may be rocky and rough, but the view is lovely.

No reservations. **Smokey Bear Ranger District, 505-257-4095.**

23 UPPER KARR

Dispersed camping popular with RVers

🚲 🚶

LOCATION: About 6 miles south of Cloudcroft
ELEVATION: 8,800 feet
NUMBER OF SITES: Dispersed
RV NOTES: No maximum length
FEE: No
SEASON: May–October
NEAREST SUPPLY CENTER: Cloudcroft
ACCESS ROAD: Paved
MAP: *New Mexico Road & Recreation Atlas,* p. 49, H7

SCENERY: ★★★	
RVs: ★	
TENTS: ★★	
SHADE: ★★★★	
PRIVACY: ★★★	
FACILITIES: ★	
CAMPGROUND ACTIVITIES: ★★	
AREA ACTIVITIES: ★★★★★	
WHEELCHAIR ACCESSIBILITY: ★	

DIRECTIONS: From Cloudcroft, go south on NM 130. Turn right onto NM 6563, also called the Sunspot Highway. Travel about 6 miles south to the campground entrance, on the left.

Upper Karr is a paved loop set among tall pines. Although the sites are dispersed and primitive, the campground is frequented by RVs. There is a toilet but no other amenities. The nearest dump station is at Silver Overflow. There is no drinking water.

No reservations. **Sacramento Ranger District, 505-682-2551.**

Rabbit tracks in the snow

24 JAMES CANYON
Roadside camp

LOCATION: 2 miles northwest of Mayhill
ELEVATION: 6,800 feet
NUMBER OF SITES: 6
RV NOTES: RVs not recommended because of the limited parking area
FEE: No
SEASON: Year-round
NEAREST SUPPLY CENTER: Cloudcroft
ACCESS ROAD: Paved to the campground entrance
MAP: *New Mexico Road & Recreation Atlas*, p. 49, G9
DIRECTIONS: From Cloudcroft, take US 82 east 15 miles to the campground.

SCENERY: ★★	
RVs: NR	
TENTS: ★★	
SHADE: ★★★	
PRIVACY: ★	
FACILITIES: ★★	
CAMPGROUND ACTIVITIES: ★	
AREA ACTIVITIES: ★★	
WHEELCHAIR ACCESSIBILITY: ★	

Once the winter snows begin in the Sacramento Mountains, this campground can be used later into the season because of the lower elevation. A simple roadside campground, James Canyon includes picnic tables, grills, and a toilet. These sites just off the highway spread out under a few trees along a usually dry creekbed. There is no drinking water.

No reservations. **Sacramento Ranger District, 505-682-2551.**

Mule deer in the nearby Sacramento Mountains

25 OLIVER LEE MEMORIAL STATE PARK

Old ranch, desert orchard, and hidden canyon

LOCATION: 14 miles south of Alamogordo
ELEVATION: 4,300 feet
NUMBER OF SITES: 44; no overflow area
RV NOTES: 38 feet maximum length; all hookup sites are in Loop A
FEE: Yes
SEASON: Year-round
NEAREST SUPPLY CENTER: Alamogordo
ACCESS ROAD: Paved

SCENERY:	★★★★
RVs:	★★★★
TENTS:	★★★
SHADE:	★★
PRIVACY:	★★
FACILITIES:	★★★★★
CAMPGROUND ACTIVITIES:	★★★
AREA ACTIVITIES:	★★★★★
WHEELCHAIR ACCESSIBILITY:	★★★★

MAP: *New Mexico Road & Recreation Atlas*, p. 49, H7
DIRECTIONS: From Alamogordo, drive south on US 70/54, veering left (south) onto US 54 just south of town. After 10 miles, turn east (left) onto CR A16, Dog Canyon Road. The campground is at the end of the road.

Nestled at the foot of the western slope of the Sacramento Mountains, Oliver Lee gives campers a true Chihuahuan Desert experience—with a few surprises. Snaking its way through a crack in the escarpment is the Dog Canyon Trail, a verdant ribbon where water flows year-round. Ferns, orchids, and water-loving plants thrive in this oasis. The canyon also served as an Apache stronghold during conflicts with the U.S. army in the 1800s. The restored 19th-century ranch of the park's namesake is open for guided tours. View the orchard of another industrious former resident, called Frenchie.

Photograph the Sacramentos later in the morning, when the sun reaches the campground. Explore the visitor center exhibits, which chronicle the area's flora, fauna, and human inhabitants. Use the campground as a base camp while visiting White Sands National Monument, Alamogordo, Cloudcroft, and the Lincoln National Forest.

March weekends are busiest for the RVs, but tent sites are usually available; bring your own shade. The visitor center, campsites, restrooms, showers, and part of the interpretive trail are all wheelchair-accessible. Group areas include four tent spots, a group shelter with lighting, and one RV space with electric hookup.

All sites have picnic tables and grills. Drinking water is available. The campground is divided into two loops. Loop A contains the 16 sites with electric and water hookups and the sites with shelters. The visitor center, which has a pay phone, is located at the top of Loop A.

Reservations at 877-664-7787 or www.icampnm.com. **Park Manager**, **505-437-8284.**

26 WHITE SANDS NATIONAL MONUMENT
Surreal, bright white desert landscape

LOCATION: 15 miles southwest of Alamogordo
ELEVATION: 4,000 feet
NUMBER OF SITES: 10; designated backcountry camping only
RV NOTES: RVs not allowed overnight in the park
FEE: Yes
SEASON: Year-round
NEAREST SUPPLY CENTER: Alamogordo
ACCESS ROAD: Paved to the campground
MAP: *New Mexico Road & Recreation Atlas*, p. 48, H5
DIRECTIONS: From Alamogordo, drive 15 miles southwest on US 70. The park entrance is on the right.

SCENERY: ★★★★★	
RVs: NR	
TENTS: ★★★★	
SHADE: ★	
PRIVACY: ★★★★★	
FACILITIES: ★	
CAMPGROUND ACTIVITIES: ★★	
AREA ACTIVITIES: ★★	
WHEELCHAIR ACCESSIBILITY: ★	

Even though White Sands does not technically offer car camping, it is worth mentioning since the park affords an opportunity to camp in one of the most amazing landscapes on the planet. In the heart of the snow-white dune fields, visitors can hike 0.75 mile along a marked trail to a backcountry camping area. The sites are in a loop but scattered among the dunes, so campsites are private. Campers must register at the visitor center by 5 p.m. The sites have no facilities, but water is available at the visitor center.

Since the area is a famous photography locale, some notes are in order. The sand really is brilliant white. Be prepared to balance your photographs as you would if shooting snow. If the white sand is the main subject of the picture, slightly overexpose so what is supposed to be white doesn't have a gray cast. If you are shooting a person or other object in a sea of white, try to get a close-up exposure reading of the subject, since the surrounding white will throw off the exposure balance. Also make sure your lens is protected by at least a UV filter, since blowing sand can ruin lens coatings.

No reservations. **National Park Service Visitor Center, 505-679-2599.**

Yucca, typical Chihuahuan Desert flora at White Sands

27 THREE RIVERS PETROGLYPH SITE

Petroglyphs in the Sierra Blanca foothills

LOCATION: 20 miles north of Tularosa
ELEVATION: 5,000 feet
NUMBER OF SITES: 10
RV NOTES: No maximum length
FEE: Yes
SEASON: Year-round
NEAREST SUPPLY CENTER: Tularosa
ACCESS ROAD: Paved
MAP: *New Mexico Road & Recreation Atlas,* p. 48, E6

SCENERY: ★★★	
RVs: ★★★★	
TENTS: ★★★	
SHADE: ★	
PRIVACY: ★	
FACILITIES: ★★★★	
CAMPGROUND ACTIVITIES: ★★	
AREA ACTIVITIES: ★★	
WHEELCHAIR ACCESSIBILITY: ★★★	

DIRECTIONS: From Tularosa, drive north on US 54/70 for 18 miles (or from Carrizozo, drive south for 27 miles on US 54) to FR 579. Go east about 4.5 miles; the site is on the left.

The simple campground overlooks an outcrop containing more than 20,000 petroglyphs created by the Jornada Mogollon people between A.D. 900 and 1400. Two trails begin in the camp: one goes into the outcrop, and the other winds to an old townsite. Campers have picnic tables, grills, and some shade from a few trees, in what is basically a large parking area with sites set along the edge. Restrooms, which have running water, and campsites are wheelchair-accessible.

No reservations. **BLM Las Cruces, 505-525-4300**.

28 THREE RIVERS RECREATION AREA

Hiking and desert views in the Sierra Blanca foothills

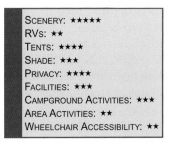

SCENERY: ★★★★★
RVS: ★★
TENTS: ★★★★
SHADE: ★★★
PRIVACY: ★★★★
FACILITIES: ★★★
CAMPGROUND ACTIVITIES: ★★★
AREA ACTIVITIES: ★★
WHEELCHAIR ACCESSIBILITY: ★★

LOCATION: 15 miles northeast of Three Rivers

ELEVATION: 6,400 feet

NUMBER OF SITES: 12; no overflow

RV NOTES: No maximum length

FEE: No

SEASON: Year-round (and a good area for winter camping)

NEAREST SUPPLY CENTER: Tularosa

ACCESS ROAD: Paved and maintained dirt

MAP: *New Mexico Road & Recreation Atlas*, p. 49, E7

DIRECTIONS: On US 54, travel 24 miles south from Carrizozo or 18 miles north from Tularosa (on US 54/70), and turn east onto FR 579 at the sign for Three Rivers Petroglyph Site. Drive 13 miles to the campground. The last 7 miles are unpaved.

As you turn off US 54 and follow the signs toward the campground, the road winds through high-desert grasslands gently rising into the western foothills of the Sierra Blanca. Along the way to the camp you pass the Three Rivers Petroglyph Site, an area containing more than 20,000 images created by the Jornada Mogollon people between A.D. 900 and 1400. The historic Santo Niño Mission Church lies just a few miles farther down the road. The campground is laid out so campsites face either the 11,977-foot Sierra Blanca Peak or the Tularosa Basin. Trail #44 leading into the White Mountain Wilderness begins in the camp. Horse corrals are available for equestrian campers. Photographers, note that sunlight doesn't reach the campground until later in the morning.

The campground is one large loop with horse corrals at the top of the loop. Sites, which are usually available, have fireplaces and tables, and some have shelters. There are vault toilets and drinking water. Campsites and restrooms are wheelchair-accessible.

No reservations. **Smokey Bear Ranger District, 505-257-4095.**

SOUTHEAST

Vast plains roll through southeastern New Mexico. This is cattle, oil, and natural-gas country, with some farming thrown in. History buffs should visit Fort Sumner, the contested burial place of Billy the Kid (see p. 241) and the site of the infamous Navajo internment camp called Bosque Redondo.

The beautiful little Bottomless Lakes are just outside of Roswell, the town famous for its supposed UFO sightings and crash sites. Near the Texas state line, the Guadalupe Mountains are vestiges of an ancient ocean reef. Visitors walk upon what was a sea floor millions of years ago; below ground, they explore the caves created by erosion after the seas receded. The celebrated Carlsbad Caverns National Park draws enthusiasts of both underground worlds and Mexican freetail bats.

Area Campgrounds

One of the smaller of the Bottomless Lakes, sheltered natural pools popular for fishing

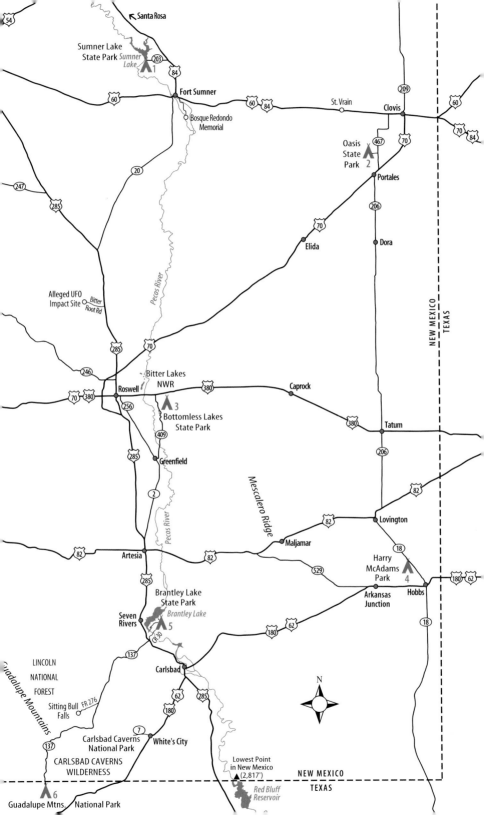

1 SUMNER LAKE STATE PARK
Swimming, biking, and Billy the Kid

LOCATION: 18 miles northwest of Fort Sumner
ELEVATION: 4,500 feet
NUMBER OF SITES: 68
RV NOTES: No maximum length; Pecos and East Side areas have electric hookups
FEE: Yes
SEASON: Year-round
NEAREST SUPPLY CENTER: Fort Sumner
ACCESS ROAD: Paved

SCENERY: ★★★
RVs: ★★★★
TENTS: ★★★★
SHADE: ★★★
PRIVACY: ★★★
FACILITIES: ★★★★★
CAMPGROUND ACTIVITIES: ★★★★
AREA ACTIVITIES: ★★
WHEELCHAIR ACCESSIBILITY: ★★★

MAP: *New Mexico Road & Recreation Atlas*, p. 44, F5
DIRECTIONS: From I-40 Exit 277, just east of Santa Rosa, take US 84 southeast for about 32 miles toward Fort Sumner. Turn right (west) onto NM 203 and travel about 5.5 miles to the park entrance.

Sumner Lake appeals to outdoor people and history buffs alike. Fish for walleye, crappie, and channel catfish. In the summer, water-ski, sail, and swim. In the winter, observe a variety of migrating waterfowl. Explore miles of old dirt roads by mountain bike. Fans of the Wild West can visit the grave of Billy the Kid at Civil War–era Fort Sumner, which houses a small museum. (Photographers should try to shoot the gravestone in the morning, since it faces east.) The fort is also near the site of Bosque Redondo, the infamous internment camp where thousands of Navajos were held after their forced "Long Walk" from their traditional homelands in the 1860s. The expanding Navajo Memorial currently has an outdoor exhibit.

Campsites are usually available, but reserve hookup sites in advance. Restrooms, showers, and the courtesy dock are wheelchair-accessible. The 30-by-20-foot group pavilion, with six tables, eight electric hookups, and grills, can accommodate 20 to 25 cars of people.

The visitor center, café/bait shop, dump station, and showers are on the east side of the lake. **Pecos** has 13 electric and water sites, and of those, six are reservable. They also have shelters, picnic tables, and grills. **Mesquite** offers sites with tables, shelters, grills, and centralized water hydrants. There are no hookups. **West River** and **East River** are more primitive. Sites have tables and fire rings, and some include shelters and grills. **East Side** has five sites with electric and water hookups, and five developed sites with only water. All have tables, grills, and shelters. A vault toilet is in the area. Primitive camping is allowed along most of the shoreline.

Reservations at 877-664-7787 or www.icampnm.com. **Park Manager, 505-355-2541.**

2 OASIS STATE PARK
Birding and fishing

LOCATION: 6.5 miles north of Portales
ELEVATION: 4,000 feet
NUMBER OF SITES: 23; no overflow
RV NOTES: No maximum length; thirteen sites are pull-thrus with electric and water, two of which also have sewer hookups
FEE: Yes
SEASON: Year-round
NEAREST SUPPLY CENTER: Portales
ACCESS ROAD: Paved
MAP: *New Mexico Road & Recreation Atlas*, p. 51, A9
DIRECTIONS: From US 70 just northeast of Portales, turn north onto NM 467 and travel about 4 miles. Turn left onto the park access road and drive 1.5 miles to the park entrance.

SCENERY: ★★★
RVS: ★★★★★
TENTS: ★★★★
SHADE: ★★★★
PRIVACY: ★★★
FACILITIES: ★★★★★
CAMPGROUND ACTIVITIES: ★★★
AREA ACTIVITIES: ★★★
WHEELCHAIR ACCESSIBILITY: ★★★★

A lovely little park in the middle of eastern New Mexico grasslands, this spot is perfectly described by the term *oasis*. With a small, stocked fishing lake as the centerpiece, the park is well-shaded by native cottonwood trees, which turn a beautiful yellow in the fall. Visitors enjoy strolling the trails that wind around the lake and hiking on the sand dunes. Birders can watch for more than 80 different species, including blue herons, ring-neck pheasants, and western sandpipers.

The visitor center, group shelter, restrooms, showers, playground, and fishing access are all wheelchair-accessible. Sites, which are usually available, are large and provide a well-raked gravel area for pitching a tent. The camping loop has electric and water hookups and a dump station. All sites have shelters, picnic tables, grills, and shade from mature trees. Drinking water is available.

Reservations at 877-664-7787 or www.icampnm.com. **Park Manager,** 505-356-5331.

3 BOTTOMLESS LAKES STATE PARK

Swimming, CCC, and UFO country

SCENERY: ★★★★
RVs: ★★★★★
TENTS: ★★★
SHADE: ★★★★
PRIVACY: ★★★
FACILITIES: ★★★★★
CAMPGROUND ACTIVITIES: ★★★
AREA ACTIVITIES: ★★★★
WHEELCHAIR ACCESSIBILITY: ★★★★

LOCATION: 15 miles southeast of Roswell

ELEVATION: 3,500 feet

NUMBER OF SITES: 69; no overflow

RV NOTES: No maximum length

FEE: Yes

SEASON: Year-round

NEAREST SUPPLY CENTER: Roswell

ACCESS ROAD: Paved

MAP: *New Mexico Road & Recreation Atlas*, p. 50, E5

DIRECTIONS: From Roswell, head east on US 380 for 12 miles. Turn right onto NM 409 and travel south for 3 miles to the park entrance.

The first of New Mexico's state parks, established in 1933, Bottomless Lakes is a string of small aquatic jewels adorning the wavy grassland. Lying below red cliffs, the blue-green lakes vary in depth from 17 to 90 feet. Anglers come here to fish for trout. Lea Lake, the largest, is open for swimming, and paddleboats are available for rent in the summer. The historic pavilion was constructed by the Civilian Conservation Corps (CCC) in the 1930s and was renovated in 2003. The city of Roswell, about 12 miles west of the park, boasts various attractions, including the International UFO Museum and Research Center, the Roswell Museum and Art Center, and the only free zoo in the state. The nearby Bitter Lakes National Wildlife Refuge is a haven for migratory waterfowl.

Since the smaller lakes lie in wind-sheltered coves, photographers can achieve nice mirror effects on the surface of the water. To emphasize colored cliff walls and blue-green water, consider using a polarizing filter.

Picnic areas, campsites, the group shelters, restrooms, showers, a playground, and the interpretive center are all wheelchair-accessible. Two 32-by-29-foot group shelters with grills, water, tables, and electricity can accommodate up to 50 people each.

Camp and picnic sites stretch along the road leading past the smaller lakes. Campsites, which are usually available, include shelters, picnic tables, and grills. The RV area adjacent to Lea Lake offers 32 sites with electric and water hookups, six of which have sewer hookup as well. All sites have shelters, picnic tables, and grills. Drinking water is available. A bathhouse and pavilion are located in the Lea Lake area.

Lea Lake area gate closed 9 p.m.–6:30 a.m. Reservations at 877-664-7787 or www.icampnm.com. **Park Manager, 505-624-6058.**

THE UFO TRAIL

When the world hears the name Roswell, images of aliens and UFOs instantly come to mind. Devoted ufologists regularly visit the area to get close to three supposed impact sites. The obligatory first stop for enthusiasts is the International UFO Museum and Research Center, at 114 North Main in downtown Roswell. Those still curious can head out to the alleged sites. Be sure to bring some ready cash.

To reach the first site, go north on US 285 and turn left onto Bitter Root Road; the alleged crash site is at the end of the road. Next, head back to US 285 and go north. Take a left onto NM 247, then another left onto County Road B7. The crash site lies about 3 miles south, somewhere off to the left of the road. Finally, continue down CR B7 to NM 246. Turn left (east) onto NM 246, then turn right onto FR 130. The last supposed crash site lies about a mile down FR 130, on the left-hand side. NM 246 will take you back to Roswell.

4 Harry McAdams Park

Gliders and golf

LOCATION: 4 miles northwest of Hobbs
ELEVATION: 4,000 feet
NUMBER OF SITES: 47
RV NOTES: No maximum length
FEE: Yes
SEASON: Year-round
NEAREST SUPPLY CENTER: Hobbs
ACCESS ROAD: Paved
MAP: *New Mexico Road & Recreation Atlas,*
p. 57, A10

SCENERY:	★★
RVS:	★★★★★
TENTS:	★★★★
SHADE:	★★★
PRIVACY:	★★
FACILITIES:	★★
CAMPGROUND ACTIVITIES:	★★
AREA ACTIVITIES:	★★
WHEELCHAIR ACCESSIBILITY:	★★★

DIRECTIONS: From US 180/62 in Hobbs, drive northwest on NM 18 for about 4 miles. The campground is on the left.

Located on the outskirts of the city of Hobbs, this park is a good place to see gliders floating on the thermals: Hobbs is home to the National Soaring Foundation and the National Soaring Championships, held each June. Set in the rolling plains of eastern New Mexico, the centerpiece of this park is a small stocked lake. An 18-hole public golf course lies just across from the park. All sites have electricity and water, and five also have sewer hookup.

No reservations. **Park Manager, 505-392-5845.**

5 BRANTLEY LAKE STATE PARK

Water sports, natural wonders, and an Old West town

SCENERY: ★★★
RVs: ★★★★★
TENTS: ★★★★★
SHADE: ★★★★
PRIVACY: ★★
FACILITIES: ★★★★★
CAMPGROUND ACTIVITIES: ★★★
AREA ACTIVITIES: ★★★★★
WHEELCHAIR ACCESSIBILITY: ★★★★

LOCATION: 12 miles northwest of Carlsbad
ELEVATION: 3,300 feet
NUMBER OF SITES: 51; overflow available
RV NOTES: No maximum length; all sites in the Limestone area have electric and water hookups and level spaces
FEE: Yes

SEASON: Year-round
NEAREST SUPPLY CENTER: Carlsbad
ACCESS ROAD: Paved
MAP: *New Mexico Road & Recreation Atlas*, p. 56, B5
DIRECTIONS: From Carlsbad, travel about 12 miles northwest on US 285. Turn right onto CR 30 and drive about 4.5 miles northeast to the park entrance.

Brantley Lake is a great base camp for exploring the Chihuahuan Desert in the southeastern corner of New Mexico. The park surrounds a large man-made lake along the Pecos River. It is a good fishing spot year-round and a refuge for migratory waterfowl in the fall. Enjoy trails and playgrounds. In addition, families can participate in a variety of ranger-sponsored events, including star parties, kite-flying rallies, and children's fishing clinics. The visitor center has phones and information about Seven Rivers, a nearby Old West ghost town. Brantley provides easy access to Carlsbad Caverns National Park, the Living Desert State Park in Carlsbad, Sitting Bull Falls via NM 137 and FR 276, and Lincoln National Forest, all within a 60-mile radius.

Be sure to reserve hookup sites in advance. Campsites, restrooms, showers, the interpretive trail, and playgrounds are wheelchair-accessible.

Limestone, perched above the lake, has sites with electric and water hookups, shelters, picnic tables, grills, paved parking, and level, gravel tent pads. Showers and one of the playgrounds are near the entrance to the camp-ground. Primitive beach camping environments are near the East Side and West Side Seven Rivers day-use areas. The boat ramp and another playground are in the East Side area as well. Unlimited group use is available in the primitive areas.

Reservations at 877-664-7787 or www.icampnm.com. **Park Manager,** **505-457-2384.**

CARLSBAD CAVERNS NATIONAL PARK

In the northern Chihuahuan Desert, cool air wafts from a great hole that draws visitors deep into the bowels of the earth. This is the entrance into the main cave of Carlsbad Caverns National Park. Within lies a veritable fairlyland of stalagmites and stalactites in a vast array of colors, shapes, and textures. More than a hundred different caves lie within the park, including the world famous Lechuguilla Cave, the nation's deepest limestone cave at 1,567 feet (478m), and third longest, according to the National Park Service. The temperature in most of the caves is a cool 56 degrees, which makes these under-ground wonders even more attractive in the heat of a southern New Mexico summer. The main cave, which is accessible via the Natural Entrance or an elevator, is wheelchair-friendly. If you are able to stick around until dusk near the main cave, you will witness the sky filling with thousands of bats as they head out for their nightly repast: insects. From the town of Carlsbad, drive south on US 62/180 for about 19 miles to White's City, turn right onto NM 7, and continue 4 miles west to the park's entrance.

Temple of the Sun in the Big Room of Carlsbad Caverns National Park.

6 Dog Canyon

Canyon wonders almost in New Mexico

LOCATION: 67 miles southwest of Carlsbad via NM 137
ELEVATION: 6,200 feet
NUMBER OF SITES: 13; no overflow
RV NOTES: No maximum length; no RV facilities; bring your own shade
FEE: Yes
SEASON: Year-round
NEAREST SUPPLY CENTER: Carlsbad. (Note that there are *no services* on NM 137, including gas.)
ACCESS ROAD: Paved to the campground entrance. Note that flash flooding areas exist along NM 137 during monsoon season.
MAP: *New Mexico Road & Recreation Atlas*, p. 56, E3

DIRECTIONS: From Carlsbad, travel about 12 miles northwest on US 285. Turn left onto NM 137 and travel about 55 miles southwest to the Texas border. The campground entrance is on the border.

Dog Canyon might as well be in New Mexico, lying at the southern end of Lincoln National Forest and the northern end of Guadalupe Mountains National Park. The range is part of an ancient marine fossil reef called the Capitan Reef. A tropical ocean called the Permian Sea covered the area millions of years ago and was home to sponges, algae, and other lime-secreting

SCENERY: ★★★★★
RVs: ★
TENTS: ★★★★★
SHADE: ★★★
PRIVACY: ★★★★
FACILITIES: ★★★★
CAMPGROUND ACTIVITIES: ★★★
AREA ACTIVITIES: ★★
WHEELCHAIR ACCESSIBILITY: ★★

creatures. As the sea receded, the Permian limestone fossil reef was exposed, forming the Guadalupe Mountains. Dog Canyon, once on an ancient sea floor, is now part of the Chihuahuan Desert.

Because of its elevation, the campground is forested and relatively cool. A network of more than 80 miles of trails links with the campground. Horse corrals are available, by reservation, for equestrian camping trips. Note that horses are not allowed to remain in the backcountry overnight, since there is no available water outside the campground.

The group site can accommodate 20 people; its restroom and four RV-sized spaces are wheelchair-accessible.

Tent campsites are walk-ins. Nicely shaded by trees, these level sites are roomy and well-screened from one another. Each has a picnic table and gravel tent pad. The heated restroom has running water. Note that no fires are allowed in the campground.

Reservations for groups and horse corrals only. **Ranger Station, 505-981-2418.**

Sitting Bull Falls lie off FR 276 on the way south to Dog Canyon from Carlsbad

NORTHEAST

The legendary Santa Fe Trail once cut across the northeastern corner of New Mexico. Minus a few towns and highways, the landscape has changed little since then. For much of the area, mesas dominate the view. The Canadian River, just south of where the Trail passed, cuts a deep gorge through what are now parts of the Kiowa National Grassland. Near Raton Pass is Sugarite Canyon, a deep valley crowned with cap rock along the rim. Capulin Volcano National Monument rises from the plains near where the remains of the prehistoric Folsom Man were discovered. And herds of pronghorn often run at amazing speeds across the flat, open grasslands.

Area Campgrounds

Mills Canyon

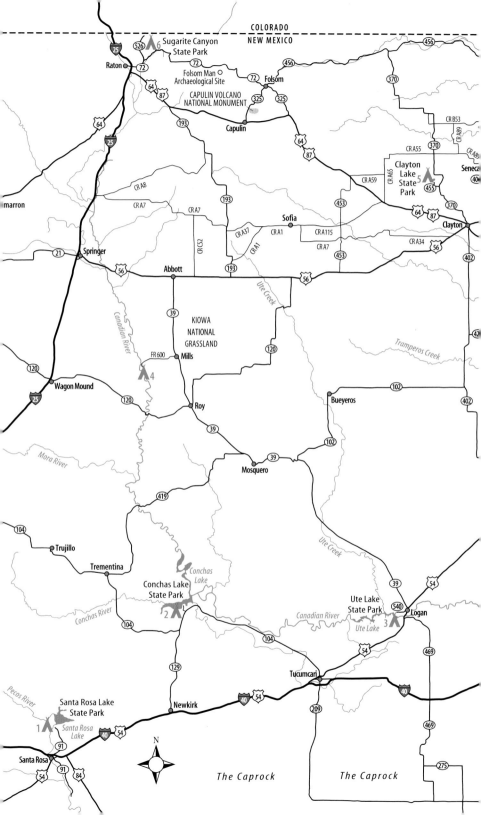

1 SANTA ROSA LAKE STATE PARK

Horseback riding, scuba diving, and Route 66

LOCATION: 7 miles north of Santa Rosa
ELEVATION: 4,800 feet
NUMBER OF SITES: 101; overflow available
RV NOTES: 50 feet maximum length; the dump station is near the park entrance; Loop A of the Rocky Point area has water and electric hookup sites
FEE: Yes
SEASON: Year-round
NEAREST SUPPLY CENTER: Santa Rosa
ACCESS ROAD: Paved
MAP: *New Mexico Road & Recreation Atlas*, p. 44, D4
DIRECTIONS: From Exit 273 on I-40, take Business 40 (Historic US 66) into Santa Rosa. Turn left on Second, cross the tracks, then turn right onto Eddy Ave. In less than 0.5 mile, turn left onto NM 91, and travel north about 7 miles to the park entrance.

SCENERY: ★★★	
RVs: ★★★★	
TENTS: ★★★★	
SHADE: ★★★	
PRIVACY: ★★	
FACILITIES: ★★★★★	
CAMPGROUND ACTIVITIES: ★★★	
AREA ACTIVITIES: ★★★	
WHEELCHAIR ACCESSIBILITY: ★★★★	

Santa Rosa offers a lovely outdoor experience. Set in the plains of eastern New Mexico, the lake beckons locals and visitors alike. A 25-mile trail open to hiking, mountain biking, and horseback riding winds around the lake. The area teems with wildlife, including eagles and migrating osprey. An impoundment along the Pecos River, Santa Rosa Lake is a favorite of anglers fishing for bass, catfish, and walleye. The Army Corps of Engineers visitor center displays information about the dam and the history of the area. The city of Santa Rosa boasts attractions including summer events; the Blue Hole, a destination for scuba divers from around the country; and, of course, an extant stretch of Historic US 66.

Wheelchair-accessible facilities include the visitor center, group shelters, courtesy dock, picnic areas, campsites, restrooms, and showers. Two group areas consist of large canopies with three tables each, plus grills, electricity, lighting, and water spigots. Memorial Day, Fourth of July, and Labor Day weekends are the toughest times to find sites.

Juniper Park sites offer shelters, grills, and picnic tables. Only the wheelchair-accessible site has water and electric hookups. **Rocky Point** has two loops. The 23 sites in Loop A all have electric hookups, and sites 1–9 also have water. Loop B does not have electric, but there are three water spigots in the area. **Los Tanos** is a primitive tent area near the entrance to the park. Sites have tables and grills; be sure to bring your own shade. The dump station and horse corrals are in this area as well. The 25-mile multi-use trail begins near the corrals.

Reservations at 877-664-7787 or www.icampnm.com. **Park Manager,** 505-472-3110.

2 Conchas Lake State Park

Dinosaurs, fossils, and fishing

Location: 32 miles northwest of Tucumcari

Elevation: 4,200 feet

Number of Sites: 145; overflow available

RV Notes: No maximum length

Fee: Yes

Season: Year-round

Nearest Supply Center: Tucumcari

Access Road: Paved

Map: *New Mexico Road & Recreation Atlas,* p. 44, B6

Directions: From I-40 in Tucumcari, take NM 104 northwest and travel for 34 miles to the park entrance.

Conchas Lake is another fine getaway in New Mexico's eastern hills. Water-sport enthusiasts can sail, boat, and water-ski, enjoying some 60 miles of shoreline and a number of islands. Anglers can fish for walleye, channel catfish, largemouth bass, crappie, and bluegill. Golden eagles, waterfowl, pronghorn, elk, deer, coyotes, and other wildlife call the park and the nearby, 770-acre Ladd S. Gordon Wildlife Area home. Rock formations scattered throughout the park attract fossil hunters from around the country, and the nearby Mesalands Dinosaur Museum exhibits dinosaur remains unearthed in the state. Note that in making photos of fossils, photographers can benefit from using a polarizing filter, which reduces light reflection on the rock surface and increases contrast.

SCENERY: ★★★
RVs: ★★★
TENTS: ★★★★
SHADE: ★★★
PRIVACY: ★★★
FACILITIES: ★★★★★
CAMPGROUND ACTIVITIES: ★★★
AREA ACTIVITIES: ★★
WHEELCHAIR ACCESSIBILITY: ★★★★

Restrooms, one RV site, the visitor center, and the courtesy dock are all wheelchair-accessible. Summer weekends and holidays are very busy, and the electric sites are tough to get. Reservations are recommended.

The **North Recreation Area** offers restrooms, a dump station, water hydrants, the marina, visitor center, a boat ramp, and the campground store and café. The reservation sites are in this area including seven with electric hookup. The **Central Recreation Area** is a tent camping and picnic area next to the dam that includes a boat ramp. The **South Recreation Area** has restrooms, a dump station, and RV camping with no hookups. There is a pay phone at the north dock marina.

Reservations at 877-664-7787 or www.icampnm.com. **Park Manager, 505-868-2270.**

3 UTE LAKE STATE PARK

Water sports and Tucumcari

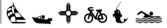

LOCATION: 24 miles northeast
of Tucumcari
ELEVATION: 3,900 feet
NUMBER OF SITES: 130; no overflow
RV NOTES: No maximum length
FEE: Yes
SEASON: Year-round
NEAREST SUPPLY CENTER: Logan
ACCESS ROAD: Paved

SCENERY: ★★★	
RVs: ★★★★★	
TENTS: ★★★★	
SHADE: ★★★	
PRIVACY: ★★★	
FACILITIES: ★★★★★	
CAMPGROUND ACTIVITIES: ★★★★	
AREA ACTIVITIES: ★★	
WHEELCHAIR ACCESSIBILITY: ★★★★★	

MAP: *New Mexico Road & Recreation Atlas*, p. 45, B9
DIRECTIONS: From I-40 in Tucumcari, go northeast on US 54 for 24 miles
to Logan. In Logan, take NM 540 west 3 miles to the park entrance.

Ute Lake is a paradise for water-sport enthusiasts. An impoundment on
the Canadian River, Ute Lake is one of the longest lakes in New Mexico at
almost 13 miles. Multiple boat ramps and a marina provide convenient water
access for motorized and nonmotorized watercraft. Anglers can fish for
walleye, bass, crappie, and catfish. There are plenty of quiet coves in which
to fish in solitude or view wildlife such as ducks, quails, and pheasants.
Bicycling is popular along the relatively level, paved roads that run parallel
to the lake. Nearby Tucumcari has attractions including the Mesalands

Dinosaur Museum. And given its location some 20 miles north of I-40, Ute Lake can be a handy stopover for interstate travelers.

Fleet-footed creatures frequent the surrounding plains and mesas. When driving to and from Ute Lake, keep an eye out in the wide-open grassy areas for deer and pronghorn, which look like small deer and have been mistaken for antelope (to which they bear no relation) for generations. Photographers should be prepared with high-speed film and a fast shutter setting.

Campsites are usually available. For sites with electric hookups, reservations are recommended. Picnic areas, restrooms, showers, and some campsites, as well as the visitor center, group shelter, courtesy boat dock, marina, and playground, are all wheelchair-accessible. The group area, accessible through the Yucca loop, contains a 32-by-32-foot shelter with picnic tables, a large grill, and four electric hookups.

North Area is the park's main campground, home to the visitor center; two loops with reservable sites, **Zia** and **Yucca**; and developed sites along the lake's edge. Zia has electrical hookups. Yucca offers paved pull-thrus and electric hookups. **Cottonwood** is a nice tent area shaded by trees along the lake's edge. **Windy Point** is less developed than the North Area but provides more space between campsites; you'll find fire rings, a restroom, and a water spigot. The **Logan Park Marina** services both boaters and RV campers, with a boat ramp, dump station, electric hookups, and showers. The top section has developed sites, some with electric hookup. **Roger's Park** is a single-loop, dispersed camp area affording secluded sites and fishing opportunities. Bring your own shade. There is a toilet and a water spigot. **South Area**, located at the Ute Lake Dam by the NM 54 junction, includes a ramp, vault toilets, and dispersed primitive sites. **Mine Canyon**, 7 miles west of the NM 54 junction, is another primitive, dispersed camp area with a boat ramp and vault toilets.

Reservations at 877-664-7787 or www.icampnm.com. **Park Manager, 505-487-2284.**

4 MILLS CANYON

Riverside canyon solitude

SCENERY: ★★★★★
RVs: NR
TENTS: ★★
SHADE: ★★
PRIVACY: ★★★★★
FACILITIES: ★★
CAMPGROUND ACTIVITIES: ★★
AREA ACTIVITIES: ★
WHEELCHAIR ACCESSIBILITY: ★

LOCATION: 44.5 miles southeast of Springer
ELEVATION: 5,000 feet
NUMBER OF SITES: 8, plus overflow

RV NOTES: RVs not recommended
FEE: No
SEASON: Year-round but may be inaccessible because of snow
NEAREST SUPPLY CENTER: Springer
ACCESS ROAD: The rocky, winding dirt road is very rough. A high-clearance 4x4 is strongly recommended.
MAP: *New Mexico Road & Recreation Atlas*, p. 38, F5
DIRECTIONS: From I-25 in Springer, take US 56 east for about 20 miles. Turn right onto NM 39 and go south for about 15.5 miles to Mills. Turn right (west) on FR 600 and follow it 9.5 miles. (Be aware that there are two entrances into the tiny cluster of buildings called Mills. Take the second right off NM 39, about 2 miles south of the first.)

Situated in the bottom of an 800-foot-deep canyon carved over time by the Canadian River, the campground hugs the river's edge. The rugged red cliffs form a dramatic backdrop to the blue-green water snaking along the bottom, providing a home to golden eagles, wild turkeys, Barbary sheep, mule deer, geese, and the occasional mountain lion. Pronghorn frequent the grassy plains above.

Holiday weekends bring more visitors than usual, but the campground is generally quiet and infrequently visited. Photographers, note that depending on the time of year, the sun won't hit the bottom of the canyon walls and the river surface until later in the morning. Hike to wider points along the river to catch the sun a bit earlier.

Sites include picnic tables and fire rings. There are toilets, but no drinking water is available.

No reservations. **Kiowa/Rita Blanca National Grasslands, 505-374-9652.**

THE SANTA FE TRAIL

Running from Missouri to the Plaza in the heart of the namesake Spanish colonial city, the Santa Fe Trail embodied frontier life and commerce from about 1821 to 1869, before the arrival of the railroads. The wagon trail followed mighty rivers, crossed vast grasslands, traversed majestic mountains, and could often be perilous. Encounters with aggrieved Indian tribes, treachery among traders in a generally lawless region, and freak blizzards and downpours all contributed to the death toll of those

Pronghorn pose near Cimarron

who plied the trail. But the pull of trade, adventure, and Manifest Destiny continued to draw settlers west, in spite of the risks, to fabled Santa Fe.

Today, visitors can roughly follow the Santa Fe Trail along New Mexico's roads in the footsteps of explorers past. The directions below roughly trace the two main trail routes, until they meet I-25 en route to Santa Fe. Note that many of these county roads are fair-weather.

Cimarron Cutoff Route: From the Oklahoma state line, take NM 410 toward Seneca, passing the McNees Crossing Monument. Head west on CR A89, which becomes CR A55. Follow CR A65 south, then turn west onto CR A59. Cross US 64/87 and continue south on NM 453. Turn right onto CR A115. Veer right at the junction with CR A7 then west onto CR A1 toward Sofia. Veer right onto CR A37. Turn north onto NM 193 and then turn left (west) onto CR A7. Turn left (south) onto CR C52. Turn right and head west on US 56. At Springer, head south on I-25 toward Las Vegas and Santa Fe.

Mountain Route: From the Colorado state line, follow I-25 south to Exit 446, just south of Raton. Take US 64 southwest toward Cimarron. In Cimarron, head south on NM 21. At Springer, pick up I-25 heading south. Access Fort Union National Monument, a major historic defensive point along the trail, north off of I-25 on NM 161 about 22 miles southwest of Wagon Mound.

5 CLAYTON LAKE STATE PARK

Dinosaurs and fishing

LOCATION: 12 miles northwest of Clayton
ELEVATION: 5,040 feet
NUMBER OF SITES: 37
RV NOTES: 45 feet maximum length; the electric sites have gravel pads; some are pull-thrus and others driveways; the nearest dump station is in Clayton
FEE: Yes
SEASON: Year-round
NEAREST SUPPLY CENTER: Clayton
ACCESS ROAD: Paved
MAP: *New Mexico Road & Recreation Atlas*, p. 39, C10
DIRECTIONS: From US 87 in Clayton, take NM 370 northwest for about 10.5 miles. Turn left onto NM 455 and drive for about 1.25 miles to the campground entrance.

SCENERY:	★★★★
RVs:	★★★
TENTS:	★★★★
SHADE:	★★★★
PRIVACY:	★★★
FACILITIES:	★★★★★
CAMPGROUND ACTIVITIES:	★★★
AREA ACTIVITIES:	★★
WHEELCHAIR ACCESSIBILITY:	★★★

The drive to this lovely campground takes you into a gorge lined with volcanic rock and then up into undulating rangeland. The Santa Fe Trail passed about 3 miles north of the park, and dinosaurs once inhabited this region. Visitors can walk an interpretive trail and see more than 500 footprints left by these creatures. (Early morning and late afternoon are the ideal times to photograph the footprints, when shadows better define the prints.) A variety of bird species migrate here, and anglers will be pleased to know that four state-record walleyes have come from Clayton Lake.

From May to August, hookup sites are usually taken; reservations are recommended. The visitor center, picnic areas, group shelter, restrooms, showers, and playground are all wheelchair-accessible. The big group shelter, located between two reservation camp areas, has six picnic tables, a water spigot, and electric and water hookups.

The park contains two reservation sections: the electric area mainly used by RVs near the park entrance, and the tent sites beyond the RV area. Follow the main park road, past the visitor center, and you'll find nicely secluded, level gravel sites along the lake with tables, shelters, and grills. Seven sites have electric hookups. Drinking water is available.

Reservations at 877-664-7787 or www.icampnm.com. **Park Manager,** **505-374-8808.**

6 SUGARITE CANYON STATE PARK

Rock climbing and butterflies

LOCATION: 6 miles northeast of Raton
ELEVATION: 7,800 feet
NUMBER OF SITES: 42; overflow available
RV NOTES: 40 feet maximum length; all of the electric and water hookup sites are in the Lake Alice area; RVs are not recommended in Soda Pocket because of the steep, winding dirt access road
FEE: Yes
SEASON: Year-round
NEAREST SUPPLY CENTER: Raton
ACCESS ROAD: Paved
MAP: *New Mexico Road & Recreation Atlas*, p. 38, A6
DIRECTIONS: Take I-25 Exit 452 at Raton. Follow NM 72 east for 3.5 miles. Veer left onto NM 526 and travel about 2 miles to the visitor center.

SCENERY: ★★★★★
RVS: ★★★★
TENTS: ★★★★
SHADE: ★★★★
PRIVACY: ★★★★
FACILITIES: ★★★★★
CAMPGROUND ACTIVITIES: ★★★★★
AREA ACTIVITIES: ★★★
WHEELCHAIR ACCESSIBILITY: ★★★★★

Running deep in a canyon surrounded by cliffs made of 12-million-year-old cap rock runs a river with two manmade lakes. This is the setting for one of New Mexico's most beautiful state parks, Sugarite Canyon (pronounced sugar-*eet*). Visitors can camp lakeside or choose a site high up in the cliffs with a spectacular southwestern view of the canyon. Mule deer, bears, and other creatures call the park home. Butterfly enthusiasts will marvel at the diversity of species in this area; peak viewing times are June and July (visit the Sugarite Canyon page at www.nmparks.com for more details). Rock climbers are welcome to scale the basaltic cap rock above the canyon. Explore the ruins of an abandoned coal mine camp, and take a short hike to the mines. The park lies only a few miles from the mountain route of the Santa Fe Trail. Within an hour's drive is Capulin Volcano National Monument, home to a classically shaped cinder cone. Visitors can drive to the crater's rim and gaze 1,200 feet down and across the vast plains. Sugarite Canyon has 15 miles of trails in New Mexico and connects to other trails across the Colorado line, less than 5 miles away.

Located at the visitor center are phones and the trailhead for the Coal Camp interpretive trail. The only showers in the campground are across the road from the center. Drinking water is available. Wheelchair-accessible facilities include the visitor center, group shelter, restrooms, showers, boat ramp, courtesy boat dock, interpretive trail, and Site #12 in Lake Alice. The **Gambel Oak** group area, in the Soda Pocket area, is a gravel loop that contains five or six sites in an oak grove, along with picnic tables, a grill, and a bearproof food-storage locker. The area can accommodate three to ten cars of people and is well-shaded. The Campfire Program amphitheater adjoins Gambel Oak.

Campsites are usually available. If you'd like to secure a hookup site, reservations are recommended. **Lake Alice** has sites with individual electric and water hookups, as well as a tent-only section. All of the sites have picnic tables and grills. Restrooms are centrally located. Trees provide good shade. Reservations are available for some sites. **Soda Pocket** boasts well-spaced tent campsites with good views. Some of the tent sites have shelters; all have picnic tables and fire rings with grills; there is one restroom. The **Lake Maloya** tent area has restrooms, a boat ramp, and a fishing dock.

For the best odds of capturing wildlife on film, particularly larger mammals, visit the creek between the two lakes at sunrise and sunset. (I happened to see not only plenty of mule deer but also a black bear.) For the most dramatic landscape shots, the Soda Pocket area is the place to be. Just beyond Site #11, enter the brush toward the mouth of the canyon at sunrise; the boulders provide a marvelous vantage point for morning shots of the canyon.

Reservations at 877-664-7787 or www.icampnm.com. **Park Manager, 505-445-5607.**

APPENDIX A: PICKS BY ACTIVITY OR INTEREST

People camp for different reasons. The categories below may help you to find features, amenities, or locations that best match your interests.

Author's Personal Favorites

Aguirre Springs
Big Tesuque
Capilla
Chaco Culture National
 Historical Park
City of Rocks State Park
Dog Canyon
Goose Lake
Heron Lake State Park
Holy Ghost
Jack's Creek
Lagunitas
Mills Canyon
Monjeau
Rio Chama
Sugarite Canyon State Park
Three Rivers Recreation Area
Wild Rivers Recreation Area
Willow Creek

Best RV Campgrounds

Bottomless Lakes State Park
Brantley Lake State Park
Caballo Lake State Park
Cochiti Lake
Coyote Creek State Park
Elephant Butte State Park
Harry McAdams Park
Manzano Mountains State Park
Oasis State Park
Quemado Lake
Riana at Abiquiu Reservoir
Santa Rosa Lake State Park
Silver Lake
Sugarite Canyon State Park
Sumner Lake State Park
Ute Lake State Park
Valley of Fires Recreation Area

Best Views

Aguirre Springs
Angel Peak National Recreation Site
Bandelier National Monument
Cabresto Lake
Capilla
Cebolla Mesa
Chaco Culture National
 Historical Park
Cimarron Canyon State Park
City of Rocks State Park
El Morro National Monument
Elephant Butte State Park
Goose Lake
Heron Lake State Park
Jack's Creek
Lagunitas
McCrystal Creek
Monjeau
Navajo Lake State Park
Orilla Verde Recreation Area
Red Rock State Park
Riana at Abiquiu Reservoir
Rio Chama
Santa Cruz Lake Recreation Area
Sugarite Canyon State Park
Three Rivers Recreation Area
Valley of Fires Recreation Area
Vista Linda
White Sands National Monument
Wild Rivers Recreation Area

Civilian Conservation Corps (CCC) Projects

Bandelier National Monument
Bottomless Lakes State Park
Hyde Memorial State Park
Monjeau
Paliza
Pueblo Park

Equestrian

Agua Piedra
Argentina/Bonito Trailhead
Cimarron
Cimarron Canyon State Park
Dog Canyon
Gila Cliff Dwellings
  National Monument
Hopewell Lake
Iron Gate
Jack's Creek
McCrystal Creek
Red Canyon
Santa Barbara
Santa Rosa Lake State Park
Three Rivers Recreation Area

Fall Foliage Viewing

Big Tesuque
Cabresto Lake
Canjilon Lakes
Cimarron
Fourth of July
Goose Lake
Head of the Ditch
Iron Gate
Jack's Creek
Lagunitas
McCrystal Creek
Oak Grove
Rio de Los Pinos
  Recreation Area
Santa Barbara
Upper Karr Canyon

Fishing

Agua Piedra
Caballo Dam State Park
Canjilon Lakes
Cimarron Canyon State Park
Cochiti Lake
Comales
Cowles
Fawn Lakes
Fenton Lake State Park
Forks
Heron Lake State Park
Leasburg Dam State Park
Mesa
Mora
Mundo Lake
Navajo Lake State Park
Orilla Verde Recreation Area
Percha Dam State Park
Quemado Lake
Riana at Abiquiu Reservoir
Rio de Los Pinos Recreation Area
South Fork
Upper End
Villanueva State Park
Vista Linda

4x4 Roads

Baca
Cabresto Lake
Capilla
Goose Lake
Iron Gate
Lagunitas
Mills Canyon
Rio Chama

Hiking

Agua Piedra
Aguirre Springs
Bandelier National Monument
Capilla
Chaco Culture National
  Historical Park
Dog Canyon
Gila Cliff Dwellings National
  Monument
Goose Lake
Jack's Creek
La Junta Canyon
Red Canyon
Rio Chama
South Fork
Trampas Trailhead
Twining
Wild Rivers Recreation Area

Native Americans Past and Present

Bandelier National Monument
Bowl Canyon Navajo
  Recreation Area
Chaco Culture National
  Historical Park
Cochiti Lake
El Morro National Monument
Gila Cliff Dwellings National
  Monument
Isleta Lakes
La Jara Lake
Manzano Mountains State Park
Nambe Falls Recreation Area
Red Rock State Park
Stone Lake
Sumner Lake State Park
Three Rivers Petroglyph Site

New Mexico History

Baca
Clayton Lake State Park
El Morro National Monument
Hyde Memorial State Park
Las Petacas
Leasburg Dam State Park
Manzano Mountains State Park
Oliver Lee Memorial State Park
Pancho Villa State Park
Storrie Lake State Park
Sumner Lake State Park
Villanueva State Park

Resort

Bottomless Lakes State Park
Cochiti Lake
Conchas Lake State Park
Coyote Creek State Park
Elephant Butte State Park
Heron Lake State Park
Leasburg Dam State Park
Navajo Lake State Park
Riana at Abiquiu Reservoir
Silver Lake
Sugarite Canyon State Park
Sumner Lake State Park
Ute Lake State Park

Santa Fe Trail

Clayton Lake State Park
Storrie Lake State Park
Sugarite Canyon State Park

Travel Stops

Interstate 10
Rockhound State Park

Interstate 25
Caballo Lake State Park
Cochiti Lake
Elephant Butte State Park
Isleta Lakes
Leasburg Dam State Park
Percha Dam State Park
Storrie Lake State Park
Sugarite Canyon State Park

Interstate 40
Bluewater State Park
Isleta Lakes
Red Rock State Park
Santa Rosa Lake State Park
Ute Lake State Park

Wheelchair-Accessible Amenities

Bandelier National Monument
Bottomless Lakes State Park
Chaco Culture National
  Historical Park
Cochiti Lake
Conchas Lake State Park
Coyote Creek State Park
El Morro National Monument
Elephant Butte State Park

Fenton Lake State Park
Heron Lake State Park
Leasburg Dam State Park
Navajo Lake State Park
Oliver Lee Memorial State Park
Sugarite Canyon State Park
Ute Lake State Park
Vista Linda
Wild Rivers Recreation Area

Whitewater

El Vado State Park
Orilla Verde Recreation Area
Riana at Abiquiu Reservoir

Rio Chama
Wild Rivers Recreation Area

APPENDIX B: ADDRESSES AND WEBSITES

For the latest information on access, conditions, and permits, contact these various land-management agencies that supervise New Mexico's campgrounds. Following the list is a selection of helpful websites that can provide detailed maps, let you make reservations, lay out fishing regulations, and give you other vital information.

Bureau of Land Management

Farmington Office
1235 La Plata Highway
Farmington, NM 87401
505-599-8900

Las Cruces Office
1800 Marquess Street
Las Cruces, NM 88005
505-525-4300

Socorro Office
198 Neel Avenue
Socorro, NM 87801
505-835-0412

Taos Office
226 Cruz Alta Road
Taos, NM 87571
505-758-8851
505-770-1600 (river information)

Indian Reservations

Isleta Lakes Recreational Complex
Pueblo of Isleta
P.O. Box 1270
Isleta Pueblo, NM 87022
505-877-0370

Mescalero Apache Tribe
P.O. Box 227
Mescalero, NM 88340
505-464-4494

Nambe Falls Recreational Area
Pueblo of Nambe
Route 1, Box 117-BB
Santa Fe, NM 87501
505-455-2304

Navajo Nation
Window Rock Sports Center
P.O. Box 2370
Window Rock, AZ 86515
928-871-6667

National Park Service

The National Park Services administers the following sites in New Mexico (Visit www.nps.gov for details):

Aztec Ruins National Monument
Bandelier National Monument
Capulin Volcano National Monument
Carlsbad Caverns National Park
Chaco Culture National
  Historical Park
El Malpais National Monument
El Morro National Monument

Fort Union National Monument
Gila Cliff Dwellings National
  Monument
Pecos National Historical Park
Petroglyph National Monument
Salinas Pueblo Missions National
  Monument
White Sands National Monument

New Mexico Department of Game and Fish

State Wildlife Agency
One Wildlife Way
P.O. Box 25112
Santa Fe, NM 87504
800-862-9310

Northeast Area Office
P.O. Box 1145
Raton, NM 87740
505-445-2311

Southeast Area Office
1912 W. 2nd St.
Roswell, NM 88201
505-624-6135

Jicarilla Apache Office
P.O. Box 313
Dulce, NM 87528
505-759-3255

Northwest Area Office
3841 Midway Place NE
Albuquerque, NM 87109
505-841-8881, ext. 627

Southwest Area Office
566 N. Telshor Blvd.
Las Cruces, NM 88011
505-522-9796

New Mexico State Parks

Santa Fe Office
P.O. Box 1147
Santa Fe, NM 87504
888-NMPARKS (667-2757)
Reservations: 877-664-7787

U.S. Forest Service

Southwestern Region
333 Broadway SE
Albuquerque, NM 87102
505-842-3292

Carson National Forest

Camino Real Ranger District
P.O. Box 68
Peñasco, NM 87553
505-587-2255

Jicarilla Ranger District
664 E. Broadway
Bloomfield, NM 87413
505-632-2956

Canjilon Ranger District
P.O. Box 488
Canjilon, NM 87515
505-684-2489

Questa Ranger District
P.O. Box 110
Questa, NM 87556
505-586-0520

El Rito Ranger District
P.O. Box 56
El Rito, NM 87530
505-581-4554

Tres Piedras Ranger District
P.O. Box 38
Tres Piedras, NM 87577
505-758-8678

Cibola National Forest

Supervisor's Office
2113 Osuna Road NE, Suite A
Albuquerque, NM 87113
505-346-3900

Magdalena Ranger District
P.O. Box 45
Magdalena, NM 87825
505-854-2281

Mount Taylor Ranger District
1800 Lobo Canyon Road
Grants, NM 87020
505-287-8833

Mountainair Ranger District
P.O. Box 69
Mountainair, NM 87036-0069
505-847-2990

Sandia Ranger District
11776 Highway 337
Tijeras, NM 87059-8619
505-281-3304

Gila National Forest

Black Range Ranger District
1804 Date Street
Truth or Consequences, NM 87901
505-894-6677

Glenwood Ranger District
P.O. Box 8
Glenwood, NM 88039
505-539-2481

Luna Work Center
P.O. Box 91
Luna, NM 87824
505-547-2612

Quemado Ranger District
P.O. Box 158
Quemado, NM 87829
505-773-4678

Reserve Ranger District
P.O. Box 170
Reserve, NM 87830
505-533-6232

Supervisor's Office/
Silver City Ranger District
3005 E. Camino del Bosque
Silver City, NM 88061
505-388-8201

Wilderness Ranger District
HC 68, Box 50
Mimbres, NM 88049
505-536-2250

Kiowa National Grassland

Kiowa Ranger District
714 Main Street
Clayton, NM 88415
505-374-9652

Lincoln National Forest

Supervisor's Office
1101 New York Avenue
Alamogordo, NM 88310
505-434-7200

Sacramento Ranger District
P.O. Box 288
Cloudcroft, NM 88317
505-682-2551

Smokey Bear Ranger District
901 Mechem Drive
Ruidoso, NM 88345
505-257-4095

Santa Fe National Forest

Supervisor's Office
1474 Rodeo Road
Santa Fe, NM 87505
505-438-7840

Coyote Ranger District
P.O. Box 160
Coyote, NM 87012
505-638-5526

Cuba Ranger District
P.O. Box 130
Cuba, NM 87013
505-289-3264

Española Ranger District
1710 N. Riverside Drive
Española, NM 87532
505-753-7331

Jemez Ranger District
051 Woodsy Lane
P.O. Box 150
Jemez Springs, NM 87025
505-829-3535

Pecos/Las Vegas Ranger District
Pecos Ranger Station
Box 429
Pecos, NM 87552
505-757-6121

Pecos/Las Vegas Ranger District
Las Vegas Information Center
1926 N. Seventh Street
Las Vegas, NM 87701
505-425-3534

USEFUL WEBSITES

Bureau of Land Management:
www.nm.blm.gov

National Park Service: www.nps.gov

National Recreation Reservation
Service: www.reserveusa.com

New Mexico Department of Game
and Fish: www.gmfsh.state.nm.us

New Mexico State Parks:
www.nmparks.com

New Mexico visitor information
and maps: www.newmexico.org

Public Lands Information Center:
www.publiclands.org

U.S. Fish & Wildlife Service:
www.fws.gov/

U.S. Forest Service Southwestern
Region: www.fs.fed.us/r3/

APPENDIX C: RECOMMENDED READING

Benchmark Maps. *New Mexico Road & Recreation Atlas*. 4th ed. Medford, OR: Benchmark Maps, 2002.

Hill, Mike. *Guide to the Hiking Areas of New Mexico*. Albuquerque, NM: University of New Mexico Press, 1995.

Julyan, Bob, and Tom Till. *New Mexico's Wilderness Areas: The Complete Guide*. Englewood, CO: Westcliffe Publishers, 1998.

Julyan, Bob, Tom Till, and William Stone. *New Mexico's Continental Divide Trail: The Complete Guide*. Englewood, CO: Westcliffe Publishers, 2001.

Metzger, Stephen. *New Mexico Handbook*. 6th ed. Emeryville, CA: Avalon Travel Publishing, 2003.

Nealson, Christina. *New Mexico's Sanctuaries, Retreats, and Sacred Places*. Englewood, CO: Westcliffe Publishers, 2001.

Patterson, David, and Tom Till. *Along New Mexico's Continental Divide Trail*. Englewood, CO: Westcliffe Publishers, 2001.

Stone, William, and Jerold Widdison. *New Mexico: Then & Now*. Englewood, CO: Westcliffe Publishers, 2003.

INDEX